ALSO BY NIGEL & MAGGIE PERCY

Dowsing Box Set

Dowsing Reference Library

Visit Sixth Sense Books at www.sixthsensebooks.com to see a description of all our books.

THE NATURE OF INTUITION

UNDERSTAND & HARNESS YOUR INTUITIVE ABILITY

NIGEL PERCY

MAGGIE PERCY

Copyright © 2019 Sixth Sense Solutions

ISBN: 978-1-946014-37-5 (Ebook version)

ISBN: 978-1-946014-38-2 (Paperback version)

Cover by Zoran Petrovic, Fiverr.com name visualarts

Cover image: ID 103353396 © Ln5555 | Dreamstime.com

Sixth Sense Books

PO Box 617

Chino Valley, AZ 86323

www.sixthsensebooks.com

To Maggie, with much love (and a whole heap of admiration)

CONTENTS

PREFACE

I've been interested in intuition for quite some time. I don't really know when that interest began, because there was no one specific moment or one specific intuition which sparked me to write this book. It's been a more gradual interest, probably because I became more aware of a problem concerning intuition as I became more interested in learning to develop and exercise another skill, that of dowsing.

Although dowsing has been used for centuries in various ways, I was interested in the fact that, despite its obvious utility, it was looked upon with scorn and derision by traditional science. Yet, if it really was useless, why was it still being used with success? From there it was a short step to realizing that dowsing and intuition seemed to have a great deal in common, which was that nobody could claim with any certainty that they knew where the answers came from in dowsing or where the information came from in intuition. Even more intriguing to me was the fact that although the experience of having an intuition is shared by practically everyone, which is not true of dowsing, hardly anyone seems to be interested in questioning what happens to allow an intuition to occur.

It seemed to me to be appropriate, for my own peace of mind at least, to attempt to discover as much as I could about intuition, this common yet overlooked experience. Although the present inquiry started as a result of an interest in dowsing, I am not overly concerned if those who defend dowsing against skepticism find any arguments to their liking in this book. What I am concerned with is exploring how such a seemingly simple and accepted facet of everyday life, as intuition surely is, can open up such an intriguing view of ourselves and the universe.

I did not really know what I was getting into when I started this book. All I knew was that I wanted to write a book about something everyone can do, unconsciously, and yet which seemed to open up some interesting questions about consciousness and awareness. I had some few ideas and some leads. The original concept I had of the book was of a relatively obvious journey: the mind, unconscious sensing, maybe a bit about how intuition was looked at by mainstream science, and then add a dash of something to do with the world and how we might be connected. It seemed to be a simple thing to begin with.

However, at some point I just knew, without knowing how I knew (a common attribute of nearly all intuitions), that this subject was much bigger and more important than I had realized. I became aware, as I was writing, of the truth of the saying that familiarity breeds contempt. The trap is in thinking that if intuition is something so easy, so obviously achievable, then it must be simple to explain. And the reverse of that is that if it was difficult to do, it must require skill and dedication and that, in turn, demands that it be studied. But intuition is not difficult (it is that very simplicity which had first intrigued me), and yet it is certainly not easy to explain.

As I became more and more engrossed in the subject, so it became more and more obvious that the study of intuition was opening up a whole new range of questions and ideas which had never occurred to me. I had to take into account time and space, consciousness and brain mechanisms, quantum mechanics and philosophy, linguistics and biophotons. I had to confront the idea that intuition challenges our thinking about ourselves and what we are capable of, and I hope I have been able to convey the excitement of those discoveries and revelations sufficiently to intrigue and interest you, the reader.

What began as a simple idea about the way the mind might work turned into a tour of the body, the mind, and the cosmos and back again. Once I committed to the study of intuition, it began to overturn everything I thought we knew about reality, about who and what we are capable of. It forces us to think of ourselves differently. To look closely at intuition, to accept what that close study reveals, will, if we allow it, show that we are amazing beings living in an amazing world doing amazing things that we take for granted. Familiarity, in the case of intuition, should not breed contempt, but wonder.

I hope you enjoy taking the journey as much as I have, and I hope you end up truly appreciating yourself as a result.

Nigel Percy

June 2019

ACKNOWLEDGMENTS

Pulling together a mass of information from a variety of sources and from various disciplines has been challenging and has taken much longer than I thought it would. It makes me wonder whether I would have started it had I known that to begin with.

I would like to thank those who have contributed to this in some fashion, notably Sonya (you know who you are), Anna (ditto), Kirk Biglione and Reverend Smyth. Most of all, I'd like to thank my wife, Maggie, who gave me endless encouragement, usually after I had been staring at the screen having run out of energy or ideas, or both, and the thought of further research was less than inspiring. She saw the potential in what had originally been something of mainly idle curiosity and urged me to stick with it when I might have surrendered and left it a shapeless mass, going nowhere and achieving nothing. Above all, her editing skills have transformed the shapeless mass into something definite and with a coherent argument I did not clearly perceive at first. Thank you!

It only remains to say that any errors remaining in this, in terms of argument, proof offered, or conclusions drawn are mine alone.

Nigel Percy

INTRODUCTION

Imagine it is a sunny day and that you are sitting on a beach. You can feel the warmth of the sun on your skin, and you can hear the waves breaking on the shore, as well as the happy sounds of the people around. You take a deep breath, and the smell of the sea is wonderful. You drag the fingers of one hand through the sand, enjoying how the warm grains feel. The other hand is holding an ice cream cone, and you are enjoying the strawberry flavor of it. You tilt your head back a little to watch the gulls overhead. It is a good day.

That is how we experience the world. Our five physical senses tell us what we need to know about it. It is natural and normal. Our eyes tell us what is around us. Our ears fill in more of the details. If we want to be certain about something, we want to touch it to make sure. If we think that smelling or tasting something will give us more information, we'll do those things. Everything around us is information of one kind or another, and all that information comes in through our five senses.

The description you have just read was processed by your brain after your eyes sent messages to it, and a picture was built up inside your head. Your picture will be a little different from someone else's, but you will have a picture created by the way you processed the words.

Everything we do and everything we experience, it seems, follows that same route: sensations sent to the brain for processing. It is a comparatively straightforward set of channels we all have, and we all navigate our way through the world in the same way.

But that is not the whole story at all.

Consider the following. You are relaxed and at home, watching something on the TV. The phone rings and suddenly, before looking at it, the name of an old friend you haven't seen in years pops into your head. There is no special ring tone for them; it's just the ordinary default tone, but you feel certain that's who is calling. You pick it up, not recognizing the number, and you were right. It really is your old friend calling.

Was that a lucky guess? But why would that name flash into your mind when there has been no contact for a long time? There were no clues at all, yet you just 'knew' who it was. There was no way you could explain to anyone how you knew it or why it felt right, but the proof was when you picked it up. There was no possible way in which any of your five senses—sight, hearing, touch, smell or taste—could have provided that information. It felt as real as anything else you had experienced, yet at the same time, you felt more certain of that information than if it had come to you via one of the five familiar senses. There could be no question of it at all. But if your physical senses didn't provide you with that information, then how did the information arrive?

Most people wouldn't have gotten around to asking that last question. One of the reasons for that apparent lack of interest is that it's only intuition. Everyone has it. It's nothing special, is it? Or, perhaps they don't want to think about it, because if they did, then everything they thought they knew about themselves or the world is on shaky ground. But it is that question and the others which naturally follow from it which is the basis for this book.

Although I gave a familiar example of intuition—that of knowing who is calling before you pick up the phone to answer—I have become aware that such a feeling or 'knowingness' was just one aspect of intuition. As a result, in this book I take a slightly broader view of intuition than others might. I consider any information obtained without the use of one of the five physical senses to be an intuition. Therefore clairvoyance, precognition, and psychometry, for example, are included.

Some might wish to use the term 'psychic' because of the broader coverage, but I will keep using the term intuition instead, as it is a word which is widely accepted to mean generally what I have just described: the arrival of information without any obvious physical medium. Admittedly, this same definition could apply to the word 'psychic', just as it could be applied to the terms 'psi' or 'ESP.'

However, 'psychic' as a term today has too much baggage attached for it to be used in this book. Its origins contribute to the confusion. It originated from the Greek word 'psychikos.' For our purposes, this word is to be found in one instance only in the Bible, at 1 Corinthians, 2:14. The usual translation is 'the natural man' (in the King James version) or the person without the Spirit, meaning a man without spiritual sensibilities, unable to receive that which comes from the Spirit of God. The term 'natural man' implies the physical aspect only, in the same way that a beast, such as a cow, is natural—entire and whole, a part of nature without any non-physical attributes. In other words, psychikos originally meant anything but the world beyond the senses, which is how it is normally considered today. The root word 'psych' comes from 'psyche' which is usually considered to mean spirit, breath or soul, because of its association with the Greek goddess of soul or spirit, Psyche, the lover of Eros. So it has connotations with being blocked from the world beyond the senses and is also associated with that which cannot be sensed: the soul or spirit—an inherently confusing set of definitions.

The term 'psychic' entered the language in the last quarter of the 19th century, where it was defined as pertaining to the human soul or mind and was more closely associated with the mental aspect than the physical. However, since then, although the word has become more familiar, it has also taken on a more pejorative or derisory aspect.

The reasons for this are dealt with more completely in this book, but it is essentially due to the cultural dominance of the empirical bias in western society. Therefore, presently, we are in the position where the term 'psychic' often implies that there is something special or different or exclusive involved, and a psychic is often perceived as someone who can do things others cannot (and who is therefore often the target of suspicion or derision—being different usually means being a target). Also, because of the pejorative atmosphere surrounding the term, a psychic is often considered to be fraudulent or dishonest. But intuition does not generally suffer from the same disparaging or condescending perspective. After all, it is what everyone has, and hardly anyone will deny that such a thing exists or that others experience it, even if not everyone can agree on what it might be (as we shall see).

As for terms such as 'psi' or 'ESP,' I have chosen to put them aside as well, for the simple reason that although they are recognizable in referring to non-physical phenomena, they are not terms which people generally use in ordinary conversation to describe their experiences. They are, however, very often used by scientists engaged in research of paranormal events, in itself a way of attempting to distance their work from the difficulties associated with the word 'psychic.'

Where psychic abilities can appear to be unusual, intuition is commonplace. Intuition happens every day. For some people it happens often and in small ways which are sometimes difficult to perceive or understand. For others, it is more occasional, but when it arrives, it can have a great effect because of the strength or clarity of the moment. The point is, it seems that intuition is available to everyone, everywhere, all of the time. It doesn't matter where you are born, how you are educated, what you believe in, or what job you do (or don't do). None of those things matter. Intuition is available to you.

And the really interesting part of this is that nobody seems to know for certain how it works. We have discovered more and more about our five physical senses—how they operate, what can go wrong with them, what they need to operate efficiently—but we have very little of that information about our intuition or our intuitive senses.

There are two parts to this book. The first will provide some of the answers about intuition by looking at research and discoveries in many different areas. From this you will gain an appreciation for intuition's complexity as well as understand that it is not something we occasionally interact with, but that it is always available in a multiplicity of forms, and that all you have to do is learn how to recognize it. It is these last points—the ready availability of it together with recognizing it—which I hope to persuade you are the most important of all.

The second part examines how you personally experience intuition and how you can improve your awareness of it and let it help you in your life. It does this by helping you examine which particular form of intuition is your strength. Then, through examples and simple exercises, you will discover how to recognize, strengthen and deepen your intuitive awareness so that it becomes a truly integral part of your life. In so doing, you will be able to fully appreciate how the discoveries and explanations of the first part apply directly to your life every day.

The end result should be that you will have a far greater understanding and awareness of just how large a part intuition plays in your life, and that it will help you to see your life as something much larger and grander than you have previously thought possible.

PART I

UNDERSTANDING YOUR INTUITION

1

INTUITION IN ALL ITS FORMS

Vivian Jaffe: Have you ever transcended space and time?
Albert Markovski: Yes. No. Uh, time, not space... No, I don't know what you're
talking about.
I Heart Huckabees (Film)

We live almost all our lives as prisoners within limits we hardly ever acknowledge, even to ourselves. Everything about us, about the world we live in, has restrictions. The boundaries of our lives which are created by our senses may seem distant, particularly because we have discovered ways of enhancing those senses with technology. Nevertheless, they are still boundaries. Our hearing is limited to a narrow range of frequencies, our sight to a small portion of the electromagnetic spectrum, our senses of touch, taste, and smell are similarly restricted. For nearly all of our lives we are content to exist within these limits. But there are moments when those limits disappear, and we know there is something beyond our senses and the boundaries they impose. It is something which our language struggles to explain. Yet it is something just as real as anything else we have experienced. Indeed, it can seem more real. We call those moments of extra-sensory awareness, when our boundaries disappear, our intuition.

Intuition is when you know something without knowing how you came to know it. It is not the usual way we gain information. It is a breaking out of the limitations of our physical senses. As we shall see, one of the problems faced in looking at intuition is that because it has one name, it is assumed that it has one cause or origin. But if we look more carefully at the wide variety of intuitions, we shall see that some of those 'hits' have different origins or causes. As a result, it becomes obvious that intuitive information arrives via different channels. This is an exact parallel to the way our senses provide information about the physical world via different channels.

In speaking of intuition, there are various terms used to categorize the ways in which it is experienced. Such terms all begin with 'clair,' the French for 'clear,' which carries with it the idea that such information is somehow more 'pure,' or at least less likely to be confused, scrambled or vague. Clairvoyance and clairaudience are the only two such terms beginning with this prefix commonly recognized by dictionaries. They were both accepted into the English language in the middle of the nineteenth century. These are two of the intuitive senses which are the closest correlates to our physical sight and hearing. Others are referred to as claircognizance (sudden understanding or knowing), clairsentience (a feeling) and—less commonly—clairalience (smelling) and clairgustance (tasting).

In general, we tend to rely upon the three physical senses of sight, sound and touch more heavily than the other two, and, in the same way, it seems that the most reported intuitions arrive through clairsentience, claircognizance, and clairvoyance (feelings, knowings, and seeings or images), with a slightly lesser dependence upon clairaudience and with clairalience and clairgustance rarely reported.

The examples which follow all focus on the three most common forms of intuitive sensing. The first and probably the most common type of intuition is that of clairsentience: feeling or sensing something without knowing precisely what such a feeling represents. Sometimes such an intuition is referred to as a 'gut feeling.' Often it is just a 'knowingness' which permeates the body. For some people it's hairs standing on the back of their neck. For others, it is a sense of uneasiness or a vague premonition, an indistinct warning.

Take, for example, Anna, a friend who shared with me an incident which happened to her in Florida. There was a music store on US 1 in South Miami which was very popular with the people in the area. However, whenever she went to the store, she felt a heaviness in her chest and a deep sadness, so much so that she always had to leave quickly. She could never stay there for very long, despite wanting to. It was only later that she discovered that the store was on the site of an earlier slaughterhouse. Anna, saying what most of us have felt, added, "The 'feeling in my gut' that you know something is just not right, even though your brain tries to rationalize it, saying, 'don't be silly, everything is OK, take no notice of that feeling': I know today to really take notice of that feeling."

This gut feeling, hunch or nudge, is also illustrated well in the story told by Conrad Hilton, the founder of the international hotel chain. In his autobiography, *Be My Guest*, he writes that, "the other name for hunch is intuition, and I think intuition can be a form of answered prayer. You do the best you can—thinking, figuring, planning—and then you pray... But the key to intuition is not in the prayer, but listening for a response. If you don't listen, you make it a pretty one-sided affair."

He then goes on to illustrate his theory by telling how he acquired a corporation which would make it easier for him to get control of a very large hotel if the opportunity arose later. He wrote, "The trustees asked for sealed bids... My first bid, hastily made, was $165,000. Then, somehow, that didn't feel right to me. Another figure kept coming, $180,000. It satisfied me. It seemed fair. It felt right. I changed my bid to the larger figure on that hunch. When they were opened the closest bid to mine was $179,800. I got the Stevens Corporation by a narrow margin of $200. Eventually the assets returned me two million."

This example is probably very close to the way many people experience intuition: a feeling that something is not quite right, that something needs tweaking, although there is no logical reason to do anything. Yet the feeling persists, and those who follow it are often able to benefit from following that feeling. And that is the important point in what Hilton said; you have to listen to the message. In his case, it was the nudge to increase his bid. In Anna's case, it was to leave the shop because it didn't feel comfortable.

Another example illustrates this underlying feeling, a sense of something not being quite right. The tale is told by Malcolm Gladwell in his book, *Blink*, of a statue acquired by the Getty Museum. It was of a type known as a kouros. A kouros is the name for a statue of a young boy, usually naked, dating from the archaic Greek period (about 800 BC to 480 BC). In this case, the museum was offered such a statue for $10 million. The documentation appeared to be good, and initial scientific analysis of the statue seemed to support the authenticity of it. This was good enough for the museum, which accepted it as genuine.

Prior to putting it on display, other experts in the period were invited to see it and, presumably, compliment the Getty Museum on its purchase. However, when it was shown to these experts, one by one, their general reaction was one of dismay that the museum had bought a fake. The experts included an art historian, a Greek sculpture expert, an ex-director of the New York Metropolitan Museum Of Art, and the head of the Archeological Society of Athens.

None of these people had the time or opportunity to look at it in detail, or even get very close to it before they each, in their own way, said that they had severe doubts about it and that the museum would be well-advised to examine it again in more detail. It was, in all cases, an immediate reaction to viewing it the very first time and not a result of close scrutiny.

Prompted by these peoples' reactions, the museum went back over the documentation and found problems with it, and then a closer examination of the statue itself found that it was made up of various styles from different places and times. When it was finally put on display (it is now in storage), the accompanying notes said that it may be dated back to 530 BC or could be a modern forgery dating to 1980.

The experts, given no clue about the statue previously, had simply looked at it, and they seemed to have an understanding which came on suddenly and which was in direct opposition to a supposedly careful and detailed analysis and examination. How did that information arrive which manifested as an uneasiness about the provenance of the statue? Not through the five senses obviously, but in some other way. (Presumably the staff of the Getty Museum were unable to allow themselves to have that same sense of unease, possibly due to the amount of money they were investing. They were not free to 'see' the statue in the same way that the other experts were.)

This vagueness about the origin of such intuitions was summed up by Albert Einstein who said, 'I believe in intuitions and inspirations… I sometimes feel that I am right. I do not know that I am." The author Dean Koontz, on the other hand, says, 'Intuition is seeing with the soul,' which really explains nothing except to reinforce the idea that the channel of information is unknown. And remember how Conrad Hilton spoke of how his decision satisfied him and that "it felt right," echoing Albert Einstein.

If having some sort of feeling, usually of apprehension or disquiet in a very general way about some immediate aspect of attention, is a very common form of intuition, then a refinement of that is a premonition, which can manifest as either clairsentience (a feeling) or, more vividly, as clairvoyance (seeing the future). The intuition itself, although linked to an event, if it is of the clairsentient variety, can nevertheless consist of vague feelings, similar to those above, but is nearly always associated with personal safety. And it is probably because these forms of intuition often can involve some sort of event or accident in the future that they are more frequently reported and remembered because they are more dramatic.

In this second group, amongst the best-known ones involve the sinking of the Titanic. Before it sailed, 55 people, or 4% of the expected total of passengers or crewmen, had canceled or changed their minds at short notice. George and Edith Vanderbilt (of the Biltmore Estate fame) left it so late to cancel that their luggage sailed without them. There are several stories of passengers having premonitions about the ship and indeed one crewman, Chief Officer Henry Tingle Wilde, wrote to his sister saying, "I still don't like this Ship. I have a queer feeling about it." He died in the accident. In fact, there are 19 documented experiences of hunches and dreams about the sinking of the Titanic.

In describing intuitions as experienced by various people, it is important not to draw some arbitrary line saying that one example is of intuition, but the next is not. The only important point to remember is whether the person who has the intuition cannot account for how they perceived it. That distinction holds true for all the examples in this chapter.

Having said that, another example of a premonition comes from an unlikely source, that of a British comedian. Michael Bentine, one of the founding members of the influential radio comedy The Goon Show, served in the Second World War as an RAF intelligence officer. In his book, *The Door Marked Summer*, he shares some of the paranormal encounters he had. One of them was how he knew which pilots would not return from a mission. He simply looked at them, and those whose faces turned into skulls ended up dead on their next mission. It was not something he could control, and he really didn't want to see such things, and he told nobody about it at the time. This was firstly a visual premonition, a form of future clairvoyance, which created the feeling of foreboding, but it was most certainly a premonition, this time about other people. His ability to somehow 'see' the future seemed to be at some personal cost, in that he foresaw the death of his son in a plane crash and the death of a friend, a politician killed by an IRA bomb. As an aside, it is possible to speculate that some people who have similar abilities do not permit themselves to see such disturbing events.

Perhaps the most impressive example of anticipation of the future, being also a most impressive example of future clairvoyance, albeit without the usual accompaniment of foreboding, comes from the British Air Marshal, Victor Goddard. In 1935, when the incident took place, he was a Wing Commander. He had flown from his base in Andover in the south of England to Turnhouse, an airfield near Edinburgh in Scotland. Nearby was an old airfield named Drem, which was in disrepair. He had spent part of the day before the incident inspecting the place and had found cows and sheep grazing there, and the buildings fallen into a near ruinous state. Leaving to return to Andover, he quickly ran into a heavy storm. He was unable to climb above it, and in the turbulence his plane plummeted 8,000 feet. Deciding to fly below the clouds to get a visual check on where he was, he knew that Drem was nearby, assuming his course was as he thought it was. It was a risk, as if he had been wrong there were hills nearby into which he would have crashed. However, under the base of the storm clouds, he soon saw the familiar sight of the old hangars ahead of him and continued toward the airfield. Now certain of his course, he climbed again into the clouds which suddenly parted before him, leaving him in bright sunlight. He saw Drem below him, but there were no cows or sheep, and the hangars looked in good repair with well-laid tarmac all around. As he looked down, he saw five aircraft: four biplanes and one monoplane which he did not recognize, all painted yellow, with mechanics in blue overalls. In 1935, planes were constructed of aluminum and Air Force mechanics were dressed in khaki. Quickly the clouds and rain returned, and he lost sight of the airfield. At his base in Andover he told some colleagues of his experience but was met with skepticism.

Within three years, however, all the details he had seen at Drem became fact. Firstly, mechanics, beginning in 1937, were dressed in blue uniforms, and training planes were painted yellow in the same year. Then in 1938, Drem was rebuilt and reopened as a flight training school. And the monoplane he had seen but not recognized was the single wing trainer known as the Miles Magister, which had its first flight in 1937.

The details of the information he saw, some of which only became obvious in later years, was remarkable. Again, this was not something he particularly wanted. In fact, his mind was very occupied with staying alive and not falling into the Firth of Forth or smashing into the nearby mountains in very bad weather. And yet, somehow he saw the future of a small plot of otherwise unremarkable land. It could not, with accuracy, be called a premonition, but it certainly shared a relationship with the future which premonitions have.

In each of these three examples, some aspect of the future became known to the recipients. In the case of the Titanic, it was vague but had a foreboding. That was probably due to the fact that the lives of the recipients of the premonitions were under threat. For Michael Bentine, the glimpse of the future had nothing to do with his own safety, but concerned those he worked with, while Victor Goddard's was the most detailed and precise and seemingly had nothing to do with the safety of himself or those he saw. And yet in each case, some information about the future—either very soon in Bentine's case, or years ahead in Goddard's—was perceived.

A third example of clairvoyant intuition does not involve the future so much as the present. For example, there once were, in Spain, a group of people known as Zoharis. These people were supposed to be able to perceive clearly what was beneath the surface of the earth. Veins of water, corpses, and treasure were all equally perceivable by these people. They were able to see in present time and present location. That this is not a lost historical ability is shown by the example of Pieter van Jaarsveld. In 1963 in South Africa, he became famous for his ability to 'see' water deep underground. The 12-year-old boy said that, to him, the water shimmered like green moonlight through the surface of the soil.

Others can see in present time but in different locations. If that sounds a little difficult to believe, then consider the story, told by Christopher Bird in his book, *The Divining Hand*, of Peter Harmon in Portland, Maine. He was a driller and a water dowser (water dowsing being one of the most familiar uses of this skill). He often used dowsing to locate the drilling site for his clients who needed a well on their properties. If it was impossible to travel there, he would work remotely with them over the phone to help them locate the best place to drill. On one occasion, speaking with a client in Oklahoma, he told the man to go to the big dog house out in the back field. Close to the north-west corner of that he would find a Coca-Cola bottle, and that would be the best place to drill. The farmer went there and found the bottle. "How in hell could you tell the bottle was there?" he asked. Harmon replied, "Well, I can see it because I'm there!" While it might not be a perfectly acceptable scientific explanation, it was as close as Harmon could get to expressing what he did.

Perhaps the clearest examples of gaining information in the present time but from a different location are those arising from the work originated by parapsychologists Russel Targ and Harold Puthoff, which was funded at one time by the CIA and later by the Air Force and Army, which then established its own program. The technique became known as Remote Viewing, and the project was known as Stargate, into which the US government poured millions of dollars over a period of 20 years.

Information about Stargate was declassified by the CIA in 1995. In essence, remote viewing under Stargate was an attempt to systematize clairvoyance. Of the many examples where a remote viewer was given very little information about a 'target,' the remote viewing by Rosemary Smith of a downed Russian bomber in Africa provides an excellent example. This act of remote viewing was spoken of by then-President, Jimmy Carter. He said, "She went into a trance. And while she was in the trance, she gave us some latitude and longitude figures. We focused our satellite cameras on that point, and the lost plane was there."

There are numerous other examples of the ability of people to 'see' over distances, not all of them engaged by the military, as Peter Harmon's story testifies. Indeed there are many examples of people with this ability being able to assist police forces uncover crimes. There is the example of the Dutch clairvoyant, Gerard Croiset, who in 1961 used only a photo, some clothes, and a map while in the Netherlands to locate the body of missing Edith Kiecorius in Brooklyn, New York.

The badly decomposed body of Steven Williams was located using remote viewing in 2006. Williams' friend, Robert Knight, was concerned about him, and remote viewing said that he was dead, and that his body was in some brackish water near Santa Barbara, California. The details proved to be accurate.

So far, we have looked at the common feelings of an intuition or hunch, as well as examples of accessing the future in some fashion and being able to 'see' remotely to gain information. If these are the most common, or probably the more commonly reported, types of intuition, there are certainly others types which exist.

Victor Goddard saw the future of an airfield in great detail as he flew over it. The historian Arnold Toynbee saw a similarly detailed vision of the past. He was later to go on and write a monumental 12-volume work, *The Study Of History*. In 1912, however, he was traveling in Greece. On

January 10th of that year he was sitting on a hill above Pharsalus (modern Farsala), where he knew that an important battle had been fought in 197 B.C. between the Romans and the army of Philip V of Macedon. It was a sunny day, but he was suddenly surrounded by a mist, the like of which was recorded on the day of the battle. Suddenly he 'knew' that the two armies were there nearby, and that they were groping their way toward each other in the mist. As the mist before him cleared a little, he saw the Macedonians charging downhill, but exposing a gap in their forces as they did so. He watched as a Roman commander wheeled his troops quickly to take advantage of the gap and fall upon the unprepared Macedonians. Toynbee even averted his eyes from the subsequent slaughter but clearly heard the screams of the wounded and dying as he saw a small group of horsemen galloping away. Then, just as suddenly, the air cleared and he was back in the brilliant sunshine, and the scene and the sounds had vanished.

It had been very real indeed to him. The battle had been plainly in view before him, and then the armies had vanished as quickly as they had arrived. The basic information about the battle, the result of study, was known to him. But this time, being at the site of the battle, he was transported to it somehow across time.

In case this sounds too much like a vivid imagination, consider also that Toynbee had other glimpses of the past. Once when in Oxford he 'witnessed' the suicide of a fugitive from Roman justice when the fugitive's wife rejected him. The event had taken place in Teanum in Italy in 80 BC.

Toynbee's interests were in the distant, classical past, and his most detailed visions were of that time. However, there are other examples to suggest that personal preference has little to do with such intuitions. For example, in Liverpool, England, there is a street named Bold Street. This street and the area immediately around it has been the scene for several different experiences of the past, going only as far back as the 1950's or 1960's. People have been walking along and seen shops and vehicles from these decades. Some have actually gone into the shops and tried to purchase items unsuccessfully with credit cards which did not exist then. The experience has been so real that, in one case, a woman took her doubting mother back to a shop she had entered the previous day only to find that it was now a bank. Once, a shoplifter, being chased by a security guard in 2006, turned into what he discovered was a dead end alley. He waited, but the guard didn't appear and so, thinking he had successfully escaped, he sauntered out but felt something was not quite right. The cars looked wrong, and traffic lights were in the wrong place. He took out his cell phone but found no signal. He saw a date on a newspaper which said it was 18th May 1967. Continuing to walk, this time a little more scared, he finally saw that his cell phone was receiving a signal. Not only that, but the surroundings looked correct. However, looking back down Bold Street, he saw the people and cars from the 1960's. When his story came out, the security guard was also interviewed, who said that when chasing the thief, he turned into the alley and his quarry had disappeared completely. The newspaper made inquiries and found that all the details related by the thief as to what he had seen were accurate. The intriguing aspect of this example is that it is almost as if the area itself is imposing a clairvoyant ability upon people such that they are entirely subsumed within it and it becomes, for a time, their reality.

Of course, such incidents as these are on the extreme edge of the usual idea of intuition, yet they nevertheless are ways in which information is gained outside the physical channels. Although all the senses of both the thief and of Toynbee were operating as normal in both cases, it was as if the body itself was not normal, in that it had somehow removed or been removed from the present. Both cases are, if you prefer, examples of whole body intuition, ones where the person, without any apparent change internally or any evidence of separate items of information being made known, is presented with a different 'reality.' Usually, it is one or more of the senses which are involved, but there is no reason to suggest that such a totality of experience cannot be considered as being an intuition.

Certainly the more common intuitions of the past are usually less detailed than the two examples above. When I was living in England, for example, I enjoyed visiting the many historic buildings which seem to dot the landscape. One particular time I was visiting, if I recall correctly,

Worcester Cathedral. I could be wrong about the building, but of the events I have no doubt at all.

I was strolling around enjoying the place, looking at the windows and the pillars and staring up at the roof. Eventually, I moved towards the crypt. This was reached via some wide stone steps and did not feel as enclosed or 'cut off' from the rest of the building in the way that most crypts are. I was standing on the steps debating whether to continue down or to end my visit and seek some lunch when I got the distinct impression of a fire blazing on the steps. I didn't feel threatened by it, I just got a quick flash of a picture. It surprised me, and I recall taking a step back. At the same time, I got the impression of death and fighting taking place there. It was nothing I could describe in detail. I did not see it, but I somehow knew of it. I knew that it had taken place, but I had no idea how I knew. The sudden flash of insight was all a bit confused but very apparent to me. I stood for a moment or two longer, trying to make sense of it, hoping I might be given further details, because it had all happened so fast, but eventually I gave up, as I could sense nothing else. Feeling a little confused, I scanned the guidebook, but there was nothing of help there.

A few moments later, still a little disturbed by the vividness of it, I was staring up at some of the arches when one of the guides approached me. Perhaps I looked lost, perhaps he was bored, perhaps it was meant to be. Anyway, we fell to talking and we soon found out that we both had gone to the same school (albeit at different times) and spoke of the buildings and the teachers we both knew. It was a very congenial chat which took some time.

Eventually, the talk turned to the cathedral and when he had begun to help out there. I casually asked if anything had happened of note in the crypt. He launched into a detailed description of a nobleman (one of Elizabeth's favorites, I seem to recall), who, having lost favor at court, and in the manner of those days, was considered a threat and was to be taken prisoner, which would have ended in his death. Naturally, the nobleman resisted and was eventually cornered in the cathedral. A fight ensued and several deaths resulted. At some point in the fracas a fire was started which trapped the supposed felons inside, and there they had died. All this, he pointed out, happened not in the crypt itself, but on the steps leading down to it.

I suppose I must have looked somewhat amazed, and I remember telling him I had felt something there, something which had given me the impression of what he had said. I mentioned that I had thought I had had the impression of flames and the feeling of violence, something I would not have told a complete stranger. He did not dismiss my observations but nodded and said that other people had reported similar sensations, although he had never noticed it himself. To him, it was just a part of the history of the place.

Why did that happen to me? I had no need of that information, yet I received it in a fashion which I could not and still cannot explain. Mine was a brief glimpse of the past in that particular spot, a claircognizance if you will, in that it was a sudden, if somewhat vague, understanding. It was a hurried snapshot together with a feeling which, combined, gave me an insight. Or, to put it another way, I received information about one event which took place in a building which has had countless thousands of events since it was built. Of course, it could also have been classed as a clairvoyant experience, given that I had seen a flash of an image.

Whilst it is easy to allocate specific phenomena to each of our physical senses, it is not quite so easy to say with precision which label should be best applied to an intuitive experience. Where my insight was a clairvoyant flash accompanied by a feeling, others might only have experienced the feeling (as Anna did in the music store) or even 'heard' the fight.

The point to bear in mind is that while it is undoubtedly true that, as we shall see, intuition has distinct channels through which it arrives at our awareness, it is not always definite which channel is predominant. Indeed, it could be said that an attempt to tie an intuitive experience to one channel is not helpful, in that it seeks to analyze and compartmentalize something which is more holistic. Therefore the terms used to categorize intuitions are not to be considered definitive, but suggestive only. However, and this is important to bear in mind, such terms do have a purpose, in that they remind us that intuition arrives in various ways, utilizing various channels, modes, or processes in the same way as our physical senses do.

Accessing the past does not necessarily always have to be in such an uncontrolled fashion. For example, the ability to 'read' information about an object is, according to Colin Wilson, who wrote several detailed studies on human potential, the best authenticated and commonest of all abilities generally labeled as 'psychic.' It is often now referred to as token-object reading but was originally termed psychometry, which is a variant form of clairsentience or clairvoyance, in that an object provides the focus for the resulting intuition. The word psychometry literally translated means 'soul measurement,' although when it was coined by an American doctor, John Rodes Buchanan in 1842, he intended it to mean 'measuring by the soul.' He found that when he passed around various chemicals wrapped in brown paper to his students and asked them to identify the contents, some of them were able to report tastes of salt or sugar in their mouths. Then he found that some of them could hold a sealed envelope containing a photograph, and they were able to give precise descriptions.

William Denton, who was a professor of geology in Boston, hearing of Buchanan's experiences, tried the same approach, but with geological specimens wrapped in thick paper. His wife, his sister-in-law and his son turned out to be extremely proficient. A fragment of volcanic rock, for example, caused his sister-in-law to have visions of lava pouring into the ocean where there were tall ships. The fragment, in fact, came from the 1840 eruption of Kilauea in Hawaii when there were ships from the United States Navy visiting.

Obviously, the earlier example of Gerard Croiset locating the body of Edith Kiecorius is another example of psychometry, but that was in the present. Not everyone can handle an object and see both present and past as well as the future. Some people, it seems, have a greater facility with one or two of these times, but not always all three.

Another type of intuition involves that of having a sudden awareness or understanding of something which had previously eluded the recipient.

This a pure claircognizance, and I have a personal example of this type involving European history.

I was studying for my history degree at the same time as I was fully employed. It required a lot of reading, and a great deal of my spare time was taken up with this. The syllabus I was following involved the whole sweep of British and European history for most of the last 2000 years. There was a lot to cover, and there were nine exams to take at the end of it!

One evening, feeling tired, I was reading for an essay on European history about the Mongol armies and their incursions into Eastern Europe in the thirteenth century. For some reason, I was only half-concentrating on the text while my mind was trying to resolve how this was going to fit in with my previous knowledge. Suddenly I was overcome with a sensation which, while not quite a vision, was a whole understanding of a vast field of history. As I sat there, I could quite clearly see how the Mongols fitted in to the development of European history, how they forced changes to occur and how Europe as a whole was changed by their appearance. It was sudden and overwhelming and incredibly clear. It lasted for a short while, and I felt as if I could see the whole development of European history from a god-like perspective. Nothing was unknown to me in that moment. Everything was related and perfectly obvious. Sadly, the vision faded and, with it, my complete understanding. It left fragments behind, but I had lost the totality. Nevertheless, those fragments which remained were incredibly helpful in my understanding.

It is important to note that the understanding I had was not intellectual, in that it was not arrived at by consciously reading and then formulating an idea or assembling previous knowledge in a new way. It was a sudden awareness or overview which I knew I could not have achieved by grinding my way toward it. Instead, it was a synthesis which arrived in its entirety, complete and encompassing the whole sweep of Europe over many, many years. And it was, for that brief moment, completely understandable and obvious. The clarity of it, the clearness implied by the prefix 'clair,' was perfectly apt.

Such insights or understandings have been reported over time by various people. One of the most famous was that of the theoretical chemist Kekulé who discovered the arrangement of the benzene atoms in a dream-like state. The formula for benzene had been known about for a time before his vision, but the structure itself was difficult to understand. After his vision, pure and applied chemistry were able to move forward very rapidly, and the German chemical industry expanded dramatically. Interestingly, seven years prior to that, he had had another dream-like state or reverie in which he had seen how carbon bonding in chemical structures worked. The understandings arrived without warning, but in his case, he was able to retain enough to continue working the problem until he arrived at a resolution.

Perhaps the most famous example of this sudden apprehension of a vision is that of Samuel Taylor Coleridge, the poet, who fell asleep reading about Kubla Khan and awoke with about 300 lines of poetry already written in his head. He managed 54 lines before he was interrupted by a man from the village of Porlock who had come to discuss a business matter. It lasted an hour and Coleridge, upon returning to the poem found, "…with the exception of some eight or ten scattered lines and images, all the rest had passed away like the images on the surface of a stream into which a stone has been cast."

Robert Graves, the poet, described his own experience when he was at school. It was a summer's evening and he was sitting behind the cricket pavilion when, in his words, he suddenly 'knew everything.' The 'everything' he knew was all aspects of his education. It was "but a simple method of looking sideways at disorderly facts to make perfect sense of them." It was still apparent to him the next morning, but he could find no satisfactory means of writing it down before it finally dissipated that evening. He called it a "supra-logic that cuts out all routine processes of thought and leaps straight from problem to answer," and he believed that we all possess a peculiar power not recognized by science.

Sudden deep insights such as these have obvious connections with an ongoing activity. Also, while premonitions might be considered to be active, in that they are recognizable by their sensations or emotions, there is also another type which might be considered to be passive or hidden in some fashion, such that although there is no specific sensation or emotion about the future, nevertheless there are actions taken which avoid a later tragedy or accident. In such cases, it is only when the incident has occurred is it possible to understand why such actions were taken.

Such a type of intuition is not easily classified in the same way as the previous examples. In the physical world, we have five senses. In the intuitive, supra-sensory world, there seems to be another type of channel for information which, as yet, has no name, but which does seem to be reacting somehow to the non-visible world. This type of intuition is perhaps the most prevalent in many ways and will be looked at more closely later on.

The most stunning example of such a covert intuition occurred on Wednesday, March 1st, 1950 in Beatrice, Nebraska. At 7:27 pm on that day, the West Side Baptist Church was demolished by a natural gas explosion. What made this of interest is that the church choir was due to practice as they always did beginning at precisely 7:25pm. They would normally assemble at 7:20 and be ready to sing five minutes later. However, on this particular evening not one of the fifteen people who should have been present at that time had arrived. Every single one of them had experienced some delay for one reason or another. One had to iron a clean dress, another stayed to finish homework. One had fallen asleep, another didn't want to leave her warm house, another had an urgent need to write and post a letter, and so on. Each had a different reason for being late, and many of them could not explain why that evening was different. None of them reported that they had a premonition, yet they all managed to stay alive.

That these people were not an exception was highlighted by a study made of train wrecks in the years 1950 to 1955. William Cox, the investigator, looked at the numbers of passengers aboard each train when the accidents occurred and then compared that number with the usual numbers. He found something very interesting. In every example, for every crash he investigated, there were fewer people riding the trains on the days of the accidents. In one car, for example, there were only nine passengers instead of the typical 60 that rode that train.

Something was telling people not to ride on those days. Presumably, some passengers had a stronger 'push' to avoid the train than others. Or maybe, as in the church in Nebraska, things so arranged themselves that they missed the train and had to take another one.

The same exact thing can be found to have happened on the aircraft which were involved in the 9/11 tragedy. In total, they were carrying less than half the usual numbers of morning commuters on those planes. Only 22% of the seats were occupied in the plane which struck the Pentagon, while those which struck the north and south towers had 26% and 19% occupancy.

These are all examples of something happening which overrode the usual activities and so avoided the accidents. It is probable that you have had a similar experience when you took a different route to work and later discovered that there had been an accident or just a huge traffic jam on your usual route. I suggest that such 'avoidance' intuition happens regularly.

This other intuitive channel is also where the information is sometimes represented as a compulsion. And compulsions can be exhibited in various ways. For example, if there is a strange compulsion to avoid something which can only be discovered later, similarly there are examples of compulsions to do or say something. One relatively famous example was when the actor Alec Guinness, on his first night in Hollywood, met James Dean, who invited Alec and his companion to join him for a meal. Before eating, he showed Alec his brand new sports car. Upon seeing it, Alec asked him if he had driven it yet. James said he hadn't. At which point, Alec begged him not to. Alec looked at his watch and saw it was 10pm on a Thursday. He said if James drove that car he would be dead by 10pm the same day next week. James Dean died in a car crash the following Thursday afternoon. It was, said Alec Guinness, entirely uncharacteristic of him and seemed almost like a compulsion against which he had no control.

If that was an example of a compulsion to speak, then a compulsion to act can be illustrated by the following story. IT systems analyst Kirk Biglione and his wife were planning a vacation to Japan in 1995 which was going to be costly. Kirk wanted to be able to converse with at least some fluency when they were there. He assessed the various learning methodologies available at the time and decided that a program called Power Japanese was the most effective. However, it was also a costly CD-ROM, being priced at somewhere around $300. This was something he felt was unaffordable at that time, considering all the other expenses. However, he still would have liked to use it. This was before websites like eBay were available for such purchases. E-commerce generally was then in its infancy. One afternoon, a rare time when he was not working, he found himself at a shop which sold old software of various types. There were racks and racks of disks. He found himself going through all of the inventory one by one, and a part of him realized that this was a strange thing to be doing, and he should not be wasting his time. But another part of him felt that he could not stop himself. He carried on in this frustrated frame of mind until the very last rack revealed a copy of Power Japanese for a ridiculously low price. There had been something driving him onward to find it when he felt he should have been doing other things. It was a compulsion he could not avoid. The compulsion itself was not of any specific information, but a way of getting him to achieve a specific goal when there was nothing to suggest that was what was happening.

All the previous examples concern people or people and places. But it is important to realize that intuition can occur between species as well. For example, Joan Ranquet, an animal communicator, has written in detail about many of the cases brought to her in her book *Communication With All Life*. She helped one client who was having problems and was being bucked off by a horse he thought he had a good relationship with. The mare informed Joan that it was because her back really hurt and that she was also upset by her owner's inability to understand her need. With this realization, the mare's back was restored to health, and the relationship between horse and rider was again a happy one. When Joan explains what she does, she uses exactly the same terms we have come to recognize as being indicative of intuition. She says, "I use telepathy (the transference of *pictures, words and feelings* (my italics)). Many people aren't aware that we are all animal communicators; I have simply developed a skill." For her, clairvoyance, clairaudience, and clairsentience are how she operates, gathered under the umbrella term of telepathy. That is no different at all from how the other intuitions described here have been experienced.

If it can work between humans and animals, then intuition can also work between humans and plants. George Washington Carver was an agricultural chemist who developed 536 plant dyes, numerous by-products of the peanut, face powders, wood stains, petroleum substitutes, and many other plant-based products. He simply said that he would walk in the woods and gain flashes of inspiration. But he also tended plants and gave them loving attention, gaining an early reputation for nursing sick plants back to health. Carver once said that "all flowers talk to me and so do hundreds of living things in the woods. I learn what I know by watching and loving everything." The key element here is that there is an obvious connection between human and plant where information flows both ways.

Here, intuition seems to be at a more basic level: that of understanding and appreciating the plant for itself and, by attending to it in the right way with the right frame of mind, it responds. That 'knowing' about how to respond, what to do for the plant, is perhaps the most basic intuition of all, one which requires only that you attend to what is before you in such a way as to make it prosper and grow.

Even at first glance, intuition appears to be an astonishing and remarkable aspect of being human. Admittedly, some of the above examples might appear to be extreme, yet in no case was there an effort made to acquire the information. If, after reading them, you feel that such feats are beyond your ability, then the rest of this book will, I hope, disabuse you of that notion and also allow you to see that, despite these outliers, intuition is always available to you in many different forms, each of them just as surprising in their own way as these examples.

From these examples, then, it seems that there are various ways in which we can access information which bypasses the usual five senses operating in the everyday world. Virtually everyone has had a feeling about something, even if it could not be termed a premonition. Some have clearer intuitions than others or have them in differing forms, but it seems to be something which is generally available to everyone. The past, present, and future all seem equally accessible, even if there is no consistency in such access.

To assume that all such stories involve the same channel of communication is analogous to saying that all our five senses are the same and operate in exactly the same way. Just as the five senses utilize access to different channels of information, so intuition utilizes different channels. The mistake is to assume all intuition comes through the same channel. By accepting that different channels or intuitive senses exist, we shall see that it is indeed possible to examine intuition more carefully, and so understand how it operates and from that, how it interacts or intersects with our daily lives.

2

WHAT THEN IS INTUITION?

Definition of a classic: a book everyone is assumed to have read and often thinks they have.
Alan Bennett (Dramatist)

Definitions help us know if we are all talking about the same thing. It is easier to explain something when everyone agrees on what is being explained. If I were to explain to you how certain ropes are made, from growing and harvesting hemp to the final coiling of the rope, even if the terminology was new to you, you would understand easily enough, because the end result is clear in your head. A rope is a rope. It has one meaning but can have different varieties, different purposes, different materials even, but it is still rope.

That is not the same when speaking of intuition. As we have seen, intuition arrives in different ways involving entirely different modes of perception. This means that one of the major problems with intuition is that, despite the fact that most people are able to guess what it might mean, and, despite the fact that many people report having intuitions, there is not one absolute definition. The reason for this is that not everyone can agree which intuitions should be included in any definition. Some, for example, would rule out Air Marshal Goddard's precognitive view of Drem airfield, while others would dismiss the Nebraska church choir—the first because it is too detailed and seemingly has nothing to do with the circumstances or contained any emotion, and the second because there were no premonitions about the explosion.

Others will speak of hunches and gut feelings as being acceptable, but psychometry as being completely beyond the pale. Some people would prefer to use the term 'psychic' for several of the examples, as if there is a subtle but definite difference between them. But, as we have seen, this term itself is not as useful as its supporters would have us hope.

It does not help to discover that there seems to be no clear and reasonable definition of intuition presently in existence. Daniel Cappon, a psychologist, writing in *Psychology Today*, for example, can argue that intuition is really only ancient instincts and writes, "Intuition is, in my view, the product of all the processed ancestral instincts of the species, through which unconditioned reflexes become conditioned and organized into patterns of adaptive behavior called instinct. Ultimately instincts coalesce into intuition, the capacity for which is stored deep in the brain." If this were to be the accepted definition, then most of the previous chapter would not fit at all, even the first examples of gut feelings.

Another approach claims that intuition is nothing more than a pattern recognition ability, and that the individual is somehow aware of the implications inherent in the pattern before them and acts accordingly. Of course, in this approach there is an awful lot of unexplained processing going on, like a black box; many patterns in the environment may lead to intuition, but the link between the two is not evident. It hides more than it reveals.

But the real problem with such an approach is that it takes intuition and wrings it dry. The fact that the Titanic's passengers and crew voiced their fears does not fit here. There are no ancestral instincts to explain them, neither could there be some discernible pattern in the fact of the ship's sailing.

Much of the research into intuition involves looking at how it is used in business, so that experiments can be more easily constructed and results correlated and compared. The danger of this approach is that if sufficient papers on the subject are published, intuition will be relegated to the world of economics and finance, and the hunches and feelings of everyday people will have to be labeled as something else.

The authors of a paper, *Unpacking Intuition*, have said, "The nature of intuition presents a particular set of methodological challenges for documenting intuitive decision processes, capturing intuitive episodes, measuring individual differences in intuitive processing, and identifying the neural correlates of intuitive processes and outcomes." In other words, investigating intuition is difficult.

One paper titled *Intuition: Myth or a Decision-Making Tool?* by Marta Sinclair and Neal Ashkanasy, suggests that intuition has three commonalities: (1) intuitive events originate beyond consciousness, (2) information is processed holistically, and (3) intuitive perceptions are frequently accompanied by emotion. The authors' three points do have a certain relationship to how most of us perceive intuition, and they also acknowledge that intuition was immune to scientific enquiry for centuries and that it was relegated to the realm of philosophy, which we will look at later.

It is worth pointing out that there are researchers who are beginning to urge that intuition itself should be considered in a new light. For example, Robert Campbell, writing in the *Journal of Communicative and Integrative Biology*, says that science, "has run the risk of becoming a purely materialistic bias itself, according no proper place to the human spirit or to intuitive insights that have guided the evolution of human cultures, even though this includes the guiding insights of the most important contributors to the sciences." He goes on to say that there is a pressing need to restore a proper balance.

Marta Sinclair of Griffith University in Brisbane, Australia has written an article with the encouraging title of *Misconceptions About Intuition*, which seeks to show that much intuition research is based on misguided ideas. (This is the same Sinclair mentioned in a previous paragraph.) One of the problems, she says, is that early intuition research had to borrow terminology from other disciplines, which has led to confusion and misconceptions. Intuition in business was often the main focus and looked more at outcomes than on processes, and the role of expertise in the business arena clouded the waters as well. In summary, Marta Sinclair is asking for a greater awareness of how intuition can reveal itself and a greater sympathy in how it is examined. This attitude can only help later research in this difficult subject.

One of the reasons for the problem of pinning intuition down is that even when people speak of it, they use vague and sometimes lightly mystical terms, as we have seen, or it is only referred to as something so obvious that it can stand by itself without any type of explanation. It is simply something that is there. Of the first type, the poet Clarissa Pinkola Estes declared that, "…intuition is the direct messenger of the soul," while Malcolm Gladwell (he of the kouros story) says, "Insight is not a lightbulb that goes off inside our heads. It is a flickering candle which can easily be snuffed out." The artist, Florence Scovel Shinn, in keeping with this difficulty of truly tying intuition down added, "Intuition is a spiritual faculty which does not explain, but simply points the way." And remember how Conrad Hilton spoke of how his decision satisfied him and that "it felt right," echoing Albert Einstein. As for simply accepting its presence, Isaac Asimov said, "The true scientist is quite imaginative as well as rational, and sometimes leaps to solutions where reason can follow only slowly; if he does not, his science suffers." And Jonas Salk has said, "It is always with excitement that I wake up in the morning wondering what my intuition will toss up to me, like gifts from the sea. I work with it and rely on it. It's my partner."

It seems, then, that intuition is something you just feel or 'know' or accept in some fashion, but that words do not have the power to capture exactly what it is. They can only chart the edges of it without ever being able to get to the center, the very heart of it. This difficulty of using language to express or describe intuition is the subject of a later chapter. Here, it is enough to acknowledge that when we speak of it, we seem unable to grasp it fully.

Given this problem, it should be of no surprise, therefore, that any definition of intuition ends up in a soup which tries to please everyone but satisfies no one. Take this example from Wikipedia: "Different writers give the word 'intuition' a great variety of different meanings, ranging from direct access to unconscious knowledge, unconscious cognition, inner sensing, inner insight to unconscious pattern-recognition and the ability to understand something instinctively, without the need for conscious reasoning."

Chambers Dictionary, for example, describes intuition as "…the power of the mind by which it immediately perceives the truth of things without reasoning or analysis: a truth so perceived; immediate knowledge in contrast with the mediate," while the *Shorter Oxford Dictionary* also has "…the immediate knowledge ascribed to angelic and spiritual beings, with whom vision and knowledge are identical." *Merriam Webster's International Dictionary* includes the following; "…the power or faculty of attaining to direct knowledge or cognition without rational thought and inference."

It seems to be very much a case of 'you pays your money, and you takes your choice.' But in all the above definitions there is the assumption that intuition is one thing only, and that the definition is applicable to all forms of definition, yet it seems that the most common of intuitions, that of the gut feeling, the sense of something, is overlooked

The word intuition originates from the Latin verb "intueri" which is most often translated as to look into, to admire, to stare, or to contemplate. Indeed, the larger dictionaries will refer to this in some fashion in the etymology of the word. The sense is that there is something, some object, worthy of attention which requires more than a swift glance, as though something under the surface will reveal itself. There is a hint of something hidden which can be seen and understood by paying closer attention. And, to a certain extent, that is true about how we tend to think of intuition; there is something more to what is going on around us, and if we look into it sufficiently carefully, more will be revealed.

Given the problems that arise from trying to pin intuition down as one thing easily defined and described and stemming from the fact that language cannot really describe it, it is no surprise to find that people have turned to talk of angels and spirits as the origin of it, as the second definition above does. The mystical is the preferred medium for many, probably because it is an easy way of equating the unknown aspect of intuition to another, equally and ultimately unknowable source. But that explanation is just as empty, because it does not explain how such a thing is possible except by saying that some other hidden mechanism must be at work in order for the 'message' to be sent and received. It also does not explain how different 'messages' in different forms arrive for different people and why some people seem never to receive some types of 'messages' at all.

It is for this reason, the varieties of definitions, that I have taken a different and broader approach. In all that follows, intuition will mean only one thing, and will have only one definition, and it is this:

Intuition is the perception of or reaction to information in any form which either bypasses the rational and logical mind, giving immediate insight or knowledge not directly associated with or mediated by the usual five physical senses, or is associated with a different time or place but is presented as being 'here and now' to the recipient.

To simplify that somewhat, intuition should be considered to be a non-rational, information-gathering system working in parallel with our physical senses, but which is separate from them and their connection with the rational mind. Neither is superior, but each is complementary.

The reason for offering such a definition is because all the previous ones seem to either act as a funnel, narrowing the term down to mean something quite precise and exclusive, or are so vague as to be meaningless. However, as intuition is, without doubt, a common experience, and that commonality involves information arriving in a direct or indirect way causing emotions or reactions on the part of the recipient, it would seem sensible to make the definition more inclusive and based on that underlying commonality. Such a definition will therefore include all of the examples in the previous chapter. In the stories where people avoided accidents and incidents such as rail crashes, their actions can be said to be a reaction to information, even if they were unaware consciously of so doing, in much the same way that the irises in our eyes react to differing light levels without us being aware of it.

Using this definition, we will be able, as in the rope analogy earlier, to talk about intuition in a meaningful way, even though there may be different modes or types of intuition in the same way that there are different uses and types of rope. If we keep clearly in mind that intuition involves information in some way, it will be easier to examine it. Information does not always have to be present in the conscious aspect of the mind to have an influence on actions.

Accepting all those stories in the previous chapter makes for an exciting and intriguing journey to understand something we all experience in one form or another. Now that we have a concrete and more apt definition, we can begin to see how intuition is a natural and inevitable part of our lives. We will turn first to examine how intuition, or non-rational information, is able to be perceived by the physical body. And then we will look at the major conundrum of the mind and how that might be involved in explaining some of the intuitive senses.

3

INTUITION AND GUT FEELINGS

When you have that gut feeling, you have to go with it. Don't go back on it.
LeBron James (Athlete)

The obvious place to start our understanding of intuition is with the physical body, as that is where we most often experience intuition as a feeling of some kind. We are reacting to something in some fashion, and reactions of our body to some type of stimulus is a survival trait. Physical reactions alert us to possible dangers in our environment. Consider how we jump at unexpected sounds, or how we go on alert when meeting a new group of people for the first time. These are just two simple examples of involuntary reactions we can experience.

In the same way, any intuitive sensing which is perceived as a feeling, whether of comfort and safety or of alertness to an unidentified threat, must have some biological value. Given that, then it is clear that intuition must necessarily be natural, that we also all have it, and that it must play a vital role in our lives in the same way that our physical senses do. What the vital role might be and how its value can be fully understood is something to examine more closely later on, after we have looked more thoroughly at what intuition consists of and the ways in which it can be accounted for.

One of the most common indicators of an intuition, as we have seen, is a feeling or sensation. Einstein said that he could feel something was right even if he didn't know it was right. Our bodies evidently have an important role to play in intuition. And when we begin to look a little more closely at them, there is certainly a sensitivity in our bodies which can surprise us.

However, for the most part we tend to view the body as a sort of machine, in that if we do certain things to it—such as eating a lot of greasy foods—then certain outcomes are predicted: we will gain weight and our complexion will worsen, amongst other things. If we want larger muscles, we use weights to stress them. If we expose ourselves to specific germs, we end up with specific illnesses. Most people hold to the belief that, as we grow older, then our bodies become less efficient and in need of extra help and support in the form of walking sticks to help our balance and locomotion, and medicines to help our organs, as well as spectacles and hearing aids for our failing eyes and ears.

Perhaps it would be fair to say that we take our body very much for granted. We put food inside it, give it some exercise and we expect it to keep working, albeit with decreased efficiency over time, until such time as it stops all the self-repair and we depart this life. It is only when our body does something we're not expecting, when we get a cold, or break out in a rash, or strain a muscle for example, do we do something different to it. Only when it does something annoying do we pay it more than casual attention.

And yet the body is an incredible thing, capable, as we shall see, of doing incredible things. If all we appreciate is that gut feeling of an intuition, that alone should be enough to make us amazed, for we have no clear understanding of how it happens. There is a sensitivity within us, or which is part of us, that is extraordinary. It is a delicate sensitivity to the physical world around us. Such a sensitivity has been identified, for example, in changes in heart rates which are associated with abnormal cosmic ray activity or geomagnetic storms in the earth's magnetic field.

Such phenomena can be measured by instruments but would seem to be remote from any interaction with our bodies. Yet the electrical activity of the brain has also been shown to be affected by these events. Indeed, abnormal variations in geomagnetic states have been shown to affect the number of acute cardiac events, including sudden cardiac death and heart attacks. Additionally, magnetically intense storms have been correlated with increased psychiatric hospital admissions.

There are people who are sensitive to earthquakes and can sense them before they arrive. Symptoms can vary greatly, but can include loud tones in the ear, migraines, mood swings, nausea and dizziness amongst others, in much the same way that some animals have been observed to become agitated or disoriented in the period preceding an earthquake. The ability to sense earthquakes is thought to be based on being able to hear the extremely low frequency (ELF) waves generated by the relatively rigid tectonic plates meeting at a fault line, or perhaps to sensing subtle changes in the Earth's electrical field caused by such events. Such ELF waves are capable of traveling great distances, and it is entirely possible that fluctuations in the Earth's electrical field could travel similar distances.

One of the most sensitive and tested people to have ear tones associated with earthquakes is Charlotte King from Oregon in the US. In fact, the ability to sense these tones has been called the 'Charlotte King Effect.' Scientists have found that she can hear in the ultra-low, very low and extremely low frequencies. That means she can hear frequencies as low as 2 to 7Hz. The normal lower range of hearing for healthy young people, for comparison, is about 20Hz, degrading with age. To make those numbers a little more understandable, 20Hz is about an octave below the lowest note on a bass guitar or is associated with the very low note of an organ, meaning it's difficult to hear. It is rare to hear anything below that. As an aside, Charlotte King also suffers pain, numbness, and headaches as a result of her sensitivity.

Even our ability to understand or interpret other peoples' intentions and make corresponding moral judgments can be influenced by a magnetic field above and behind the right ear applied in as short as 500 millisecond bursts. This was revealed by first identifying the area of the brain where we process other people's thoughts, intentions, and beliefs. This area, known as the right temporo-parietal junction (RTPJ) varies slightly from person to person. The magnetic field was applied by a method known as transcranial stimulation, and the result was that the subjects of the experiment were told stories and were asked to judge if they were morally objectionable or not. After stimulation by the magnetic field, it was found that they ignored the intentions of those involved and focused more on the end result. As a result, they found the stories that were used to be more morally objectionable than those who were not so stimulated. And all from a very short magnetic stimulus to a specific part of the brain.

We are sensitive to our environment in many ways. We have to be in order to survive. The ways in which we are sensitive are sometimes more obvious than not. About the most obvious example of our sensitivity is how we react to the sun. Our eyes detect light, and some of the signals generated pass to a small area within the hypothalamus (itself a tiny area deep within the brain) to two very small, wing-like structures called the suprachiasmatic nucleus (SCN), composed of thousands of nerve cells which fire according to the perception of daylight, effectively re-setting our clocks every morning. Signals from the SCN are passed through to the pineal gland (more about this gland later), which generates melatonin. Melatonin is thus regulated by this day/night, 24-hour cycle and, in the late evening there is a surge in production of this hormone which signals organs to slow down and repair themselves.

Rapid Eye Movement (REM) sleep has a 90-minute cycle, for example. Our brain waves change during this period and signals to our limbs shut down to avoid us acting out our dreams. The reason for these recurring periods of sleep and precisely what occurs then is unknown. All we do know is that the absence of sunlight is the beginning of the whole process. The hormones we have floating around inside us are released according to our inner clock. They boost or curb processes as appropriate. When we sleep, our body temperature drops and our bowel movements are suppressed. Our blood pressure increases as we awaken and, after being awake, bowel movements are more likely. The light of sunrise causes our bodies to prepare for the coming day. The sun is, without doubt, our body's main regulator.

If we stay with the body-as-machine analogy for a moment longer, we can gain a better, although still wildly imperfect, understanding of our body if we assume that it consists of various differing aspects, all of which, like a complicated clock, are interconnected in some fashion. They are separate entities which can be removed and replaced to the benefit of the whole, much as we could replace or repair some cogs inside a clock. Heart and lung transplants, blood transfusions, repairing fractured bones, as well as hip and knee replacements are all examples of this.

Our common attitude toward ourselves as a purely mechanical set of systems is, however, deeply wrong. It would be difficult to ascribe sensations of a 'gut feeling' to such a machine. However, decide to change how we look at this body we inhabit, and we can then begin to see that there are some fascinating possibilities, especially with regard to understanding our intuition.

Physically we are aware of the presence of others, even if we are not always conscious of our reactions. For example, we have a natural reaction to anything which is in our personal space, even if we don't necessarily gain precise intuitive information from it. August Kinzel, a psychiatrist, investigated what he called body buffer zones. Our body buffer zone is the area we consider to be our personal space, and we are aware of anyone who enters into it.

This personal space is most obvious when observing birds on a wire. They maintain a regular distance between each other; swallows, for example, have a space of six inches. Seagulls, on the other hand, require about twelve inches, and flamingoes, about two feet.

For us, however, our emotional state will dictate the size of our body buffer zone. For a normal, relaxed individual, Kinzel found that the zone was roughly cylindrical and extended approximately eighteen inches in all directions. However, when he explored this idea with violent prisoners, he found their zone was much larger. It extended about three feet in front of them and nearly four feet behind them. Any encroachment into that zone was met with hostility which increased as the distance lessened. However, we have also learned generally how to control this space and can, therefore, crowd together into trains and elevators, suppressing our hostility and angling our bodies away from each other.

There is, it seems, an inherent awareness of what is around us, as well as a natural reaction to who is present. For example, if there is a group of people holding a meeting, there is a sense of that group's combined zones. If someone leaves the group there is a subtle but detectable change in how it feels, just as there is when someone new arrives. At this basic level we have an awareness of changes which impinge upon our personal space. In essence, we know what is our space and what is not.

Our bodies are obviously more than mere mechanical automata. A machine tends to be thought of in isolation; it works by itself. But Sayer Ji, a natural health expert, speaks of the ways in which we human beings are closely connected with everything else. MicroRNAs are present in the food we eat. (MicroRNAs are a subset of RNA. RNA is a messenger from DNA that regulates the genome and controls the synthesis of proteins which are essential for virtually everything happening in our body, from the structure of our bodies to holding our genetic code. The term for this activity is gene expression.) When we consume the food, the MicroRNAs enter our blood and alter our gene expression. Sayer Ji says, "Basically, we're finding that over the course of evolution we have literally outsourced gene regulation to the plants in our environment, and also there's other passengers on this journey with us. Bacteria produce microRNAs, for example. And they help to orchestrate the complexity of our being… there is interspecies communication occurring through the mechanism of MicroRNAs, such that the biosphere is actually all one, on some basic molecular level."

Obviously an interconnectedness does exist, otherwise we would fall apart and die at the least little change within us. But the parts themselves are far more complicated than we imagine. Not only that, but they are not even the same type of 'thing' as the 'us' which they make up. But, as Sayer Ji said, a great deal of what makes us up, which constitutes us as human beings, is not necessarily what we would consider human to begin with.

If that sounds too much like an exaggeration, consider the following. Research microbiologist Kiran Krishnan says, "We've got 150 times more bacterial and viral DNA in our body than human DNA. It's looking like 99% of metabolic function, things that we do on a daily basis that make us human, are coded for by bacterial and viral DNA. We can barely do anything for ourselves. We need the microbial DNA to conduct necessary functions to live, to digest food, to breathe. Even how our emotions and view of the world are concentrated and how they're characterized are dependent on the types of microbes and microbial DNA we have in our system… We're really a walking, talking ecology. We're like a walking, talking rainforest. There's a massive amount of structure to the ecology. Different parts of the body, different ecologies within the body have to communicate with one another. We require all of their help in order to be human."

One of the largest concentrations of these microbes is in our gut. This is made clear in a paper, *Gut Feelings: The Emerging Biology of Gut-Brain Communication,* where it is stated that, "There are between 200 and 600 million neurons in the human ENS (Enteric Nervous System), which is equal to the number of neurons in the spinal cord… The size and complexity of the ENS is not surprising…: it interfaces closely with our largest body surface (the intestinal surface area, which is approximately 100 times larger than the surface area of the skin), with the largest population of commensal microorganisms of all body surfaces (100 trillion microorganisms from 40,000 species with 100 times the number of genes in the human genome), with the gut-associated immune system (containing two-thirds of the body's immune cells) and with thousands of enteroendocrine cells (containing more than 20 identified hormones)."

The figures are surprising and bear repeating. Our gut contains *40,000 different species* of microorganisms which have between them *100 times more genes* than is in our genome. And that is normal. We do not usually consider that we are populated by a vast number of non-human microorganisms. But their existence (and their importance to us as functioning humans) can also help explain one aspect of intuition. Think of how intuitions can be referred to as 'gut feelings,' 'a sinking feeling in the stomach,' 'butterflies in the stomach,' 'stomach in knots,' or 'a gut reaction.' The microbes in your gut weigh about the same as your brain. Indeed, the gut has often been called the second brain. It can function independently of the brain, unlike every other organ in the body. As mentioned above, it also has a dense nervous system of its own, the enteric nervous system. The brain and the gut can communicate with each other. As Krishnan says, "The bacteria within your gut can actually produce chemicals like neurotransmitters, peptides (the building blocks of proteins), things that could influence your thought and the way you react to the world around you and directly send it to your brain through the vagus nerve and the enteric nervous system."

If we have non-human DNA inside us, then the next step is to understand how that collection of bacteria could explain the gut feelings of intuition. That this is indeed possible has been known about since the latter half of the twentieth century.

On February 2nd, 1966, an event took place which clearly showed that non-human organisms were able to respond to external, non-physical stimuli: in this case a threat in the form of a thought. On that date, Cleve Backster thought to burn the leaf of a plant in his office which had been wired up to a polygraph (lie detector). He had hooked it up originally to see how long it would take water to reach the tip of the leaf where the electrodes had been attached. The thought of burning the plant's leaf caused the polygraph pen to jump off the top of the chart. Backster had previously worked for the US Army Counter Intelligence Corps and then the CIA, during which time he became interested in interrogation techniques and the use of the polygraph. He formed his own company to advance the understanding and use of the polygraph and developed the Backster Zone Comparison Test, which is the worldwide standard for lie detection. In other words, he was an expert in the equipment he was using, and what he saw convinced him that something important and previously unknown had occurred.

The realization that a plant could be proven to respond to a mental image led Backster to devise further experiments involving, in the end, plants, shrimp, eggs, yogurt, sperm cells, and white blood cells, all of which responded not only to thoughts and emotions of people, but also to the deaths of other organisms as small as bacteria. It led him to develop the theory that what the plants and others were responding to could not be called extrasensory perception (as they lacked most of the five senses to begin with). Instead, he referred to it as primary perception because it took place at a more basic level.

In essence, what his work showed was that all cells and all organisms were able to react to their environment, to threats, emotions, and thoughts. He proved, for example, that white blood cells were still capable of reacting to their donor as much as three hundred miles away. All of those reactions were recorded electronically. In other words, primary perception was able to send electrical signals, in the same way that nerves impulses operate.

We have a variety of cells and bacteria in our bodies, and Backster's experiments have shown just how sensitive they all are and how they all share this basic primary form of perception. As we have seen, the gut is full of a huge number of such organisms. It is perfectly acceptable to assume that our gut microbiota will react to various stimuli in the outer environment, just as Backster proved, and that such reactions will trigger emotional responses within us due to the gut-brain connection. It would seem, therefore, that we have identified a system operating within us which can easily account for that common sense of an intuition, a 'gut feeling.'

Dean Radin, the Laboratory Director at the Institute for Noetic Sciences in California, asked attendees at a conference if they had often or frequently experienced gut feelings about people or events. Of the nearly 500 respondents, 89% of females and 72% of males said that they did have such responses. As Radin warned, sometimes a gut feeling is nothing more than emotional turbulence or a bad burrito. But the strength of the response was sufficient to encourage him to set up an experiment whereby one person, the sender, in front of a computer set up to show random scenes or music, attempted to contact the receiver and send the emotions evoked by the pictures and sound displayed. The results showed that the receiver had changes in the electrophysiology of the gut responding to both the happy and sad emotions of the sender. The odds against chance for these responses were 1,100 to 1. In other words, following on from Backster's work, there does seem to be the ability to 'pick up' on other peoples' emotions, even at a distance, and it is likely that the gut is intimately involved in this process in some fashion. Of course, the question then turns to how such information might be apprehended. Sayer Ji spoke of the entire biosphere, of which we are a part, as being one. Perhaps we should instead use Backster's term of primary perception, even if we cannot yet fully understand the precise mechanism.

But gut feelings, which are basically a form of clairsentience, are not the only way in which we experience intuition. If the gut is the source of that basic, primary intuition of a vague feeling, then intuitions where there is a little more depth, a little more information, are to be found, in the physical body at least, in the heart and the brain.

4

THE HEART AND THE BRAIN

The intricate connections of mind and body must exceed our imagination, as from our point of view we are peculiarly prevented from observing them.
John Desmond Bernal (Scientist)

If the gut has specific properties which explain some of our intuitive hits, then the heart may also have some relation to intuition as well. If we can have gut feelings, we can also 'know in our hearts' about something, that is, knowing without intellectual or rational analysis.

The heart has a very strong electromagnetic field. According to Rollin McCraty of the HeartMath Institute, the heart "generates the largest electromagnetic field in the body. The heart's electrical field as measured in an electrocardiogram (ECG) is about 60 times greater in amplitude than the brain waves recorded in an electroencephalogram (EEG)." The field the heart generates is 5,000 times stronger than that of the brain. It is able to be measured several feet away, as well as between two individuals who are physically close. This extension of the field of the heart might help to explain how we can size up a person quickly. Richard Branson, the highly successful entrepreneur and founder of the Virgin

Group, has said, "I tend to make up my mind about people within thirty seconds of meeting them."

That assessment has to be based on something other than a carefully considered analysis. Branson's example is one, perhaps, we can all relate to. We have all probably met someone of whom we have formed an opinion within about thirty seconds, based on nothing obviously tangible. In such situations, we usually refer to it as making our minds up about someone, although there are occasions when we might refer to 'having a feeling' about the person. Branson specifically referred to making his mind up, rather than having a gut feeling. Information, in some form, has to have been transmitted and received between Branson and the person he was meeting. Some of that information could, of course, have been through conversation, but often it is not what is said, but the way it is said, which is important, and that, added to another carrier of information, another transmission if you will, would 'fill in the blanks' of meeting that person and 'making up your mind' about them.

The field of the heart could be responsible for that additional information. As the field is electromagnetic, it is exactly the same type as that used by a cell phone. And a cell phone, as we all know, can send and receive information in the form of voice, images, and text. What the field of the heart might contain is hard to define, but there is no reason not to suppose that such a strong field could contain some type of information about the person. It could be that this field is only concerned with the emotional state, or it could also contain something more detailed about the person as a whole. What is received or interpreted may also depend on the specific sensibilities of the receiver, of what they are expecting to receive, or what they are looking for, as well as what they are capable of.

An example of this is provided by a friend, Anna, the same Anna who had a bad feeling about the music store. At the time she was a therapist using a protocol called Body Talk. This is a system which seeks to address the whole person: lifestyle, genetics, and history, the emotional, physical and environmental influences, in order to evaluate what is needed to bring about health and well-being. Using kinesiology—a method whereby specific muscle resistance is used to assess answers to specific questions—the underlying issues can be revealed. However, in

Anna's case, sitting with a client, she not only got answers in the usual way, but started seeing movies in front of her eyes which helped her to understand more about the problem the client was having. In the example she related to me, she said how she saw a young child drinking milk in a room with a small dog on the floor nearby, leading her to define one of the issues as a milk allergy. Given the closeness of such a therapist/client relationship, it is certainly possible that, because Anna was open to an understanding of her client and was in a highly receptive state, she was able to extract significant and useful information from the client's electromagnetic field emanating from the heart. The image she saw was indeed a scene from the client's past, suggesting that all of the past of each one of us is encoded and held in some fashion within us.

Perhaps such insights and intuitions in cases of close proximity might almost be considered to be examples of biological psychometry. Instead of holding or touching a physical object, it is the electromagnetic field of the person which is touched. In fact, to take the analogy further still, perhaps all intuition is nothing more than variations of forms of psychometry, in the sense that we are inevitably, always connected with the world around us.

The gut and heart, then, are two organs we associate with feelings about intuition, and there seems to be at least some idea of how they might be involved in this, even if the mechanisms are not yet fully understood. However, it is the brain itself which appears to be more heavily involved, in that the brain is where we get the sights and sounds, the perceptions of an intuition. We should also understand that we can translate intuitive perceptions from any source as being in our minds.

However, we should be aware that the brain and the mind are not necessarily the same thing. When we have an intuition, we might experience it in the mind, but that does not automatically mean that it occurred in the brain. The brain is the primary processing center. The vast number of connections within it, somewhere around 100 trillion it is thought, provide for a still-not-fully-understood complexity. The workings of the brain can be subject to physical measurement and analysis to some degree in a way which is very different from the mind. The mind is often considered to be a product of the brain's activity. Both are involved to some degree in processing information, no matter whether it is from the physical senses or the intuitive senses, but it is to the mind to which we first turn.

The study of the mind has a relatively short history. Such a study was not possible until the seventeenth century, when Descartes split the mind and the body into separate areas of study with his statement, 'I think, therefore I am.' This was the basis he worked from, for the only thing he could assure himself of in all the world was that he was able to think. The activity of the mind, of thought, was the foundation from which he built up an assurance that the world actually did exist. But, by so doing, by focusing on the activity of the mind, on thinking and perceiving, he allowed the mind to be studied separately from the body. Prior to that, it was man as a whole which was the subject of enquiry: Man and Nature, Man and God, Man and Justice, and so on. There had been no real investigation of the role of the mind before Descartes said that it was the most important aspect of man, in that it alone could be used to explain the world, and that what went on inside it was hugely important.

Such a split allowed the mind to be studied by itself without reference to anything else. Thoughts, dreams, beliefs, madness and the like were now viewed as being held within and perhaps caused by the mind. It is also important to acknowledge that such a split, along with the discoveries of the likes of Copernicus, Galileo, and Newton, also saw the development of science and empiricism: the drive for experimentation and measurement at the expense of a more holistic and subjective experience of the universe. The scientific side of that split, with its emphasis on the impersonal examination of reality, has been increasing in importance more and more ever since, such that the opposite side of the divide, that of the personal viewpoint and its relation to that which resists measurement and analysis, has become devalued and, often, derided. Such things are considered mere illusions by those on the scientific side of the divide, an illusion being that which is not real.

The desire to understand and explain and measure has not, however, made huge inroads into coming to terms with the mind. Indeed, there are more difficulties than would at first appear. Part of the reason for this is the problem of what is meant by the mind. It is, in many ways, the same problem as defining intuition; everyone thinks they know what they are talking about, but a closer inspection quickly reveals the scope of the problem. Different disciplines will have different definitions or interpretations. To a philosopher inquiring into the mind, the main concerns will be those of memories, personal identity, the very personality of the individual. A whole school of philosophy, that of phenomenology or the study of direct experience, has developed from Descartes' split. To some, the mind is also where the logical and rational faculty resides. To a psychologist, the study of the mind is intimately connected with the study of how people behave. To other scientists, the mind is where thoughts, ideas, attitudes, and beliefs are to be found, and they are more concerned with how such things arise than with their effects upon people. Close physical examination of the brain and detailed measurements are the ways in which such theories are developed. And for a religious person, the mind can be where the spirit, that which seeks to be closer to God, is to be found. Dictionaries, as we have seen, merely reflect the current uses of the word and offer a rag-bag of possible definitions which together cover a vast range of human activity.

It may be that you have never given the word much thought yourself, but have a sort of basic approximation of what the word 'mind' means to you. It might be the thing which defines you as being different from every other person, or it might be that your mind is where thoughts occur and nothing else, or where emotions originate. But how then *should* we think of it? 'Mind' is such a common term that we tend not to think carefully about what it might mean to us. The fact that the word is used in different ways does not help us to think clearly about it: 'Looking for peace of mind,' 'I'll give him a piece of my mind,' 'Make up your mind,' 'Open your mind,' 'A powerful mind,' 'Be mindful of others,' 'In two minds.' All of these common sayings infer that the mind is important in various ways, but do nothing to say *how* it is important or what it is specifically concerned with.

One of the intriguing concepts arising from this difficulty of definition, is that the mind, whatever it might be now, has changed. It has been suggested that the mind was not always as it is now, that it has developed or changed in some fashion. The English psychologist Stan

Gooch, for example, suggested that present-day humans are the result of Cro-Magnon and Neanderthals interbreeding, and that Neanderthals were not the big-browed, stocky, virtually non-verbal individuals of popular imagination. We tend to think of them as inferior cousins, lurking in caves and living short, brutish lives. Gooch, however, maintained that they were far more advanced than that. Indeed, he said that they had a language of their own, a suggestion which was ridiculed at the time. Archeological remains, however, now point to the Neanderthals as having sophisticated tools, wearing jewelry, and having a deeply religious sense of the world around them. The idea that they had a developed language has since been given credence by the discovery of the FOXP2 gene in Neanderthal DNA. This is a gene which is associated with language abilities; a version of that same gene is found in us modern humans. Then there is the discovery of hyoid bones amongst their skeletons. The hyoid anchors the tongue among other things and is indicative of language ability. Indeed, the sophistication of some Neanderthal sites has led an archeologist, João Zilhão, to say of Neanderthal remains in Spain, "The one thing these finds make clear is that Neanderthals were behaviorally modern. They were not like early modern humans anatomically, but they were cognitively as advanced or more so."

The more aggressive Cro-Magnon man, the eventual successors to the Neanderthal, met and mingled with them over a period of about 10,000 years. During that time, Gooch believed, there was interbreeding. Although this idea was originally thought impossible, it has since been proven that the modern genome of peoples of Eurasia contains between 1% and 4% of Neanderthal genes. Neanderthals are still alive in us.

Stan Gooch believed that the Neanderthals were well-advanced in many ways and that their culture "was a moon-goddess-worshipping, matriarchal, food-gathering society, where women governed all matters." Incidentally, this is a view supported by the work of the Professor Emeritus of Archaeology at UCLA, Marija Gimbutas. She studied Paleolithic and Neolithic cultures and religion and wrote extensively on their being female-centered.

The importance of this in our quest is that Gooch believed that this society was able to use intuition. Indeed, he went so far as to say that they gained their knowledge of the world, not through scientific means, but intuitively, implying that there was far less rational analysis of the environment. He preferred the term 'alternative consciousness' to subconsciousness, but also used the term 'intuitive mind' and said that this intuitive mind's function was to convert information into experience. Therefore, if Neanderthals gained their knowledge intuitively, then it would seem, from Gooch's viewpoint, that they felt their way in the world. For example, perhaps they would 'know' that a plant was poisonous, or that a good supply of fresh water was just a little way ahead, even though they were in new territory. If we compare how we, today, sense things, then we cannot necessarily explain how we came to have a particular feeling, only that we have it and trust it, without a 'scientific' analysis. And that would be very much how Gooch said the Neanderthals traversed their world.

Does this mean that we can claim our intuitive inheritance from them? Gooch would certainly have argued so. For example, the human brain has both a cerebellum and a cerebrum. The cerebellum is smaller and sits underneath and to the rear of the cerebrum. The cerebrum is associated with logical and rational thinking, while the smaller cerebellum, according to Gooch, "is responsible for trance states, for dreams, for telepathy, for psychic healing, for spontaneous wounds, for poltergeist phenomena, and all other such matters. It is also the source of and the impetus for religious belief." In other words, it is where you would expect intuition and non-rationality to be found or expressed. Although both Cro-Magnon and Neanderthals had both types of brains, the cerebellum was much larger in the latter, suggesting that they passed on their intuitive relationship with the world to their conquerors, the Cro-Magnon, and so to us. In modern humans, the cerebellum represents about ten percent of the brain's volume but contains fifty percent of the brain's neurons, making it a small but potent area. Modern women, anecdotally more psychically able and more associated with intuition—'a woman's intuition'—generally have larger cerebella than men.

Most of us have become accustomed to an alternate theory about brains which Gooch's ideas do not accommodate. His theory about how the parts of the brain work and what they are involved with goes against the popular 'split brain' theory, which is not now supported by the majority of scientists, as it appears to be too simplistic. Nevertheless, it does highlight how the brain is conceived to work in general; different regions are responsible for different tasks. Anatomically, the brain is more or less divided into two very similar halves, joined by a thick network of tissue. This division has, of course, been of interest for a long time. What was its purpose? When did it develop? Is it essential to proper function? Are the two halves of the brain the same or different and does this connection, this bridge, act as some sort of mediator between the two?

The split brain theory was put forward by Roger Sperry in 1968 after the examination and testing of eleven patients who had had the two halves of their brains separated by surgery in an effort to mediate their severe epilepsy. Their various responses showed that each half of the brain seemed to be dealing with different issues. In general, the left cerebral hemisphere is considered the seat of logical, rational and analytical thinking, and the right hemisphere is the seat of artistic, creative, and intuitive functions. So, a person with a split brain looking at a picture with his right eye (which would be the responsibility of the left hemisphere) and then asked to say what he has seen is unable to, as the speech center is (usually) in the right hemisphere and, because there is no connection between the two, information about the image does not pass from left to right.

There is a tendency to be quite definite as to what is controlled by which hemisphere, whereas there is actually a degree of flexibility. For example, it is not always the truth that the right hemisphere is where language is processed. It can be the left hemisphere. Therefore, it is important not to accept as unalterable truth which hemisphere does what. However, having said that, it appears that the left hemisphere's dominant functions tend to be logic, calculation, and language, while the right hemisphere's dominance tends to be in spatial awareness, facial recognition, visual imagery, and music. Note that intuition does not appear in either list, because that is conjecture based on the concept of creativity, which is presumed to be part of the visual imagery and music dominance of the right hemisphere. Sperry's experiments were not concerned with identifying where intuition might lie.

Julian Jaynes, an American psychologist, perhaps stimulated by Sperry's work on the two halves of the brain, proposed a theory that consciousness did not develop until very late in human evolution. In fact, as late as between 1400-600 BC. He put forward this theory in 1976 in his book, *The Origin Of Consciousness In The Breakdown Of The Bicameral Mind*. He based this theory on the examination of the Greek work '*The Iliad*' where it does not seem, to him at least, that there are any subjective thoughts and that people acted more or less as automata. He suggested that, prior to those dates, people would hear voices in their heads which they claimed were from the Gods, but which Jaynes said came from the other hemisphere, presumably via some rudimentary connection. It was only after the two hemispheres were fully joined, he claims, that consciousness came about. However, that would require a very rapid development in the brain to complete the complex connection of the two hemispheres.

Of course, the problem of defining consciousness rears its head in this argument (something we shall look at in more detail later on), and Jayne's book has stimulated much discussion about the concept of self and what role his theory might play in working with various mental disorders. In a sense, it does not necessarily matter which argument is used: bicameral brain or the cerebellum's role. Both can be used to help explain intuition to one degree or another. Neither, of course, can be said to be definitive in any way, but Gooch's suggestion is given extra weight by the other proposals he made which were later born out by evidence. For example, he said that Neanderthals were red-headed, which has been corroborated by science, as well as the previously mentioned verbal ability, and his assertion, originally considered outlandish, that Neanderthals and Cro-Magnons interbred.

There is also another area of exploration of the brain concerning consciousness (and unconsciousness) which poses interesting questions and might help us to understand where intuition might be found, and it is in the sleep research of Professor Andreas Mavromatis of Brunel University. He was interested in the hypnagogic state, that period when we are about to fall asleep. (The morning period, when we are not really awake, is technically known as the hypnopompic state, although the term 'hypnagogic' is often used for both periods.) These periods—the names simply refer to either entering or leaving sleep—are when we can clearly see images, hear sounds, and experience other illusory sensations while knowing that we are not yet asleep. It is almost like dreaming whilst awake.

The people Mavromatis studied in hypnagogic states seemed to move in and out of what would be 'normal' space and time and had experiences with strange imagery, even entire adventures unfolding very rapidly. Mavromatis argued that hypnagogia was linked to the 'old brain,' or the subcortical area. One of the subcortical structures is the cerebellum which so fascinated Gooch. The older brain structures, Mavromatis argued, take over in the hypnagogic state. There is where imagery, symbols, and analogy happen, rather than structured thought, again much as Gooch suggested.

Mavromatis said that the subcortical processes are always active, and that it is the dominance of the neocortex which suppresses them. However, as they are always active, he argues that they can be allowed to become present to us by holding back the cortical awareness through relaxation or meditative techniques sufficiently for us to experience the subcortical brain.

The subcortical area contains, amongst other structures, the thalamus. For Mavromatis, the thalamus was the 'center of consciousness' and was the probable source of hypnagogic phenomena. He considered it a vital element also because it is linked with the three parts of the brain (the triune brain) which are: the reptilian (the central core), the limbic (early mammalian brain), and the cerebral hemispheres. Also, of particular interest to our investigation: within the thalamus lies the pineal gland, which we will be looking at later.

This relaxation allowing the barriers within the brain to break down could help explain some of the intuitions illustrated in the first chapter, particularly my vision of Europe and Kekulé's insights. There are also those intuitions which appear in dreams and which are able to do so due, in all probability, to the relaxing of the control of the rational mind.

Such intuitive dreams are well illustrated by a story told by Anna Capaldi-Gilbey in her book, *Many A Mile To Freedom*. She had been a volunteer at a children's home where she felt a close bond with a particular two-year-old boy. Whilst she was debating whether to apply to adopt him, the boy, Michael, was taken for adoption by another couple. Anna was heartbroken but could do nothing about the situation. In her words, she said, "A year later, I had a dream that seemed to be a premonition. In it, I was sitting at a small desk in front of a classroom where there was a translucent figure that seemed to float. It was writing on a huge blackboard and each word would then start to disappear after each letter was formed. 'Call HRS' it said. (HRS was the department that handled foster children and adoptions.)

"The following morning I was torn as to what to do. My head was telling me that it was ridiculous, but my instinct told me to ring the department, so after an hour or two of indecision, I telephoned, not knowing what I was going to say. When I mentioned my name, the woman was so surprised and said she had just been trying to find my phone number. Michael had come back into the foster home and I could come and get him the very next day. Because of that dream, I learnt to follow my intuition and not always listen to my logical thoughts."

Anna's dream is an example of information that is of a type of compulsion to do something, but which arrived during sleep. And note how she spoke of the difference between her head and her 'instinct,' a word which is suggestive of something deep and natural. There have been other examples of predictive or precognitive dreams which have been more dramatic, but they may be said to be visions of the future, such as that of Drem airfield, but which happen during sleep rather than wakefulness. Two such famous dreams were those of President Abraham Lincoln and Mark Twain. The president dreamed of his own death, and Twain dreamt of the death of his brother, down to the details of the coffin and the flower arrangement on it. In essence, the information is exactly the same as the various types of precognition discussed in the previous chapter, whereas the more gestalt understanding suggested by

Mavromatis' studies happened prior to sleep and were of a different type altogether.

The gut, the heart, and the brain seem to have some sort of relevance, directly or indirectly, to intuition, although the precise mechanisms are not yet clear. These are the physical aspects of the body but, as anyone who cares to think even a little about intuition, there has to be something non-physical about the body which is also involved.

There has to be some aspect of ourselves which extends beyond our skin, beyond our normal senses, if we are to begin to explain how we know, for example, that there has been an argument recently in a room. The body buffer zones which Kinzel researched are one simple example of an everyday experience about something which is part of our body, but is not really physical. Our personal space seems to lie in that indeterminate area of physical and non-physical sensing.

When we speak of non-physical aspects, it is sometimes hard to know exactly what is being referred to. The obvious reference would be to something which is non-visible, but yet which connects us with the world beyond our sense of touch, for instance. But the non-physical can also mean that there are aspects to what we conceive of normally as our bodies which are far more changeable than we would think.

If we say that our bodies can do certain things—see so far or so close, have a need for food and water and so on—then anything which challenges those beliefs would tend to stretch our ideas of what our physical bodies are capable of. In that sense, such instances can be regarded as non-physical aspects. It is these non-physical aspects of the body, the invisible part of ourselves, as well as the apparently malleable aspects of our bodies, which we shall turn to look at next as a way of understanding those intuitions which appear to come from beyond the range of our usual five physical senses.

5

INTUITION AND YOUR NON-PHYSICAL BODY

All human beings are interconnected, one with all other elements in creation.
Henry Reed (Writer)

If the physical body has fields which can transmit or receive information between people or the environment, then that only goes so far in explaining intuition. From the examples we have seen, some types of intuitive information will not be entirely defined by those examples. The heart and brain fields extend only so far, and the gut biome, according to Backster and Krishnan, is in contact with the world around us. Even if those fields contain information from the person's past, it is only associated with that person present at that time. Yet some intuitions are not of the immediate present or associated with a person presently before you and would seem, therefore, to require other mechanisms to explain them. We need to look beyond the physical body as it is generally thought of and look at two distinct areas which might help us uncover more about our intuition.

The first area to look at is how the body can be changed or extended in some fashion so that it does more than we think it can. The second area to look at is, if the body can be far more sensitive than is usually considered, then where does that extension of ourselves begin to be something non-physical, and what does that imply for our understanding of intuition? From the examples we've looked at, information obviously comes to us from beyond our 'normal' physical senses. What we need to do next is examine what that might mean in practical terms.

Previously we have looked at how the body can be seen or treated as a machine, made up of parts which operate together to make us human. That concept was shown to be inadequate, in that the body is not something isolate and alone, but is inevitably in contact with the surrounding environment. An alternate view of the body is that it has a physical form and physical abilities associated with it. The form can be changed a little and the physical abilities have limitations; we can only run so fast, see so far, jump so high and so on, with the outliers such as Charlotte King and her sensitive hearing. It is this view of the body—that it operates within an accepted and narrow range of abilities—to which we turn next to examine how true that might be.

There are those who can change their bodies in ways which seem almost inconceivable. Bodybuilding and fasting are two obvious examples of changing the physical characteristics of the body, but there are other types of physical change which are more dramatic. Although we can alter our bodies using simple physical exercises, it is clear in what follows that the mental aspects are of probably greater importance.

As we live and grow from birth to adulthood, we may change what we believe in and how we act, but there is a constant thread throughout our lives—of memories, of associations—which defines us as being 'us.' However, when that thread of continuity disappears, problems arise. The most distinct of these problems used to be called Multiple Personality Disorder, but is now referred to as Dissociative Identity Disorder (DID). In many such cases, not only does the personality change, but the physiology can change as well. This has led Dr Frank Putnam, a psychiatrist at the Laboratory of Developmental Psychology at the National Institutes of Health to say that, "A given state of consciousness has its biological reality."

What this means is that dramatic biological changes can be observed as different personalities emerge. Differences in handwriting as well as which hand is dominant; differences in allergies; differences in responses to medication (which is why this disorder is never treated with drugs); and differences in eyesight are among those recorded. This is in addition to scar tissue or other skin features appearing and disappearing. These are, of course, the extreme range of symptoms, but it is thought that somewhere between 1 to 5% of the world experiences some form of DID. Whatever the effects on those suffering from it, the underlying point is that the mind can and does have a direct effect upon the physiology of the body. The body is malleable. The body and the personality are not necessarily fixed.

What the above examples illustrate is that changes in the mind can change the body. This correlation has been known for centuries. Perhaps the most famous and certainly the earliest exposition of the connection between mind and body is to be found in the writings of the Indian sage, Patanjali. His *Yoga Sutras* (written some time between 500BC and 400AD) detail the various advanced capabilities which can be expected through diligent mental discipline. Essentially he taught that these capabilities, or siddhis as they are termed, arise naturally from the ability to hold a deeply absorbed meditative state. The *Yoga Sutras* refer to a number of these abilities. The precise number is difficult to state, because although 25 are mentioned, it is not entirely clear how much overlap there is between them. However, it can be said that amongst such siddhis are the ability to have incredible strength, to see at a distance, to see microscopically, to live without food or water, to levitate, and to know the future and the past. Other similar texts of the same period add other siddhis, including the ability to bilocate (be in two places at the same time), and to have control over the elements, including the weather. While these may seem superhuman, Patanjali emphasized that they were to be considered normal.

That such abilities are within the reach of everyone can be illustrated by the story of Dmitry Lykov. Although not exhibiting a strictly siddhi ability, he does illustrate one extreme of what a body can be capable of. Dmitry was born in the wilds of Siberia to parents who followed a fundamentalist Russian Orthodox faith known as the Old Believers. His parents had fled into the wilderness in 1937, away from the atheistic government, ending up 150 miles (about 240 kilometers) from the nearest settlement. They lived for the next 42 years in complete isolation from all other humans. Dmitry, growing up in this harsh environment, learned to chase and hunt game as well as sleep outdoors in temperatures reaching 40 degrees below zero. Knowing no better, not being told it was impossible and the fact that hunting was essential to the family's survival obviously made him able to endure such privations without the benefit of warm clothing; most of the family were clothed in patched potato sacks when discovered in 1978.

There are other examples of siddhi abilities in other cultures. The medieval period throws up many tales of people sending their doubles to different places in order to spy on their enemies or to gather information. The Anglo-Saxons, for example, had a precise term, a 'fetch,' used for a person's double or wraith. A tale told in the 18th Century described the double of a Sami, an inhabitant of Lapland, leaving his body. At the request of the Archbishop of Uppsala, this 'magician' fell into a trance and visited the archbishop's house to report on what his wife was doing. When he recovered from the trance he told of her preparing food and that he had deliberately hidden her wedding ring. When letters were exchanged, the wife was able to recall the date clearly, because it was the day she had lost her wedding ring and had briefly seen a vision of a well-dressed Laplander in her kitchen. The Sami, as a culture, had a belief in the concept of bilocation, and there are many stories of them being able to visit other places when in a trance.

Emmanuel Swedenborg was a Swedish scientist, mystic, theologian, and philosopher who died in 1772. In his later life he began to experience visions and gained a reputation as a clairvoyant. The most well-known example of this occurred in Gothenburg, about 250 miles (400km) from Stockholm. It would normally have taken about two to three days for news to travel that distance. Nevertheless, at 6pm on Thursday, July 19, 1759, Swedenborg became agitated and told those who he was with (he was having dinner with some friends) that a fire had broken out in Stockholm and that his house there was threatened by it. Two hours later, he declared with relief that the fire had been stopped three doors from his home. The fire was well documented, and the reports of various authorities in Stockholm confirmed the exact time and severity of the fire and that it had approached his home as he had said. There were several other instances of his ability to know things clairvoyantly, but in none of them did he obviously have the same need to go into some form of trance state as the Laplander did. The cultural conditioning of the Laplander more or less demanded that, whereas Swedenborg seemed to have a natural ability to use his clairvoyant ability without any obvious preparation.

It would seem that there are those people who have a natural talent for such things, whilst others may only gain it after considerable effort, or feel that they have to expend such effort to reveal their talent. The chief difference between Swedenborg and the Sami is that where the former was able to 'see' at a distance without his body being visible at the remote site, that was not true of the Sami's approach. The former is now termed remote viewing and the latter is better known as bilocation. However, both were able to access information remotely. This has obvious similarities to the remote viewing project originated by Russell Targ, but without the protocols of his version.

Today, there are many examples of people proficient in various energetic techniques, such as QiGong and Tai Chi, being able to emulate the siddhis described 2,000 years ago. There are studies of such masters being able to start fires with nothing but their bare hands, alter the temperature of their hands by several degrees, or move objects without touching them. A Native American medicine man, Rolling Thunder, who died in 1997, not being trained in any such techniques, was known to be able to command thunderclouds as well as heal people, amongst other things. Daniel Dunglas Home, probably the most famous medium in the nineteenth century, was reliably recorded by many people to be able to levitate.

Dean Radin, in an interview about siddhis said, "...be aware that many simple siddhis will occasionally happen spontaneously, so they shouldn't be regarded as outrageously surprising, nor should they be taken as anything more than revealing what has always been there, just not previously noticed. To attain super-siddhis, like levitation, not only takes a great deal of practice, but also talent. The former is under your control; the latter is not." Furthermore, in his book, *Supernormal*, he adds, "For a Western-trained academic, the mere existence of, say, telepathy would be considered supernormal and thus wildly extraordinary. But for an experienced yogi, it's just a boringly normal minor siddhi."

If there are sufficient examples to show how the physical body's senses or abilities can be extended, then the existence of other fields emanating from or forming an intrinsic yet non-physical part of the body should also seem to be plausible. In the previous chapter we learned of the strong field of the heart, as well as of the changeable nature of personal space, but in fact there are many fields emanating from the human body. This is not surprising given that there are billions of nerve impulses in the body and that those electrical impulses are constantly creating complex fields. But the other non-visible part of us, often termed the energetic or subtle body, has been acknowledged and described in different ways by various cultures, yet there are similarities amongst them.

The reason for looking at what has been said about this subtle body is that it appears to have a relationship with more than the immediate environment, which is the purview of the physical body's senses. And because of that, such a relationship might help us to understand how we can explain such things as premonitions or understandings— claircognizances—which defy rational analysis.

The idea of an energetic body associated with the physical one is gaining credence in the modern, industrialized west, but has long been accepted as fact in the east, as well as in various other cultures around the world and in different historical times.

So far, we have seen that the non-physical fields of the heart and brain, those generated within and emanating from the physical body, can be considered to be of great importance in the sense that they are capable of carrying large amounts of information beyond the body. It is possible that these fields are involved, in some fashion, with accessing similar information transmitted from others. Whether they operate only in transmitting or in both transmitting and receiving (which rationally seems far more likely, as we shall see), they provide one channel of information concerning the immediate environment not available to the physical senses. They do not, it seems, receive information from beyond the body (the immediate environment, that is). However, the beliefs about some form of connection with the world beyond the body are concerned with the idea that there are centers within the physical body which allow interaction with unseen influences or fields, and it is those influences which act primarily as controlling factors in our health and well-being. More than that, however, it is claimed that such interaction is not limited to the immediate surroundings, but that there is some sort of connection beyond that, with the world and even the universe.

The most widely known of these non-physical connections is that of the chakras. These are generally conceived of as being circular or conical or as vortexes which spin and have as their function the ability to 'pull' energy in from outside the body. This energy is thought to be all around us permeating everything, a concept we will look at later in a different context. The chakras are considered to be a conduit between the physical body and the energy of the universe at large.

In the Hindu system, the most widely known of the different variations, there are considered to be seven major chakras running up the center of the body from the base of the spine to the top of the head. Each of these major chakras is also associated with an endocrine gland and organ or organs. Thus the fourth chakra is associated with the thymus, heart and lungs, the fifth with the thyroid, parathyroid, larynx, and so on. Apart from the major chakras, there are said to be many, many other locations where the interface between the subtle and physical bodies occur. In this system, the belief is that it is important that the chakras remain healthy, or there is danger of the associated organs showing signs of disease. It is thought that diseases or imbalances will first manifest in the chakras before they become evident in the physical body.

The belief that there is a naturally occurring invisible connection with something outside of the body is repeated by the various cultures who have their own versions of the chakra system. Tibetans, for example, have a six chakra system which they believe links them with varying realms of existence. Their oral tradition claims that it originated 17,000 years ago.

The Maya of Central America (credited by some with bringing the chakra energy system to India) believed they originally came from the stars. This base belief therefore permeated their understanding and interpretation of how they were energetically connected with the universe. Their subtle energy system was based on the idea that their spirit came from a solar energy and that the chakras (or chaclas as they termed them) were related to the Milky Way.

The Inca also had their own energetic system. Instead of it revolving around a relationship with the universe beyond, they believed that around every person was an energy field which transferred information to and from the physical body. This is remarkably similar to the role of the heart and brain fields in relation to intuition. The chakras, in their opinion, were situated within this field and had threads of light which connect us to the natural world. They brought more focus to a relationship with this world, rather than with the universe at large. However—and this is a departure from the concept of the heart field—they also believed that these light threads allowed a connection with the past as well the future. Again, such a connection, however it might be conceived to operate, would be one metaphysical explanation of how intuitions reaching beyond the present time could occur. The seventh chakra in the crown—there were nine in total in this system, the last two not directly connected with the physical body—was associated with wisdom, transcendence, and illumination, the same as the Hindu system. Also similar to the Hindu system was their belief that the crown chakra was associated with the pineal gland, which we will look at in more detail in the next chapter.

The Cherokee or Tsalagi people, like the Maya, track their origins to the stars, in their case more specifically to the Pleiades. There is, they believe, a connection between themselves and the stars, an energetic connection which can be fully realized via activating the chakras, with the topmost or crown chakra being responsible for connecting to a higher consciousness. For them, as for other cultures, there is the belief that the human body is manifested from the spirit energy, and that the earth itself has a complex web of energy with which the human body interacts. (In essence, this idea is the scaled-up version of the body's heart and brain fields, only this time the interaction is with the planet as well as each other.) Here it is important to note that it is through care of the chakras, the subtle energy aspects, that a more thorough connection with 'higher consciousness' is possible: an awareness above and beyond that which we experience everyday, which is a reasonable interpretation of what intuition is. It is a given that we humans are part of the subtle world of energy. This is a central concept of intuition examined more fully later.

This idea of connection with the universe beyond ourselves and not restricted by space and time was also a part of the belief systems of the ancient Egyptians as well as the Zulu. Each believed there were energy bodies as a natural and inevitable part of existence, and that it was via these bodies that we are connected to the universe and to wisdom or prophecy at the very least. The Egyptians, for example, referred to the sekhem or life force running through the body and that certain types of breathing would prove beneficial in enhancing or strengthening it.

Australian Aboriginals, taking the idea of connection a little further than the above systems, consider that there is no separation between the physical world of objects and the world of creative energy. They see themselves very much as part of the earth, not distanced from it. Everything—animate and inanimate, plants and rocks, animals and people, the Earth and the universe—is interconnected and cannot be separated. They 'feel' their way through the world to a degree which white people would find difficult to follow or emulate, using songlines which tell of how the various creator beings formed the land, the plants, and the animals. By knowing the songs and singing them in correct order, they can navigate the land across vast distances and know what happened where and when without the use of books, compasses or atlases. The land is very much alive to them, and they are an integral part of it in a way which is hard to understand for a non-aboriginal. Although they do not have the same clear divisions of physical and non-physical, the fact that the two are blurred to our way of thinking merely emphasizes their close connection with the world beyond the body.

While this brief survey is interesting in itself, what relation does it have to our exploration of intuition? Obviously, all of these systems emphasize a connection with the larger universe which is not strictly physical. Information arrives from beyond the reach of physical senses. In return, through various disciplines, a person can gain insight, understanding, or wisdom, the exact same thing we gain through intuition. And, as has been said before, intuition is nothing more than gaining information of various kinds which apparently does not arrive in our consciousness via any physical process. Does this mean, then, that intuition operates via the chakras, and that is the end of the trail of exploration?

The obvious answer is no, firstly because we have, as yet, no way of explaining how the chakra system might mediate the flow of information. But it is also because our intuition is shaky and intermittent and gives us distinct feelings, such as premonitions; brief visions, such as my experience on the Cathedral's steps to the crypt; and even distractions such as experienced by passengers on trains and planes which are going to experience accidents. Certainly there might be some intuitions which could fit with such energetic systems, but equally there are others which do not. The energetic body and the chakras are simply another way in which information can come to us. Such things are one more channel or mode of communication, in the same way as eyesight and touch are two different channels or modes of communication with the world around us.

Intuition, as we normally experience it, is more prosaic, more day-to-day, in that it tends to help us with problems, or gives us insights into the world around us. A medical intuitive, for example, can help to diagnose or understand a disease process, but that intuition does not automatically bathe her in some wondrous appreciation of her place in the universe, such as is emphasized in the above cultures.

Certainly it is true that some people are able to see aspects of the energetic body. For example, the subtle human energy field, or at least, one of the major ones, is known as the aura. Some people can naturally see this as a cloud of shifting colors around the person. Seeing it can, in some cases, allow them to perceive illness or past disease or imbalance in the person, reinforcing the ideas above about the health of the non-physical body being important and that we are surrounded by an energy body, or field, which carries information about us. In the case of those people who can read auras, it is the location and color of the aura which they have to translate into words, rather than Anna's vision of the child and the milk which arrived complete and whole. Nevertheless, it is obvious from the example of skilled practitioners that they are quite capable of gathering detailed information from examining the aura which, to many people, remains invisible.

A connection between ourselves, between everything in fact, can perhaps be illustrated by the unlikely story of the crystallization of glycerin. Glycerin is used in medicine, the manufacture of explosives, and as a lubricant. It has been known about for nearly 300 years. But although well-known and much used, chemists had a very hard time in crystallizing it. It was assumed that it did not have a solid form at all. No matter what was done to it, it remained a liquid. Until, that is, a barrel was being transported from Vienna to London. Something happened to it on the journey so that when it arrived, it had crystallized. Although it was annoying for the purchaser, it proved very useful to chemists who borrowed bits of it from the barrel and used them to seed their own glycerin. It proved remarkably easy to crystallize glycerin with such help. However, two scientists reported that although they had successfully crystallized a sample they were working on in their laboratory, they found out that spontaneous crystallization had occurred in all their other glycerin samples, including those in air-tight containers. Suddenly, for no apparent reason, glycerin 'decided' to become crystallized. Either the knowledge that such crystallization could occur was sufficient (and somehow also suddenly made ubiquitous in the universe) to allow it to influence other sealed samples, or the glycerin itself passed on such information to its other 'selves.'

However you choose to explain it, there was a connection which cannot be explained in ordinary terms, but only as something representative of the interconnection of all things. The story of glycerin is perhaps another example of Backster's primary perception at work. It would seem that the idea of the physical body having limitations as to how far it might reach or be connected via the physical senses may be just as inadequate a concept as the previous 'body-as-machine' idea was. The siddhi powers —overcoming gravity, seeing in extreme close-up, or controlling the weather, for example—show that the human body is not restricted by our 'normal' view of the world. Added to that are the various cultural ideas that the body contains energy in some fashion and that there is also an invisible web of energy permeating the world all around us, and that we are able to connect to that as a natural part of our being.

Again we come back to the idea of a connection existing between ourselves and the world around us. In terms of information carried within that connection, intuition can be accounted for by the actions of the biomes in our bodies, by the fields generated specifically by the heart and the brain, and by the wider fields of energy in and around our bodies. This latter idea would seem to suggest that there is more to intuition than mere survival (although that might have been the origin of intuition, perhaps dating back to Neanderthal times) making it something which deals with higher functions, in much the same way that our physical senses have evolved from primarily identifying threats and finding food sources.

But for the connections referred to in this chapter, there is a common idea shared amongst various cultures which is that there is something about the higher energy centers in the body, particularly in the head or on the crown of the head, which is different. The lower energy centers deal more with the physical body. But the higher ones are considered to act as a connection with something bigger or beyond ourselves. Some called it wisdom, others termed it 'higher consciousness.' The Hindu believed that the pineal gland was the vital part of such a connection, and so it is to the pineal gland we turn next, as that appears to offer another channel of supra-sensory information.

6

THE ROLE OF THE PINEAL

Watching television is like taking black spray paint to your third eye
Bill Hicks (Comedian)

In the previous chapter, we saw that the energetic connection with the universe, and through it to a wider awareness, was considered to take place in some fashion in the head, more specifically via the pineal gland. The pineal has usually been linked with one of the upper chakras or energy centers and, as a general rule, the higher the chakra's placement in the body, the more likely it is to be associated with a connection with the energetic world beyond the body. The various cultures' ideas concerning such a connection did not directly refer to the pineal gland as being vital, only that it was associated with the higher chakras, and that association brought with it the possibility that it was some form of mediator between the physical and the non-physical.

The philosopher Descartes asserted that the pineal is "the principal seat of the soul and the place in which all our thoughts are formed." He therefore believed that the soul contained consciousness, and that it resided in the pineal gland. How the soul and the body interacted was, however, never determined. His main contribution, as we saw, was to separate the mind and body into two distinct areas of consideration.

It was the founder of Theosophy, Helena Blavatsky, who associated the pineal with the concept of the third eye, specifically at the brow chakra, an idea which has become firmly rooted in metaphysics ever since. She believed that humans were originally far less solidly physical and were more energetic beings. According to her beliefs, during the long ages of this evolution where humanity descended into the physical body, the third eye, as she referred to the pineal, disappeared, as it became sunken in the head and became an atrophied organ.

This small gland, located in the center of the brain between the two hemispheres, above and behind the pituitary, lies outside the blood-brain barrier, which is a membrane restricting the passage of certain substances which could infect the brain, yet allows nutrients to enter from the bloodstream. The pineal, therefore, has its own plentiful blood supply, so much so that it is second only to the kidney in the amount of blood flow per cubic volume in that respect. It is named from the shape it has, being that of a pine cone ('pinea' in Latin). It is quite small, approaching ten millimeters in length in adult humans. The pineal first appears in the fetus 49 days after conception.

For its small size, the pineal gland has had a large influence on human culture, showing up in sculptures and paintings around the world and throughout the centuries. The Egyptians thought the gland important enough to preserve it separately in the embalming process. Representations of it can be seen in Egyptian, Roman, and Greek art as well as in Masonic symbolism. Each culture associated it with illumination or esoteric understanding.

The reason for our interest in this small gland is that, as we have seen with theosophy, it has been called the third eye, the connection with the energetic world, and has been associated with extraordinary vision, the ability to go beyond normal eyesight. As such, it seems to have intriguing possibilities of a connection with intuition and with siddhi powers. It has cells which resemble the back of the retina, and it reacts to the circadian rhythms of light and dark. Current understanding is that the pineal, despite being buried deep within the center of the head, can react to light, because the original reaction to light is sent along the optic nerve to an area in the hypothalamus, and from there nerve impulses travel via the sympathetic nervous system in the spine before finally ending up at the pineal, a roundabout process.

It is now known that the pineal gland regulates the release of melatonin that helps maintain our body clock or the circadian rhythms we looked at earlier. Its association with chakras and energy bodies is due to the fact that it can be stimulated by certain practices such as meditation and can, apparently, give rise to perceptions of 'other' or extended realities. Therefore, it has been argued, what our perceptions of 'normality' might consist of could be due, in some part, to the function of our pineal gland. The fact that Blavatsky named it the third eye and associated it with a much earlier stage of evolution has no doubt had an effect on the modern metaphysical approach to this gland with relation to 'seeing' other realities.

This view that some perceptions might be controlled by this tiny gland has been given some truth by research which has shown that it can produce a molecule called DMT (dimethyltriptamine), which has been called the Spirit Molecule or God Molecule, because it is essentially a powerful psychedelic drug. If you were to take this into your system through your mouth and digestive system, you would experience strong hallucinations, and often, a deeply spiritual awareness would develop.

In fact, DMT is found in the Amazonian plant mixture commonly called ayahuasca, which provides altered states of consciousness. Ayahuasca is taken in order to communicate with nature and 'see' over long distances, much as the powers professed by the siddhi abilities. The mixture has long been used by Amazonian medicine men to assist in their dealing with clients. It has now become more widely available to those who seek a method of enlightenment or spiritual awakening, even though it has apparently a very unpleasant taste and texture, and it often induces vomiting. Nevertheless, the effects upon consciousness are considered to be enough to offset such unpleasantness. The pineal gland, on the other hand, secretes this chemical naturally and without the unpleasant physical effects.

The pineal also contains magnetite which, it is conjectured, helps us to find our direction, much as birds do when they are migrating. Additionally, the production of melatonin has also been found to be affected by changes in the Earth's magnetic field. Given our bodies' sensitive abilities, it is possible to conclude that the Earth's magnetic field could have a direct influence upon us via this gland. We have seen previously that our heart rates and the brain's electrical activity are influenced by changes in the earth's magnetic field. It seems perfectly possible to suppose that the function of the pineal gland could be similarly affected.

It would seem so, given the experiences of Dr. Rawls. Dr. Walter Rawls was an investigator interested in the effects of magnets on living things (bio-magnetics). He and his associate, Dr. Albert Davis, discovered that different poles of a magnet had different effects on such things as earthworms, plants, and rats. One pole, the South pole (that is, the pole which is really the north-attracting pole and usually marked N on magnets), increased growth and general activity, whilst the opposite pole acted in the opposite manner.

He was also interested in seeing how humans might be affected by magnets. Rawls intended to see if the concept of a 'third eye' was valid or not and decided to try an experiment on himself whereby he placed a north magnet, held in place by a mask, over his pineal gland. This, he decided, would stimulate it and so perhaps bring about some understanding of what it was capable of. He intended to have the magnet in place for between ten and thirty minutes a day over a period of about a month.

During the first week, he was working at his desk when he saw a vision of a man, looking ghost-like, who appeared through the wall of Rawls' office, walked across and vanished through the opposite wall. He was seemingly unaware of Rawls. During the second week, the man appeared again, looking a little more solid this time, and he glanced at Rawls, or appeared to. The third week was when it took another turn. This time, instead of the man walking through and disappearing, Rawls looked up from his work to find that the entire wall of his office had disappeared, and that the same man he had seen previously was sitting with a woman beneath a tree. After a few moments, the man looked up and appeared startled when he looked at Rawls, as if he recognized him. The wall slowly re-appeared, and Rawls decided not to continue with the experiment any further, after which the 'sightings' ceased. It seemed that there was a correlation between stimulation of the gland and the ability to perceive beyond everyday normality.

The fact that the pineal gland can be stimulated in this way might also help to explain why some people sense or feel things when they are within magnetic fields such as can be found at certain megalithic sites like Avebury in England or Carnac in France. Such places have been found to have quite specific channeling of electromagnetism within and around the stones. This directing of electromagnetism varies throughout the day, so it is not always the fact that being near such places will automatically stimulate the pineal. Brittany, where the impressively large number of Neolithic stone avenues of Carnac are located, has the highest rate of seismic activity in France. The stones there are mainly of granite containing significant amounts of quartz. Quartz, if stressed mechanically, will produce electricity, which will create a field of energy. Given the seismic activity in the area, there is a gentle vibration of the stones, causing a piezoelectric effect in and amongst them. This could most certainly be considered to have an effect on the pineal gland of those visiting the area and who are sufficiently sensitive to such influences.

Megalithic monuments have been found to have varying degrees of electromagnetic energies associated with them. One of the most well-researched stone circles in this regard is the Rollright stone circle in England. Detailed surveys of this site over a period of some years revealed that magnetic force was channeled into the circle where it spiraled into the center. Additionally, the level of intensity of the geomagnetic field was lower inside the circle, suggesting some form of shielding taking place.

Avebury, the well-preserved and very large megalithic monument in England, has also revealed some interesting findings with regard to earth energy, in that it has been found to conduct electricity into the surrounding ditch before it enters into the circle. Voltage and magnetic variations have been shown to alter with the dawn and dusk.

Readings taken of some menhirs—large, solitary standing stones—have shown that pulses of energy can be monitored over a period of about 70 minutes, extending to about 30 feet away. It is unlikely that such effects were accidental. It is probable that the builders of these monuments were able to perceive such flows with greater clarity than we presently can unaided.

As to the specific purpose of such engineering, that is much harder to consider and, in any case, it lies outside the scope of this investigation. However, that there is a complex of energy, some of which can manifest physically to people, throwing them off balance, giving headaches or altering perception, is well documented in Tom Graves' book, *Needles of Stone*. And, as Dr. Rawls discovered, stimulation of the pineal gland can bring about different perceptions. As the pineal contains magnetite, then simply entering the naturally-occurring electromagnetic fields of some places might well trigger differing perceptions for some people, leading them to have an intuition about that place. However, it is not certain from Dr. Rawls' experience what such an intuition might relate to.

The flow of electromagnetic energy is not necessarily restricted to just these places, however. It has recently been discovered that every eight minutes a magnetic portal opens up on Earth connecting it directly with the magnetic field of the Sun, allowing particles to pass through easily. These portals tend to form over the equator and roll over to the north or south depending on the time of year. Additionally, the flux lines of Earth's magnetic field are being constantly interfered with by the sun's strong magnetic field. The base resonance of this interference—0.1 Hertz —has been found to be exactly the same as the rhythm of the human heart when it is coherent. Or another way of saying that is that when we are feeling good, happy, well-adjusted, our hearts are resonating at the exact same frequency as the Earth's primary resonant frequency. Of course, that base frequency of the Earth is not constant, as the sun alters and as the Earth rotates. But there is no reason not to suppose that there are times when such a connection via the natural magnetic field of the Earth happens at the right time with regard to our sense of well-being, and that information can easily be transmitted and received by us. What that information might consist of is open to question, but the channel or connection itself certainly exists. Indeed, such a connection might also prove to be the answer to the Random Number Generator results—investigated in a later chapter—or how people can perceive earthquakes or can 'know' that someone they know and love is in trouble on the other side of the globe. Perhaps this natural field of the Earth operates in a similar way to how regions of the ionosphere bounce radio waves over huge distances, in that it can allow a direct contact between two people even when on different continents.

Obviously, such sources of magnetism, whether from the Sun, from gently vibrating quartz-bearing rocks, or from megalithic monuments, and the ways in which electricity and magnetism flow through and around them in varying strengths and at varying times, could have direct and observable effects on the pineal gland. These effects would also vary according to the time of day as well as the time of year, making any investigation far more involved than wandering around with a couple of measuring instruments for a day or so. Such effects could be of visions such as were experienced by Dr. Rawls.

The work of Mavromatis would also tend to suggest a more visionary type of intuition, as would the beliefs of Gooch we looked at earlier, both of whom believed that the subcortical area was important in understanding intuition. And the subcortical is, you will recall, where the pineal is found. Given these factors, it should not be surprising to find that reports of sudden insights, feelings, and sensations, all of which are varieties of intuition, are frequently remarked upon at ancient megalithic sites.

However, such intuitions would be limited to such places where electromagnetic fields are strong enough or directed enough to stimulate the pineal. But, as has been made abundantly clear, intuitions arrive seemingly at any place and any time. This chapter has only examined the possible effects of stimulation of the gland with regard to the subtle energy body. But it certainly does suggest how other forms of stimulation, such as meditative techniques or exercises to strengthen specific chakras could also result in similar intuitive insights.

No matter how you look at it, the tiny pineal gland has a definite role to play in how our intuition works. It certainly does seem to play an important role in gathering information when used as a focus for extending awareness into the supra-sensory world by those who are drawn to the spiritual life. The role of the pineal, that of acting as a link between the physical and the non-physical worlds, illustrates another aspect of intuition: that it is part of the language of such spiritual seekers.

It seems that our bodies are capable of transmitting and receiving information amongst ourselves. It is also apparent that we are connected with our environment and the wider world in some fashion. If intuition is the accessing of information in various forms, using various channels or modes, then there has always been the problem of how to account for the source.

In early investigations, intuition was thought of as knowledge. It led to asking if such types of knowledge were different in some way. If so, how can that be accounted for? Intuition, the arrival of knowledge seemingly from out of nowhere, has to be accounted for in how we think of the world, for such knowledge should have some location, some way of being accessed, shouldn't it? It is to these and other similar questions we turn to next.

7

OTHER WAYS OF THINKING ABOUT INTUITION

The human body is essentially something other than an animal organism.
Martin Heidegger (Philosopher)

Certainly we can learn and acquire information about the physical world as a natural by-product of our existence here, but what of the world beyond the physical? What information might be accounted for there? So far we have been looking at the physical and energetic aspects of intuition. But the broader subject of how we obtain information or knowledge of the world has, not surprisingly, also been of interest to philosophers for a very long time.

The term philosophy translates as 'love of knowledge,' and as intuition certainly does provide knowledge in some fashion, philosophers have tried to come to terms with it, with varying results. How do we acquire knowledge? Is the reality we perceive always true and consistent, or is there something else, something beyond this reality, and how can we determine what it might consist of? How do we know anything anyway? These are the sorts of questions which have attracted thinkers over the centuries. And, considering that we already understand that intuition does not arrive through our usual physical senses, the questions they pursued and the answers they arrived at will be of great interest and use to us.

One of the earliest approaches to explaining this subject was made by Aristotle. Incidentally, the term we use for the study of various non-physical subjects, 'metaphysics,' is associated with this philosopher. The word 'metaphysics,' which can mean many things, but usually includes the study of abstract concepts such as time and space (of great interest to our own study of intuition), originated in the sixteenth century. Translated, it means 'what comes after physics,' referring to the sequence of Aristotle's works and identifying those following his work on physics. Aristotle's Physics was really about the physical senses. The metaphysics, as originally defined, involved the study of first principles, including how we come to have knowledge of the world, a natural progression from the physical senses. Aristotle said that there were four ways of knowing anything: scientific knowledge, practical wisdom, philosophic wisdom and intuitive reason, but that only intuitive reason was able to grasp first principles, that is, the things from which everything else derives.

Scientific knowledge, for example, can explain things through logic and reason, but it is intuitive reason which uncovers the eternal facts of the universe. In other words, there are some things which we cannot demonstrate or explain or realize through mental effort. Those things are, according to Aristotle, the eternal unvarying facts. He does not explain what those might be, but he recognized that there were things which we just 'know' somehow and cannot easily explain. That may sound like a difficult concept to embrace, but consider the following. Think of numbers. They are really only concepts. In order to understand these concepts, children are taught to visualize them in different ways, using examples they can find in life. Three oranges are not the number three, but a representation of that number.

Certain forms of mathematics are concerned solely with concepts. Concepts do not have a physical existence, being only an idea. As such, researchers have discovered that being blind may actually improve mathematical abilities. Blind children are often taught numbers using abacuses so that they can 'feel' where the numbers are and how they relate to each other. More than that, however, when it comes to geometry, the blind person has an unspoiled intuition (the exact words in a report on this subject) of three-dimensional space, whereas a sighted person is trying to gain a three-dimensional understanding from a two-dimensional representation on a page. Further, there have been some significant mathematicians who were or became blind.

Leonhard Euler, for example, became blind later in life toward the end of the eighteenth century, but that did not reduce his work output, which is remarkable, as he is generally considered the most prolific mathematician of all time. It has been said of him that approximately one-third of the entire corpus of research on mathematics and mathematical physics and engineering mechanics published in the last three-quarters of the eighteenth century was from him. Nicholas Saunderson, blind soon after birth, became Lucasian professor of mathematics at Cambridge (the post held by both Isaac Newton and Stephen Hawking). But perhaps the best example of this ability to understand intuitive concepts is provided by Bernard Morin, a maths professor blind since the age of six, who became a master in topology (the study of geometric forms in space) who was renowned for his study of turning a sphere inside out without cutting or tearing it. (Other examples of blind mathematicians are to be found in the American Mathematical Society's Notices, Vol 49, Number 10.)

These examples may perhaps help us to understand what Aristotle was speaking of when referring to intuition as being capable of revealing eternal, unvarying facts. Concepts, like numbers, which have no physical reality, are nevertheless able to be conceived of, visualized, and made accessible through what he would call the true application of intuition. This view of intuition, that it is of things you simply 'know' without knowing how, is similar, on the surface, to how we generally tend to think of intuition. However, Aristotle's view is somewhat restricted, as it deals only with concepts, which are often the building blocks upon which philosophers build their investigations and theories, rather than being whole and complete in themselves, as we tend to think of and experience intuition.

Another explanation of intuition, and one which has remained in force in one way or another for several centuries, was proposed by Saint Thomas Aquinas. However, it should be remembered that when Aquinas was speaking of intuition, he was referring to a specific sort of knowledge. As he put it, "A truth can come into the mind in two ways, namely as known in itself, and as known through another. What is known in itself is like a principle, and is perceived immediately by the mind...It is a firm and easy quality of mind which sees into principles." To explain this further, imagine that I am speaking to you about three dogs named Albert, Belle, and Charlie. They are labradors, and Albert is yellow, Belle is chocolate and Charlie is black. I can tell you that Belle is lighter than Charlie but darker than Albert, and you can understand that. You don't need to see them to understand that. You only need to know the concepts of darker and lighter to make sense of it. Those concepts are what Aquinas said "come into your mind… as known to itself."

He further said that angels have the ability to know things by direct intuition (as you know the different relative colors of the labradors), and that therefore intuition is the highest mode of knowledge man can have. In fact, because of the angelic intuition of things which can only come from God, the use of intuition therefore is the most perfect way of being for man. This, as a reminder, is how the *Shorter Oxford Dictionary* defines intuition: "…immediate knowledge ascribed to angelic and spiritual beings, with whom vision and knowledge are identical."

Now, it must be remembered that the intuition Aquinas was writing about is the intuition of concepts, not the same type of intuitions which cover premonitions of disaster or visions of the past or future. Nevertheless, his writings influenced how people have viewed intuition. This is mainly due to the importance of Aquinas in religious— specifically Catholic—thought for generations. But the fact that he said that intuition, the complete understanding of things, originated in God, has colored many, many peoples' views or explanations about the origin of intuition.

Intuition is still considered as something mystical, often religious, in origin. Indeed, people will often refer to an intuitive 'hit' as being a message from their guardian angel. One woman, Rhonda Taylor, whose younger sister was pregnant in a different country, sent money to her on an impulse which turned out to be life-saving for the new-born. As Rhonda said, "We felt that this was a message which was clearly Divinely inspired." And she is not alone in ascribing intuition to the realm of God and the angels.

Although there is no mention of intuition as such in the Bible, the closest is in Proverbs 2:6 which says, "For the Lord gives wisdom; from his mouth come knowledge and understanding," which is very much what Aquinas was arguing: that perfect knowledge, the knowledge of things acquired without the use of reason and intellect, comes from God.

One experiment reported in the *Journal of Experimental Psychology* asked people about their belief in God and then tested their attitude toward, and use of, intuition. The results suggested strongly that those who were more intuitive in the way they think and decide are more likely to believe in God. As one of the researchers, Amitai Shenhav of Harvard said, "Some say we believe in God because our intuitions about how and why things happen lead us to see a divine purpose behind ordinary events that don't have obvious human causes."

One philosopher who did more than any previous one to reduce human intellect to only the rational aspect was Descartes. We saw earlier how important his ideas were in the development of science and the scientific approach, and how it broke away from seeing man as a whole. The modern split between mind and body as two distinct and separate entities, if not started by him, can be said to certainly have been made much plainer than before. It was he who said, "I think, therefore I am," implying that anything which was not associated with rational thought or susceptible to such thought was outside the scope of human intelligence and understanding. About intuition he said that, "Intuitive knowledge is an illumination of the soul, whereby it beholds in the light of God those things which it pleases Him to reveal to us by direct impression of divine clearness in our understanding..." In other words, he was in broad agreement with Aquinas several centuries earlier: God is the source of all knowledge and understanding, and we get to see and understand that which He allows us to see.

Philosophers, those "men whom too much learning and thought have made mad," according to a seventeenth century Moravian nobleman, Michael Sendivogius, approach everything from a rational and empirical point of view. If it cannot be deconstructed, analyzed and debated over, it cannot be understood. Therefore, their view of the world cannot encompass anything which is not susceptible to rational analysis. Not surprisingly, if you ask such people to consider intuition as illustrated by the examples in the first chapter, then it is either ignored or reduced to a set of systems, reactions, chemicals and personality traits.

This state of affairs, where the understanding of general concepts was all that intuition consisted of, remained as the dominant force in philosophy, while the unexplainable insights which many people had was thought of as being given over to God or the angels. In other words, there was no real attempt to understand what so many people have experienced, until the beginning of the twentieth century.

Up until that time, intuition was still something which allowed us to understand general concepts. The debates which took place were merely rearranging the scenery, not altering the location of the arguments. Thus Immanuel Kant's views on intuition in the eighteenth century stated it as being the only way in which the reality of concepts such as space and time could be used as verification of reality outside of ourselves. For him, these were forms of intuition, and we apply the concepts of space and time to everything we perceive. He said, "It is our mind that processes information about the world and gives it order. Our mind supplies the conditions of space and time to experience objects." In other words, he was saying that there is something going on in our heads or, more accurately, in our perceptions, which determine how we see the world. This idea of space and time being purely mental constructs is a theme we will take up later, as it has an important bearing on intuition in general.

Schopenhauer in the nineteenth century adjusted this theory of intuition from which arise general concepts by saying that this was not necessarily true, as there was a type of intuitive cognition or knowledge of perception which allows us and many animals to find our way through the world without such concepts as space and time. In other words, he, along with people like Locke and Berkeley, and Hume, was suggesting in a roundabout way, that reality, or the stuff 'out there' which was not us, was in some fashion created by our senses or, ultimately, our minds, an echo of Kant's statements, but broader in perspective.

Locke, for example, said that there was intuitive knowledge such as that of our own existence or of obvious nature, as in knowing that one object is black and is therefore different from an object which is white, or a snake is not the same as an orchid. Hume also spoke of intuition as being of relationships between things such as time and place, and that it occurred in the mind.

Bishop Berkeley, taking a different tack, suggested that instead of knowing concepts and struggling with space and time, there were only the objects we perceive and nothing else. In other words, if you don't perceive it, it isn't there, which he summed up in Latin as "Esse est percipi" (To be is to be perceived). However, although this, at first sight, is remarkably close to ideas we shall look at later, he realized that he still had to account for God in some fashion. After all, he was a bishop! In his thesis, if we do not look at a table, it continues to exist only in the mind of God, as God was infinite and contains everything, and it is He who allows us to experience matter according to His will. To Berkeley, all reality is effectively mental. He was, in effect, disagreeing with Descartes' division between the mental and the physical world, saying that everything was mental.

As a side note, Dr. Johnson, he of early encyclopedia fame, was reported by his biographer, Boswell, as having a discussion of Berkeley's ideas outside church one day. Boswell said that Berkeley's doctrine was impossible to refute. "I never shall forget the alacrity with which Johnson answered, striking his foot with mighty force against a large stone, till he rebounded from it, 'I refute it thus'." Although it is dramatic and memorable, it was ineffectual, as it certainly did not refute the idea of reality being created by the senses, as a kick was still only a physical process interpreted by the senses as having movement, force, and duration.

It was not until the twentieth century philosopher Henri Bergson came along that any real progress in a new direction could take place. Bergson was a famous and influential French philosopher in the early part of the century who sought to overcome the paradoxes and divisions, such as rationalism, empiricism, idealism, and realism, which were the results of earlier arguments amongst philosophers. His view was that philosophy as a whole was based on intuition.

By this he meant that intuition was the only way in which reality could be apprehended. That might sound somewhat similar to earlier ideas, but he meant something different. Intuition was, he said, an "immediate consciousness" or direct awareness of reality, where previously it had been concerned with underlying concepts upon which reality could be based.

Rational thought and analysis were what happened only after reality was grasped, but the intuition itself was very difficult to express by the intellect. As he wrote, "One part of the mind has the power to encounter reality as simply and directly as drinking a glass of water. The other part can only come to terms with reality by strapping it into a kind of rigid iron framework and measuring it with clocks and rulers." He was against the strictly deterministic interpretation of evolution, saying instead that there was a life force (the *élan vital*) which penetrated matter, and it was that which was driving evolution to higher and higher forms of complexity and freedom. And it was this same *élan vital* which was at the heart of everything which we are able to perceive via our intuition. To Bergson, it was evident that the understanding gained through this intuition had either to be spoken about using metaphors or not spoken of at all. Reality, then, was inexpressible but understandable.

Now the idea that reality was understandable but not capable of being expressed might sound strange but, without diving into how physics or spirituality views reality, it does go some way towards how we, as non-philosophers having intuitive hunches, fail to clearly express those hunches themselves. They are incredibly difficult to convey to others, and we fall back, time and again, on how Conrad Hilton expressed it: 'it feels right.' This problem about language and intuition will be looked at in a later chapter.

For Bergson, then, the most valuable, the most important things, cannot be thought about, but only experienced. This state of affairs, where philosophy sees intuition as a form of knowledge of reality, is only so helpful to us. It does not involve or consider what we, the general public, might wish to call intuition. However, it does help us to see that, even where the philosophers do not agree with us, they agree that there is something beyond the familiar in the act of intuition. It also begs the question of what is meant by reality anyway? The reality which intuition points at for philosophers is clearly not the same as the reality as you and I conceive of it in our daily lives, although we will find interesting parallels with the scientific view we shall be examining later. But does intuition as a source of knowledge then have a distinct or separate reality? If so, does that then match, to some degree, the philosophers and their interpretation of reality? Are there underlying truths in the universe and about ourselves which are only accessible via intuition?

Of course, when we non-philosophers speak of truths about ourselves and the universe, we tend to think about the truths or otherwise which arrive via our senses. In other words, we speak about our perceptions of the world around us. We observe the colors in a sunset, we smell the flowers which grow in our yard, we revel in the touch of a lover, we hear our favorite music, and we taste the flavors in a carefully prepared meal. Those are the basic sensations which make up our world. They are our reality. But there are questions to be asked about this.

For example, can I be sure that I am seeing the exact same colors as you in a sunset? Might I not see more orange or red than you? And what about listening to the same piece of music? Maybe I cannot hear the top notes as easily as you. Or maybe it is the lower notes you are missing. The same problem exists for each of our five senses. Only I know what I perceive. Only you know what you perceive. And the reason for these differences might lie in different physical constraints we each have—my eyes might not be as sensitive as yours, your ears not as receptive as mine, and so on—but there is another consideration. No matter what I perceive, everything around me is filtered through my brain. The processing of the world you and I live in takes place only in our brains.

As Marcus Aurelius, the Stoic Roman emperor, wrote in the second century AD, "Everything we see is a perspective, not the truth." The poet

William Blake wrote: "If the doors of perception were cleansed every thing would appear to man as it is, Infinite. For man has closed himself up, till he sees all things thro' narrow chinks of his cavern." His words were echoed in the twentieth century by the Swiss psychiatrist and psychoanalyst, Carl Jung, "It all depends on how we look at things, and not how they are in themselves." The personal viewpoint is pre-eminent. We might be standing side by side, looking at the same scene, and yet have totally different experiences. This is confirmed by comparing witness reports of accidents; there are often wild variations in what was perceived, making it difficult to piece together the actual sequence of events and discover what did happen.

So what happens if my brain doesn't process the information it receives the same as yours? This difference in brain processing would, it seems, lead to different views of reality. If you cannot see the color orange as I see it, and you see it as purple instead, then that changes how you see the world. If your hearing is so sensitive that it makes being near anyone speaking a torture, you will surely have a different perception of music from me.

If the brain is a filter for us, how much does it filter out? Instead of seeing a different color or hearing a different range of sounds, might there not be other filters at work, filters which we are not necessarily aware of? There are some lines of thought which would suggest that is the case.

If we recall the philosopher Henri Bergson, he said that intuition was a way of gaining insight into the reality of things. But he also went on to say the brain was the "organ of attention to life." He said that the brain only works in that way by "shutting out from consciousness all that is of no practical interest to us." In other words, Bergson was saying that there is a whole lot more going on around us that we never get to experience, because our brain decides what it should engage with and, therefore, what becomes of interest to us.

In physical terms, Bergson was absolutely correct. The mediation of our physical world is done through the reticular activation system (RAS). This is a narrow two inch bundle of nerves at the top of our brain stem through which all the senses, with the exception of smell, pass. The RAS filters out much of what is perceived, so that we are not overwhelmed. Maybe it is possible to persuade the brain to change its decision-making process and allow us to extend our perception. Maybe we can alter the way the RAS filters our senses. That certainly could explain some of the results of mystical experiences gained after deep meditation.

The huge amounts of information around us in the physical world are subject to filters to our conscious awareness. It is more than likely that such a filtering system is also at work for our intuitive awareness, and this may account for differing intuitions amongst people at certain locations, or explain why someone experiences a feeling in the gut when the next person catches a flash of insight.

It would seem, therefore, that the ability to have such intuitive experiences is a natural part of our being. Everything seems to point to that: our intuitions, the variety of experiences, all make that an unarguable observation. But saying that says very little indeed. It takes us no further in our journey. But it also makes us refer back to the brain or some associated process or processes as being responsible for that variety of experiences and intuitions.

The philosophers have pointed out to us that there may well be different types of knowledge, of information, in the universe and that our perceptions are largely responsible for our understanding of the universe, our reality. This means, for our purposes, that in order to make further progress, we need to examine how the brain and reality coincide, as well as dig a little deeper into what reality might or might not consist of.

Andreas Mavromatis and his research into hypnagogic states has given us one possible idea, that there are parts of our brain reacting differently to the world and which present differing views of reality: the logical neocortex with sense perceptions and the older subcortical processes using imagery and symbolism as a way of communicating. One is more externally focused and the other more internally. Both are happening simultaneously, but usually we are aware of only one at a time.

In the case of my sudden awareness of European history, the fact that it faded and I could not put it into words but had to let it go from me would suggest that I experienced a hypnagogic state where images are predominant but analysis and logic are not. It was a deep awareness within me. There was nothing external about it. It was imagery, and it was sweeping in scope and seemed to take huge swathes of time but happened in seconds. These are all hallmarks of such a state.

Therefore we appear to have one type of intuitive experience within our grasp. But it also leaves something unanswered. For me to have had that experience, that intuition, I needed to collate vast amounts of information covering centuries and put them into some sort of order. How is that possible if it really was only the subcortical structures, those non-analytical parts of my brain, which were involved?

There is something else which needs to be accounted for. Even if we accept that a hypnagogic state gives us insights, it still does not allow us to come any closer to explaining how we get feelings of the future or explicit visions of the past and future. Neither does it explain how an absence of definite information contributes to missing a train or a plane about to crash. That absence of information provides a space in which we can find ourselves avoiding an accident of some sort such as the choir members avoided, without any apparent effort or awareness.

The philosophers we looked at were interested in uncovering basic concepts from which they could begin to develop theories of the world and our interaction with it, as well as theories explaining how we tend to think and act. These considerations would not allow them to come to terms with such problems as the sudden sweep of understanding or of premonitions, and therefore we must look elsewhere for help.

However, because of their conclusions and our earlier investigations, we are forced to acknowledge that we are surrounded by and connected with a vast array of information which is presented to us in various forms. Our physical senses are tuned to certain frequencies or to specific stimuli in order to interpret the information contained therein. Our intuitive senses are similarly susceptible to a wide range of information accessible to us in various forms via different channels: our biomes, the em fields we produce and interact with, the pineal and its associated connections, as well as some sort of ultimate reality not within the bounds of the physical world but mediated by us in some fashion.

It is that mediation or processing to which we must turn next. For that we need to look more closely at our consciousness and how that operates, as that will have a direct bearing on our intuitive insights, as consciousness is central to everything about us.

8

THE ROLE OF CONSCIOUSNESS

I would argue that nothing gives life more purpose than the realization that every moment of consciousness is a precious and fragile gift.
Steven Pinker (Scientist)

___

As we looked earlier at the mind, which is also a key component in accessing the intuitive knowledge promulgated by the philosophers, so we need to to look at an associated area where, supposedly, the processing of all information takes place. As we saw, the mind is difficult to pin down to one simple meaning. However, there is an attendant aspect of mind which, if anything, is even more complex and frustrating to investigate, yet it is one which would appear to have a direct bearing on our intuition in one form or another because of its overwhelmingly important role in our lives. I refer to consciousness.

If the mind can mean different things to different people, the concept of consciousness can appear even harder to grasp. There is a problem with defining consciousness, never mind locating it in any one specific area. If the mind is hard enough to pin down as meaning one thing, then examining consciousness gives rise to an intractable problem. This difficulty is what is known as the 'hard problem' of consciousness.

Briefly, the hard problem is as follows. You know that you can sense things such as colors and sounds and smells and sights and textures. And in all of those things we all do every day of our lives, we know, without a doubt, that we are the ones doing them. We are conscious beings, conscious of our own existence. We are self-aware. And the hard part of the problem is that there is no way of explaining satisfactorily (at the moment) how such conscious awareness arises from the physical matter which is our brain and is, for some, where the mind resides. For example, if consciousness is simply nothing more than something which happens in some fashion in the mind, then how is it that consciousness is aware of the mind? And, when we are unconscious, that is, when we sleep, how do we know that we are the same person when we awaken? Consciousness is, without doubt, a very tricky thing, and the extent and depth of its trickiness has only come about since the mind itself was able to be studied. Descartes again!

A Rutgers University philosopher, Jerry A. Fodo, flatly states, "Nobody has the slightest idea how anything material could be conscious. So much for our philosophy of consciousness."

One of the most extreme reactions to this lack of understanding is to suggest that the whole idea of consciousness itself should be dismissed. It is, for some, an unnecessary concept. Indeed, Daniel Dennett, a Tufts University cognitive scientist, has said that nobody is conscious. Others, not going quite so far, assert that everything—thoughts, emotions, mental states, etc.—can ultimately be explained by chemical reactions, molecules, cells and so on, which make up the brain. As Francis Crick, the co-discoverer with James Watson of DNA's structure, said: "'You, your joys and your sorrows, your memories and your ambitions, your sense of personal identity and free will, are in fact no more than the behavior of a vast assembly of nerve cells and their associated molecules." Such a situation led Sir John Eccles, a Nobel neurophysiologist, to remark that "professional philosophers and psychologists think up the notion that there are no thoughts, come to believe that there are no beliefs, and feel strongly that there are no feelings."

Even if we cannot pin consciousness down but accept its existence, it is worth asking, as well, just how much brain is required in order to have consciousness appear? There are well-documented cases where people live perfectly normal lives with very small brains. For example, a 44-year-old man, a father of two who worked as a civil servant, complained of mild weakness in his left leg. During examination, he revealed that he had hydrocephalus as a child (water on the brain) and had had a shunt inserted to drain the water. That had been removed at age 14. The doctors decided to check on the condition of his brain and were astounded when the scans revealed that, instead of the usual narrow chambers—lateral ventricles—which would be filled with cerebrospinal fluid, his were vastly enlarged. These ventricles, which are two curved openings within the brain filled with the fluid, act not only as a cushion for the brain but also help to remove waste and circulate nutrients. This particular man's lateral ventricles were so enlarged that one doctor estimated that the fluid had reduced the volume of the brain by between 50% and 75%.

Another example was that of a mathematics graduate with an IQ of 126 who had only a millimeter or so of brain tissue between the ventricles instead of the usual 4.5 centimeters. An autopsy on a young man who had died suddenly revealed that he had "only the most paltry rind of brain tissue." It was assumed that he had been severely dysfunctional as a result, yet he had a job and was considered to be bright. Finally, there are people, such as a young woman in China, who are born without a cerebellum, yet who function normally enough, albeit in her case with a slight speech impediment and minor lack of motor control. It was mild dizziness and nausea which caused her to seek medical attention.

In other words, the brain is not some simple organ where specific functions or abilities are always connected to specific areas. This was hinted at when considering Sperry's split-brain theory, when it was noted that language is not always processed in the right hemisphere. The brain has a plasticity which makes it possible to overcome problems in one area by allowing the brain to develop compensatory growth in another. In stroke patients, some functions which were lost can be slowly regained as cells around the damaged area take on new functions. Given sufficient stimulus, certain areas of the brain may enlarge in order to deal with specific types of processing.

One notable example of this is in the brains of London taxi drivers. They have to learn and memorize all of the streets of the city if they want to gain a green badge which allows them to ply their trade anywhere in Greater London, specifically within a six mile radius of Charing Cross. This encompasses thousands of streets as well as landmarks. The requirement to learn such a vast amount of information was started in 1865.

As anyone who has visited the city can attest, it is a muddling maze of different streets and alleys with no discernible pattern to them. The memorizing of this confusion of roads and places is called, not without some irony, 'The Knowledge.' There is nothing like this requirement anywhere else in the world, and passing the various stages of the tests is still a requirement to drive a black cab, even though there are now many electronic navigation aids available. Training for this test can take three to four years. It requires a formidable act of memory. The cab drivers have to know how to get from any one place to any other place in the capital in the most direct way, so that even if there are roadworks or other obstacles, they can adapt and adjust accordingly without a glance at a GPS screen.

When compared to London bus drivers, who have fixed routes to follow and therefore do not need extra details, the area of the taxi drivers' brains called the hippocampus is enlarged. The hippocampus, named for its resemblance to the shape of a sea horse, is a small area buried deep within the brain, roughly above and slightly in front of the brain stem. It is the part of the brain which deals with memory, with learning, and with spatial awareness amongst other things. The effort of memorizing so many streets and landmarks causes a measurable change in that area.

The brain, then, is a quite remarkable organ. Its central role in the perception of the world around us has been the source of much interest over time. The work of Oliver Sacks and other researchers into neurological problems provide many striking examples of strange processes or disorders in the brain. Amongst them, for example, is the story of a woman who, when she had mild seizures in a specific part of her brain, clearly heard old tunes and songs from her childhood playing continually. Another story Sacks shared in his book *The Man Who Mistook His Wife For A Hat* was that of a woman who had suffered a severe stroke which had not altered her intelligence or sense of humor, but had made it impossible for her to have even the concept of the left side of her body. She could not see anything to the left, even food on a plate, and had to rotate 360 degrees to her right to bring it into view. Sacks also wrote of a man who did not recognize his own leg as belonging to him and tried to throw it out of bed, leading him to fall on the floor.

Such stories and research allow us to see how the brain might distort or otherwise confuse our perceptions of reality. Whilst the mind and the brain, as we have seen, appear to be two different things entirely, some would prefer to discover consciousness as arising directly from aspects of the structure of the brain, so that it might be entirely describable from existing knowledge. Yet, how that view survives the above examples is hard to say.

Nevertheless, there are many other theories attempting to explain consciousness. One, for example, is the single neuron theory, whereby it is assumed that every single neuron in the brain has some level of consciousness. There must be, it is argued, a means of communication between them despite the fact that there is no physical connection and that connection could be consciousness. This might sound ridiculous, but it does echo the results of some experiments we shall be looking at later.

Another theory of consciousness is that a certain level of complexity of information will naturally develop into consciousness as a result of the amount of processing involved. Of course, if this is correct, then an inevitable development of this theory is that any sufficiently complex system—think of artificial intelligences—will develop consciousness. In opposition to this view there are those who predict that it is impossible, and always will be, to use a computer to model consciousness, as human brain processes are not compatible with a computer model and its ability to retain sufficient data due to compression and resulting data loss.

Finally, there are those who claim that the brain acts as a quantum computer, and that allows consciousness to arise. This is an area which we will look at more closely in due time.

Roger Sperry, he of the split brain discovery, said that, "In searching brains for clues to the critical features that may be responsible [for consciousness], I have never myself been inclined to focus on the electrons, protons, or neutrons of the brain, or on its atoms…it has always seemed rather improbable that even a whole brain cell has what it takes to sense, to perceive, to feel, or to think on its own."

Consciousness, then, seems to defy easy explanation. It seems to be part of the mind, but the mind does not seem to be part of the brain. Not only that, but there is no way that you can be sure that anyone else is conscious. You cannot touch it or share it. You cannot prove conclusively that anyone else is conscious, because any proof would have to pass through your own consciousness, not theirs. It is taken on trust and it is utterly personal. Yet it would seem important for us to have some idea about it, as without it there would seem to be no intuition. Intuition is, in some form, related to consciousness. There is an awareness of feelings, sounds, sights—the 'phenomena'—during an intuition, and it is phenomena which are the defining characteristics of consciousness. We are aware that we have an intuition, therefore we are conscious of it. But where is consciousness to be found?

It is a question which could only have arisen after Descartes, because it seeks to find something which is not obvious within the body. He believed that the soul contains consciousness, and that the soul resides in the pineal gland. If we do not hold to the idea of the soul being where consciousness resides (to do so would add an unnecessary layer of complication to this inquiry), then we are still left with the problem of the location of this frustrating concept. It is much easier to see examples where consciousness is altered, through injury or drugs for example, as in the works of Sacks, than it is to see how it might be working normally.

It is because of this that some researchers have taken to trying to identify which parts of the brain could be involved in everyday awareness. The underlying assumption is that if such areas are identified, then naturally consciousness itself is located in the actions and connections of those areas. But this is merely locating those areas which facilitate consciousness, not what consciousness itself consists of. It is similar to deciding that one switch amongst many, when closed, makes a light appear, without considering the electrical current which flows as a result of the switch being closed.

General theories about the location of consciousness tend to favor the mechanistic view, that it is a function of the brain rather than of the mind. And yet the nature of intuition, of the people on the Titanic, or the choir members who avoided being killed, or the people who missed trains or planes which had accidents, precludes such a mechanistic view. Those intuitions make no sense in a strictly mechanistic world, because they seem to defy both time and space. Such intuitions cannot happen if we consider the brain to hold consciousness, and that it can therefore be located and defined in both time and space within the brain.

A psychiatrist, Sally Satel, in the book *Brainwashed*, says of the use of machinery such as Functional Magnetic Resonance Imaging (fMRI), which is used to watch what happens in the brain and then make hypotheses, "fMRI shows *only* correlation between task and brain activity, *not* which part of the brain is causing a behavior." In other words, despite seeing activity, we cannot know what causes anything we do, we can only see the results. And that holds true for consciousness in general.

These questions about the mind and consciousness, about their locations and functions, could be said to be questions of the west. Only the western approach to understanding could have brought about such a query. The desire to dissect and measure in order to understand is a function of how the west, generally, has developed intellectually.

The eastern hemisphere, however, has long taken a more holistic view of these aspects. In a sense, it is, in some ways, the opposite side of the evolution of understanding which, in the west after Descartes, resulted in empiricism, but which in the east continued in its more personal and inclusive approach to understanding. (It is of passing interest to note that there are very few antonyms of 'empiricism,' with most dictionaries failing to provide any examples, and those which do are well-represented by the following examples: 'loss,' 'negativity,' and 'unsensational.' Such a lack clearly illustrates the difficulty of even beginning to express the opposing view of the relationship between the individual and the world in this western culture.)

It would be a difficult and unnecessarily complicated task to go into particulars about how different religions have considered the problem of awareness. However, it is possible to give a summary. As a generalization, it is safe to say that consciousness and mind, in the east, are considered to be separate. Whereas in the west we tend to think of consciousness as being ever-present, except when we sleep for example, in the east consciousness is something to aspire to. Unconsciousness is the norm. The day-to-day experiences are brought to awareness by the mind and the senses, which is not what consciousness is, according to this eastern view.

We have seen that, for the west, the mind is not seen as one specific thing. It varies in relation to the different approaches taken. But in the east the mind is that which has intention, and by disciplining the mind through exercises such as meditation or yoga, consciousness can be obtained. Reaching such a goal means that consciousness will then reveal that which is beyond the ability of the mind to perceive. In other words, the mind through discipline can achieve consciousness, but consciousness is not within the mind, nor part of the senses, nor of the heart. It is that which can reveal much more than the mind alone. At such a point one is no longer unconscious.

In the east, with such a view, it would be pointless to look for specific areas in the brain to locate consciousness, and the very fact one is alive and noticing and reacting to the world is proof enough of the mind. Why try to subdivide either of them further? Consciousness then comes to mean a far greater awareness than the immediate physical world. In essence, it embraces not only the person and the body, but the relationship of the body and the mind with the whole of the universe.

Instead of seeing a separation between the body and the universe by measuring and dissecting, such an approach to consciousness seeks to bring the body and the universe to a closer relationship by controlling the mind to bring it into a place or form where a deeper appreciation and understanding is possible than through the immediate physical world of the five senses. Both approaches seek to understand the greater realities of existence, but whereas one seeks the answers through experimentation, impersonal observation, measurement, and analysis, the other seeks it by willingly allowing the individual personality to be subsumed within something far greater in a way which makes measurement and remote observation impossible.

Ananda Coomaraswamy, an eminent Indian art historian, metaphysician, and philosopher who sought to interpret Indian culture to the west, summed up the essence of this view of the awakening of consciousness. "Life is an 'awakening' from nonexistence; 'sleep' is an awakening from life." By sleep, he meant a meditative state where the powers of perception and action are controlled, and through which it is possible to transcend this world and 'the forms of death' (the various ways in which the individual can experience loss of life, such as death of others, death of childhood and so on).

The reduction of the processes from a mechanistic view in favor of a more holistic approach does, it must be admitted, seem to fit more generally in with the feelings, the phenomena, associated with an intuitive 'hit.' It is not centered necessarily in any particular part of you, but it is known throughout your being.

While it is helpful to acknowledge that a different approach gives a feeling of 'that's nearer the truth of it,' it does not help us to proceed much further. If we want to dig a little deeper into this more holistic sense, the sense that there is something which our consciousness can perceive but which our five senses cannot, then we must turn next to another area of exploration.

Before we do, however, it will be useful to summarize how this idea of consciousness fits in with what we have examined so far. Intuition has been shown to consist of a series of different phenomena as perceived by our consciousness, utilizing different channels to provide those phenomena. Yet how those intuitions arrive or where they originate from is not yet clearly understood.

Consciousness is, without a doubt, central to our intuition. If we insist on seeing consciousness only as a by-product of the brain, we are left with the difficulty of understanding how perceptions arising from our consciousness can be altered in some fashion (as in Sack's patients, as well as how such malleable perceptions can explain intuitions). If, on the other hand, we adopt the view that consciousness is that which arises from mastery of the mind, allowing us to gain deeper insight into the phenomenal world, then we are left with the problem again of understanding what such insights consist of and where such reality might be said to exist. Plus, of course, in none of the examples offered at the beginning of this book was there any indication that there had been attempts to master the mind in terms of deep meditation. Intuition seems to be spontaneous and not necessarily the result of dedication and practice. Using either the western or eastern approaches leaves us with questions concerning reality: is it the personal apprehension of it (western) or the nature of it (eastern) which defines it?

No matter which we choose, most of our perceptions of the world rely upon what we consider to be two major properties inherent in it: space and time. If these are basics of the world, then some of the examples make it difficult to believe that space and time are indeed constants. Toynbee's vision of the Battle of Pharsalos, for example, or Air Marshal Goddard's of the future Drem airfield make our accustomed ideas of space and time seem inadequate, as do the psychometric readings of William Denton's sister-in-law's vision of Mount Kilauea or the experiences of people visiting Bold Street in Liverpool. These and many other examples of our apparent ability to 'step outside' of time in some fashion must give us pause to reconsider what we think we know. As Kant said, "It is our mind supplies the conditions of space and time."

How do we account for them? Which of the observations are real (assuming that is a useful term): the steady movement along the continuum encompassing the future, present, and past, or the possibility that time is able to move at different speeds, maybe even remain static or flow backward? If we remove our focus on the body and how it operates, then we must look next at how we understand the body in relation to both space and time.

Although an examination of space and time would seem to offer interesting avenues of exploration with regard to intuition, attempts to examine both concepts together would be confusing and muddled. Let us, for the moment, allow ourselves to consider that the future and the past are really accessible to us, albeit erratically. In the next chapter, we will look at time and intuition.

9

PAST AND FUTURE: THE PROBLEM OF TIME

Go to your bosom: Knock there and ask your heart what it doth know
William Shakespeare (Dramatist)

Intuition, as I hope is now evident, is the accessing of information via various channels, and although the sources may vary and the information be different, we tend to assume that time is a constant in everything, and that time is the standard against which our world and everything in it is measured. Time passes. That is the nature of it, from our experience of birth, growth, and decay.

Yet although we know what is happening now, and we have formal ways of accessing the past, that does little to explain the premonitions or glimpses of the future or visions of the past. Perhaps the reason for the concept of time as being static, even though we may 'feel' the future or 'see' the past, is because our bodies are anchored in the present. Yet even that is not consistently true when we consider the example of Bold Street in Liverpool, where people appeared to physically enter the past. It would seem that time is open to different perceptions or, given the previous chapter, different forms of consciousness. If our consciousness really is the determining factor in our perception of time, then it is vital that we examine time more closely, as it will then fill in our developing picture of intuition.

Carlo Ravelli, a physicist involved in quantum gravity research, in his book, *The Order of Time*, says, "The nature of time is perhaps the greatest remaining mystery." But before we take a closer look at time, it is worth asking about our relationship with it today, specifically about our relationship with clocks and watches. Why do we have them? Modern society demands that we have a clear idea of what the time is to keep everything running smoothly. Of course, some scientific experiments demand precise timekeeping in order to broaden and deepen our understanding of the physical world. But the first is a side effect of having clocks, and the second example doesn't really need to encroach on 'normal' life outside the laboratory. So, why do we have them in such numbers in our lives? And why do we really need the incredible precision on offer now where your wall clock can link to an atomic clock elsewhere, and it will only lose one second in 100 million years? Such exactitude is an indication of how minutely controlled our lives are by timepieces.

The necessity for accurate knowledge of time was paramount in ocean-going navigation. It was relatively easy to find out how far north or south you were—your latitude—by the height of the sun above the horizon at noon, or by using similar measurements of stars. Local noon on board ship was provided by the measurement of time using a 30 minute glass with each half hour made known by the ship's bell being struck an appropriate number of times. Eight bells was either twelve midday or twelve midnight. This worked tolerably well for local noon. However, the problem was with fixing one's longitude.

On land this was relatively simple by the use of Jupiter's moons, discovered by Galileo. But taking such delicate measurements at sea on a moving deck proved highly problematic. The problem seemed disarmingly easy at first glance. The Earth rotates at a fixed rate. Therefore, if you know what the time is at a distant fixed point, you can also know how far east or west you are of that point. As we have seen, it was easy enough to fix your local time (when the sun rises and sets), but not so easy to know how far away you were from the place you started out. What was midday where you were might only be mid-morning or three hours later at your starting point. Not knowing what that difference was became a problem, especially for voyages beyond the sight of land and its landmarks.

Lack of such knowledge meant ships relied on guesswork, and sometimes such dead-reckoning ended in disaster. Without knowing how far east or west you were (for which you needed an accurate timepiece tied to the time at your point of departure), you could be far closer to a shoreline than you thought. Added to that was if the sun was obscured for several days when you needed to measure its elevation to help you determine how far north or south you were, you could end up in dire trouble.

One such event happened in 1707. The so-called Scilly Naval Disaster occurred when severe weather coupled with lack of precise knowledge of their location led to 1,550 lives being lost when four warships of the Royal Navy (of a total of 21 under the command of the magnificently named Sir Cloudesley Shovell) foundered on rocks in the Isles of Scilly. It seems they presumed they were off the coast of Ushant, an island near Brittany in France, rather than the rocks of the Scilly Isles, a difference of 80 nautical miles (about 150 kilometers, or over 90 miles!). This, one of the worst disasters in British maritime history, led to calls for a way of accurately measuring time at sea with the passing of the Longitude Act of 1714.

This Act offered a sliding scale of rewards for increasing accuracy, up to a value of 20,000 pounds sterling (worth approximately 3 million pounds today) for being accurate to within half of one degree of longitude. (One degree of longitude varies according to how far from the equator the measurement takes place, for the meridians converge as they approach the poles. At the equator a half of a degree is about 60.1 nautical miles and at 10 degrees latitude that becomes about 59.2 nautical miles. As you can see, the accuracy demanded by the Longitude Act would not give modern sailors much comfort!)

Existing clocks were incapable of such accuracy, especially given the motion of the ships and the varying weather which created problems in the machinery. Eventually, however, such a timepiece was created, and navigation subsequently became safer. John Harrison, a Yorkshire carpenter, over a period of 31 years ending in 1761, eventually designed a marine chronometer accurate and reliable enough for use at sea.

Therefore, for very good reasons of safety at sea, a more precise measurement of time was effected. After that, time became regularized for large numbers of people with the coming of the railways, where the time was carried along from town to town so that everyone knew that 3:00pm, for example, was exactly the same at the next station along no matter how high or low the sun was. This was after November 18, 1883, when time zones were established in the US. Prior to that, each state had its own clock, and railroads had their own time zones, making long-distance travel a nightmare in terms of making connections. After that date, railroad timetables in America could then be printed so that people, taking the time from the station clock, would know precisely when the next train would arrive. (The problem of time zones did not arise in the UK.)

Prior to that, churches rang bells to call people to prayer, and monasteries, which had services at regular intervals throughout the day and night, had candles or primitive clocks to make sure that worship was carried out with reasonable regularity. Yet even those times of worship were strictly local and variable, and depended on the season of the year, as well as individual quirks of the time-keeping apparatus. The monasteries, with their daily cycle of prayers and vigils, prior to the early mechanical clocks, would have experienced as much as three hours difference in their early morning prayers depending on whether it was winter or summer.

If you have ever gone without wearing a watch, without having to rely on precise time, you will have found that there is a looseness in your day, less of a need to 'clock-watch' and, instead, to enjoy the opportunity to 'take *your* time.'

There are ways of measuring duration other than by a clock. Cooking, an activity which often requires some form of timekeeping, used to be regulated according to activities. For example, the length of time a dish needed to be cooked would be measured by saying the Lord's Prayer a number of times, or sending someone to walk the perimeter of a specific field, or by singing a particular song a certain number of times.

The sun, the moon, and the stars, flowers opening and closing, the seasons, hunger and thirst are all excellent ways of knowing how time passes without the use of a clock. In modern society, the clock seems to act more as a way of restricting ourselves rather than liberating us. It might be something you want to try for yourself, getting rid of timepieces and finding other ways of measuring the days. The sense of time in such cases is altered.

On such occasions, it is not enough to say that the *sense* of time is altered, rather that it is as if time itself is altered. The passage of a day is differentiated by various activities and by the bodily sensations and not by the hands of the clock. Time, in essence, still can be something personal, something which only you experience and understand, and that understanding is related to what you do, not what the clock does.

A wheat farmer, for example, might have a different sense of time: he thinks in longer, cyclic terms of harvest and annual cycles. In fact Hesiod, a seventh century BC Greek farmer and poet, wrote detailed descriptions of how to know when to perform various agricultural activities by noting where the stars were in the sky and what was happening in nature. The time for such things was long and slow, the stars gently moving into position, the plants slowly opening or closing. There is no suddenness in such time, no mechanical precision.

On the other hand, a day laborer (whether on an annual salary or not, but one who has varying daily tasks), whether in an office or working in the fields or in the streets, looks forward to the end of the day or the end of the week, with little regard for nature's movements. It is a quicker pace of time due to the shorter period of measurement.

It could be argued that there is an inherent need in Man to measure time in some fashion. The Biblical Genesis with its seven days of creation and lunar calendars scratched on bone dating back 30,000 years are just two examples. But that does not imply that time was perceived in the same sense throughout history. Indeed, Mircea Eliade, a historian of religion, argues that there was no distinction between the past and the present in the minds of our ancestors; ritual enactment of gods' and heroes' deeds meant that they were still alive in the moments of the rituals. This is echoed in the Catholic mass and the belief in the transubstantiation of the bread and wine into the body and blood of Christ.

If we do not take into account the cultural systemization of time as evidenced in calendars used for social and governmental purposes, then time, as measured by different individual people, seems to be elastic. It has been found that time is also dependent upon the size and metabolic rate of an organism, according to a study published in the journal *Animal Behaviour*. Flies, it seems, experience time more slowly. The same is true for children. How often have you thought back to your childhood and it seemed that the days were longer? The fact is, because you were smaller and your metabolic rate was higher then, your experience of time was different from how you experience it now. Time was slower for you then. (This has been proven with experiments using atomic clocks. For everything that moves, time passes more slowly (in microseconds) than that which static. It can also be shown that the passage of time varies (also in microseconds) according to altitude.)

There is also no one universal time we are forced to follow when we are alone. We can make our time be what we want it to be. We can think of it in differing ways for differing reasons, yet mostly we choose not to, relying instead on following the pacing of the hands of a clock or the changing figures on our phones or computers, making us conform in our thinking about, and appreciation of, time.

"Time is what stops everything happening at once," goes the saying (variously attributed to Albert Einstein, Richard Feynman, and Woody Allen, amongst others). Einstein once said that spending an hour with a pretty girl seems like a minute, and putting your hand on a hot stove for a minute seems like an hour. That was his way of explaining relativity as simply as possible. And it is something to which we can all relate.

We, each of us, have had moments which seemed to fly by, and others where the clock seemed to have moved at a snail's pace. Obviously, we are perceiving the passage of time differently in each case, just as Einstein said. And always, time seems to move forward, so that we experience a present moment, but ahead of us is the future and behind is the past. Both of them, according to our clocks, our measurements, are unobtainable. They are separate from us; the past is irretrievable and the future unreachable.

We tend to take those examples where time flies or time crawls as aberrations, anomalies in the usual way we measure time. After all, we have clocks and watches and sundials and all the rest, and we can see the march of time. Any such deviations from the monotonous ticking of seconds must be due to some problem within us. (Yet, of course, such mechanisms are only our efforts to measure a concept which is not universal, despite our wishes. The differences in time according to speed or altitude are examples of this.)

But even if we accept that dismissive excuse for our ability to distort time, still we have to accept that it does happen. Bergson, the philosopher, had noticed this when he said, "One part of the mind has the power to encounter reality as simply and directly as drinking a glass of water. The other part can only come to terms with reality by strapping it into a kind of rigid iron framework and measuring it with clocks and rulers." In other words, he was saying that if we want to see reality as a flow of time, then that's what we will see. But the truth of things, the 'real' reality, is not something which can be strapped down and measured. It must be experienced differently.

Itzhak Bentov in his whimsically titled *Stalking The Wild Pendulum* suggested that it was possible, through practice, to 'stretch' time. (The title, by the way, was because, according to Bentov, "…everything in the universe that is visible or manifest behaves like a pendulum moving from one point of rest to another. In other words, all matter vibrates.") In order to demonstrate this stretching of time, he said you should have a clock with a second hand in front of you and you should sit and be relaxed.

Once you have the rhythm of the clock in your head, you should close your eyes and allow yourself to bring to mind a favorite scene, such as being at the seaside. It is important, he said, to visualize this as clearly as possible. The sounds, the sights, even the smells, should be as vivid as you can make them.

Having achieved that state, then you open your eyes and casually glance at the clock, but in a very disinterested, remote fashion. He said that if you have followed these steps well, then you will see the second hand stick or slow down, even hover momentarily.

However, as soon as you consciously become aware of what it is doing, it will return to its original rhythm. The more you practice this, he said, the better you will become at stopping the second hand. For myself, I have been immersed in something such as reading a book which has taken all my attention, and I have blotted out the world beyond as a result. Looking up at the clock without really being aware of what I was doing, I have seemed to wait a long time for the second hand to move. Once it started, there were no longer any hesitations. My conscious mind kicked in and everything reverted back to 'normality.'

What makes time so interesting, and especially so for us in coming to terms with intuition, is that in the vast majority of cases of intuition, either the future or the past is involved. Sometimes only the immediate future, as when you know who is on the phone before picking it up, sometimes the long distant past, as with Toynbee at Pharsalos.

Of course, we have to ask how is that possible, if time is simply flowing along, the future ahead of us becoming the present before disappearing behind us into the past, and we are simply stuck in the present unable to hold on to either? The same problem holds true for each and every time we have had a feeling or foreboding about something in the future. It holds true for the passengers and crew of the Titanic who voiced their premonitions.

For all of these examples, for each of our own premonitions, whether they are seen in great detail or they manifest only as a 'bad' feeling or an uneasiness, the central problem is time. There seems to be something in us which can perceive the future. And, if that is the case, then presumably we can also perceive the past, something hinted at when Anna felt uncomfortable in the music shop which once had been a slaughterhouse.

The thing about time is that we seem to be immersed in it, but we also seem to be unaware of how we can somehow ignore the commonly accepted concept and jump back and forward in it even when we don't know we are doing any such thing. Do we, in fact, possess some amazing natural ability to ignore, interrupt or alter the flow of time?

In 1955, Michele Besso, a great friend of Einstein, died. Writing a consolatory letter to the family, Einstein said, "Now he has departed this strange world a little ahead of me. That signifies nothing. For us believing physicists, the distinction between past, present, and future is only a stubbornly persistent illusion." Ravelli, the quantum gravity expert, expands upon this by noting that in the fundamental equations of his area of study, there is no variable for time, because it is not necessary. The world can be described without using time.

The proof of such an assertion that time is merely an illusion can, it seems, be found in experiments carried out whereby participants were shown random images, some of which were beautiful and calming, whilst others were designed to shock or arouse. Upon reviewing the physiological responses of these many tests, it was discovered that the body was reacting to the *next* image in the sequence. Dean Radin, the scientist in charge of the experiments held at the University of Nevada in Las Vegas, saw that there was a drop in blood pressure in the extremities about a second before a disturbing image was shown. These were when the highest responses occurred, less so prior to a calming image's appearance. A similar reaction was observed in card game participants who somehow 'knew' at a basic physiological level they would be getting a bad hand before they were given any cards.

Daryl Bem of Cornell University, writing in the *Journal of Personality and Social Psychology,* reported on an experiment in which the subjects were asked to remember as many words as possible from a long list. Later they were asked to type a random selection of words taken from that list. He found that they were significantly better at remembering words they would later type. The future was affecting the present. The paper, reflecting this unexpected process, was called, *Feeling the Future: Experimental Evidence for Anomalous Retroactive Influences on Cognition and Affect.*

Further, similar experiments carried out by Rollin McCraty of the HeartMath Institute have also shown this precognition at work. In his experiments, subjects were shown random pictures, either calm or designed to provide an emotional response. Sat in front of a computer showing a blank screen, they pressed a button and six seconds later one or other of the type of pictures was shown for 3 seconds before the screen blanked again. A range of physiological readings were taken throughout.

What the results showed was that the heart was responding to what was *going* to be seen; the heart rate increased prior to an emotional image, or remained even prior to a calm image appearing. These reactions were happening up to six seconds ahead of the event. Stop what you are doing now and let six seconds elapse. It is a long period of time when you are doing nothing. But it has been shown that your heart, or rather the field of the heart, can perceive the emotional future at least that far ahead.

The experiment only accounted for a six-second period of premonition. We do not know exactly how far ahead the heart can sense, or whether such sensing is only possible in the immediate environment, or whether another mechanism is responsible for sensing something at a distance. Of course, it might not fully explain much longer-term premonitions, such as those mentioned concerning the Titanic, but it does help to explain at least some of the varieties of experiences we all share.

These results should also be considered in light of the previous discoveries about the size of the heart field and how it might contain much information. Of course, the precognitive heart rate does not have to be the same source as the heart field or consist of the same data which that could contain. But what it does show, quite dramatically, is just how important the heart is in terms of intuition, either in conveying information or anticipating it.

There are some results which suggest that this ability of the heart to perceive the future on an individual basis is something which is common to us all concerning the planet we live on. More than that, these results suggest that when sufficient numbers of people are monitored, there is something like a collective mind at work. Indeed, this collective mind not only is aware of global events, but is aware of them prior to their happening.

Placed around the world are seventy small contraptions known variously as RNGs or EGGs. The latter name comes from pushing the words electroencephalogram and Gaia together. (Gaia was the name the scientist James Lovelock chose to represent his hypothesis that Earth was a living being.) The other term, RNG, is what they really are: Random Number Generators. The idea behind them is that such randomness can be altered and made more coherent by the unified attention of many minds on specific events.

Note that the RNGs are not themselves the focus of the people, but are reacting to what the people are sensing elsewhere. This effect was originally noted in laboratory experiments intended to monitor remote healing abilities. However, upon examination, the RNGs showed a greater coherence (less randomness) than expected at peak times of the experiment. Further analysis of RNGs elsewhere showed that, in this case, those located nearest to the experiment showed a greater degree of coherence. In other words, the researchers realized, it was possible that both living and non-living objects could be influenced by focused attention.

From this basis arose RNGs being monitored by the Global Consciousness Project. Instead of there being focused attention such as sending healing, it was believed that sufficiently large numbers of people sharing or experiencing emotions in general would show up in the data as greater coherence, less randomness in the numbers being generated. Global sporting events and deaths of influential figures and so on were considered to be useful data points.

The data, which are publicly available, reveal that there is an element of precognition occurring. Prior to such a significant event as 9/11 for example, there is evidence that there was a premonition about something (in this case the attack on the twin towers, up to four hours prior to it happening). Instead of the heart rate and other physiological readings of a comparatively small sample being used to provide the data, here it is the global population which makes up the experiment size, and electronic random number generators are what are being affected.

Studying the results and placing them in context with significant moments has revealed over 400 events which seemed to have been predicted or be the subject of premonitions in some fashion. Such events ranged from tsunamis to volcanic eruptions to aircraft crashes to the death of Princess Diana and even the opening ceremony of the Olympic Games. Chance would suggest that such results would be more or less random, say 1 in 2. However, according to their analysis, to have this number of correlations happen randomly would be closer to one in a million.

One such event was the tsunami of December 26th, 2004, the third largest earthquake recorded on a seismograph, and one which resulted in the deaths of nearly 250,000 people in 14 countries bordering the Indian Ocean, the majority of them in Indonesia. Although it showed up as a greater coherence in the RNGs, there is also the testimony of a friend, Sonya, who remembered the day before, Christmas Day, very clearly. She was sitting at home in England, surrounded by her family when she suddenly said, "There hasn't been a major disaster for ages. I can sense there is going to be one." As is by now common, she had no idea why she said it, except that it "just came out." Her family made comments about how cheery that was on Christmas Day. Such a large earthquake could possibly have been detected in some fashion around the globe, but the wording was specific about a coming disaster rather than offering a general feeling of unease about the future. It is highly probable that Sonya was indeed 'picking up' in some fashion what the global mind was latching onto. That she had a sensitivity to such a consciousness had been shown before, on May 22, 2002. On that date, again for no specific reason that she could recall, she said, "There's going to be a plane crash. A big one." On May 25, 2002, China Airlines flight 611 disintegrated in mid-air and crashed, killing all 225 people aboard. There is no possibility of sensing that in the same way as an earthquake's low frequencies might be sensed. There seemed to be a genuine precognition of specific events in the same way that the RNGs were showing. As an aside, she also mentions that her family now take any of her predictions seriously.

For these RNG results to occur, it must be assumed that there is a connection of some sort which exists between the RNGs and the people in much the same way that the glycerin example of an earlier chapter seemed to be connected. This connection is an important point which we will return to later.

Incidentally, this idea of a large number of minds having an ability beyond that of an individual mind is echoed in discoveries of how crowds of people are better able to predict outcomes than talented individuals. Here the focus is on knowledge, not just of the future, in a general fashion, but of a more specific kind. The common assumption of crowds is that they are mad or without reason. Such ideas are seemingly confirmed with images of riots among rival supporters of sports teams. In such cases, the words of the English historian, Thomas Carlyle, who said, "I do not believe in the collective wisdom of individual ignorance" would seem to be accurate.

However, if we exclude the crowds which gather together in a passion to oppose or support something, then his words are wrong. This was first proved in Plymouth, England in 1906. In that year, a statistician named Francis Galton, who was also obsessed with the idea that better breeding amongst people (as well as animals) was the answer to a brighter future, attended an agricultural show. In one area, there was a large ox on show. Members of the public (about whom Galton had decidedly misanthropic views concerning their general stupidity) were invited to guess the weight of the ox after it had been slaughtered and made ready for sale. 800 people took part, paying for the privilege in hopes of winning a cash prize if they were nearest to the actual weight. Galton's views on the entrants can be guessed by what he wrote afterward in his report in the journal *Nature*. "The average competitor was probably as well-fitted for making a just estimate of the dressed weight of the ox, as an average voter is of judging the merits of most political issues on which he votes." After the competition was over and the prizes were awarded, Galton asked for and collected the tickets to analyze the results. Amongst other things, he calculated the mean of the total guesses. What he found amazed him. He thought if people were dumb, then the end result would reflect that. Instead he found that the average of all the guesses put the weight at 1,197 pounds. The actual weight was 1,198 pounds.

Galton had accidentally stumbled over a fact which has been proven to be correct over and over again in different ways: that collectively, people have an ability which as individuals they lack. This exact same ability has been shown in locating sunken submarines, predicting stocks and shares, and betting on sports, not to mention the outcomes of elections and academy awards.

It does seem, therefore, that people en masse have an ability which individuals might exhibit only on occasion or fitfully. One of those abilities includes, it seems, something within us which is able to sense the future. Perceiving the future in some fashion can be tested and results obtained. But what of the past? Intuitions reveal information of the past, but is it possible to set up experiments or provide evidence that we can react to the past in much the same way as we can the future? How do we explain sensing the past, as in Toynbee's vision in Pharsalos or glimpsing Hawaii and the eruption of Mount Kilauea?

There would seem to be two possible approaches to answering this question. The first possibility is that past events are somehow imprinted or embedded in objects or places in some fashion and that they can be 'triggered' somehow by some people. The second possibility is that we are capable of reaching back in time in the same way as we can reach forward into the future. There is, of course, a third possibility, which is that we have absolutely no clue at all about what time really is, and we are basing everything on incorrect assumptions—a dead-end, in other words.

If we consider the first option, that of the past as a recording, then it might be that there are in some places an ability to store information in some fashion. After all, we can store information using a long wavy groove, as on a record, or using tiny pits on DVDs and CDs and magnetically manipulating an oxide on a tape. There are also photographs created using various chemical and now digital processes as well as sculptures and paintings. Even a tree, in the way it has grown, not only in the growth rings but in the shape of its growth, exhibits its past to us.

The past is available to us in a variety of forms, some more detailed or more specific than others. It is reasonable to suppose that, in some fashion, certain aspects of the past, perhaps those with greater emotional intensity, could be held by the environment and accessed by those with sufficient talent or the correct mental attitude, or even by being in the right place at the right time for certain, as yet unknown, circumstances to coincide.

Such does seem to be a possibility in the case of battlefields such as at Naseby in England or Gettysburg in North America, where people, over a considerable period of time, have reported hearing the noises of battle as well as of seeing ghosts. If those are at the extreme end of such possible recordings, then Anna's feeling of unease in a record store, the site of which has been a slaughterhouse, could be considered to be the norm of our reactions. (Of course, the earlier examples of the influence of piezo-electricity and the natural earth magnetism of megalithic monuments may also be a way of storing aspects of the past.)

Interestingly, there have been studies on the effects of emotions upon the environment. Research has shown that carbon dioxide and nitrogen in the soil alter where predation has taken place, specifically where an animal was killed. Equally, those same changes have been shown to take place where the *fear* of being eaten existed. In other words, measurable physical changes can be found in the ground to reflect past emotional issues of the animals on it. There is no reason not to think that presently unmeasured or unrecognized changes in the environment might also be stored and accessed, providing an explanation for seeing or hearing old battles or feeling specific emotions at sites of violence.

The philosopher Henri Bergson who believed intuition was the way of getting to the heart of reality and said that a part of us can only deal with reality by measuring it with clocks and rulers, also believed our brains are effective filters. What we sense, he said, was only that which our brains allowed to come through to us. The past, he thought, "still exists." It was still present "to our consciousness in such a manner that, to have the revelation of it, consciousness has no need to go out of itself....It has but to remove an obstacle, to withdraw a veil."

While that might be a helpful belief, it does not speak to the central issue of proof. Is the past accessible from the present, not simply as memory, but as something malleable? Or, to put this all another way, what if all precognitions were due to influences or mental states of the future, instead of the present perceiving the future? What if we are creating our own time, our own experience of time, due to our future actions? When stated like this, it seems inconceivable. Yet we are quite content to accept that somehow we can peer into the future. Peering into the future is, however unlikely, 'normal,' especially in intuitions. The strangeness of the idea only happens because we have become accustomed to expect that the past is the past and cannot be changed. It has happened. That's the very implication behind the past tense: there is something (history), which is now set in stone due to it having happened prior to this present moment.

Here we get to the second possibility about accessing the past: reaching back in time. The obvious question which arises from such a conjecture is, if the future is mediating the present, can there be proof of such a thing? If so, that would constitute an argument for accepting that the past is as accessible as the future seems to be. While that might seem to be an impossible hurdle to overcome, there are several highly convincing experiments which show that we are able to reach back in time and alter it. If those are true, then it would seem that the present is simply a label for something which is fluid and subject to change at a moment's notice. The past is then accessible.

To explore the idea of influencing the past, a German parapsychologist, Elmar Gruber, converted random everyday events into a series of clicks. For example, when people in a supermarket crossed a photo beam, or cars entering a tunnel in Vienna did the same, or when gerbils moved around their cage or rotated their activity wheel a certain number of times, each movement or activity was converted into a click. These clicks were then stored on tapes, copies of which were kept to eliminate fraud. These tapes were not listened to until later. In the case of the gerbils, he asked volunteers up to six days later to listen to one of the tapes and, as they listened, try to influence the gerbils to move faster than usual or to break the beam more often. In the case of people and the cars, the volunteers didn't listen to them until up to two months later. Again, they were asked to attempt to influence the speed of the people and the cars on the tapes. Success would be measured by a greater number of clicks than usual. This was ascertained by comparing the tapes; the ones listened to and the copies which had been stored. The results were then analyzed statistically, and an effect size was given. An effect size of 0 means that there is no change between the two tapes. Normally an effect size of between 0.3 and 0.6 is considered medium, and anything above that is a large effect.

Gruber was astounded to find that the effect size was, for all of the experiments, between 0.44 and 0.72. To put those figures into some sort of comparison, it has been pointed out that the well-known drug Aspirin, then considered as a successful heart attack preventive, has an effect size of 0.032. That's ten times less of an effect than Gruber's results.

But measuring clicks and applying statistical analysis to them, while interesting, feels empty of human emotion and difficult to relate to in everyday terms. However, in 2000, another experiment was carried out which was about people, not clicks. Here a double-blind experiment was set up (one where information which could influence any of the parties involved is kept hidden) whereby about 4,000 people in hospital who had developed sepsis were selected to see what effects, if any, could be attributed to prayer. The patients were split randomly into two groups, and only one of those groups were prayed for. This was done by giving the names to someone to pray for them and for the health of the group overall. Three results were looked at: the number of deaths in hospital, the length of stay and the duration of fever. In examining the results, it was seen that the group which had been prayed for suffered fewer deaths (but not enough to be statistically significant), and also suffered fewer days of fever and had fewer days in hospital.

What makes this of interest to us are two things. First, the experimenter was Leonard Leibovici, an Israeli professor of internal medicine who wanted to prove that alternative medicine could not withstand the scrutiny of carefully applied scientific experiments. In this, it could be said, he failed. Because the second point of interest is that while the experiment was carried out in the year 2000, it was carried out on people who had been in hospital between 1990 and 1996. In other words, the prayers were said anywhere from four to ten years after the sepsis occurred. (The full details of all these experiments with time can be found in Lynne McTaggart's book, *The Intention Experiment*.)

Perhaps we should be more aware of what T.S. Eliot said in his poem, *Burnt Norton*:

> *Time present and time past*
>
> *Are both perhaps present in time future,*
>
> *And time future contained in time past.*

Statistically and experimentally, not to mention anecdotally, it seems that we can prove that we can sense the future and sense as well as influence the past. Yet what science, as a generality, holds to be true, the basics of what is taught in schools at least, appears to have no way of reconciling these views of space and time. To quote one investigator, Dean Radin, "it suggests that what science presently knows about the nature of the universe is seriously incomplete."

Indeed, everything we have examined in relation to intuition can be said to have overturned the traditional scientific view of the universe. It now seems evident that if intuition is to have any comprehensive theory, then it must encompass an understanding that how we see the universe is not how it actually is. There are intuitive senses operating at the same time as our physical ones and utilizing a variety of channels in the same way that sight and smell and touch utilize different channels to acquire information. But the intuitive senses seem not to be operating under the same rules as the physical ones.

To revert back to our consideration of what were always assumed to be the fundamentals of our world—time and space—then quite obviously time is not what we think it is. In which case then, what of space? The past and the future can be accessed by our intuition. But space, or distance, as in Sonya's awareness of tragedies half a world away, also seem to offer no barrier. Space also appears to be as fluid a concept as time.

10

THE FAILURE OF CLASSICAL PHYSICS

Quantum physics is a bit of a passion of mine. It's extraordinary. There's a branch of mathematics based on lunacy, and that's wonderful.
Bob Hoskins (Actor)

If time is one of the ways in which we normally measure our world and our lives, then the other foundation of our existence is space. And, in intuition, we have found that distance is no barrier to acquiring information. The stories of Peter Harmon 'seeing' the coke bottle on his client's land or Gerard Croiset locating a dead body while on the other side of the Atlantic seem to indicate that space, like time, is no barrier to ourselves and thus to our intuition.

Time and space are how we understand relationships between objects. Indeed, the concepts of space (how objects relate to each other) and time (in what order things happen) are central to physics, particularly the physics which we are all taught in school.

However, this 'school physics' with which we are so familiar has obvious limitations when we think of the different examples of intuition.

If time and space seem to impose no limits to intuition, then it seems very likely that much else of what we traditionally learn in schools about how science explains the workings of the world could also be wrong. Science and the scientific tradition that we are taught have imposed a template upon the physical world into which have been squeezed much of the everyday phenomena. It is referred to as the 'classical' model of physics. Yet, time and again, intuition, the everyday supra-sensory apprehension of the world, does not seem to fit into this template easily.

If the classical model does not help us to explain intuition, then we must look to another model instead. But, in order to understand the difference between the two, it is necessary for us to comprehend what the classical model consists of and how it provides us with a concept of the universe. Once we understand that concept clearly, then we can begin to appreciate that a different model is necessary if we are to better understand intuition.

There are five assumptions contained in the classical model of physics, and it is these five assumptions which are the background against which we form our reality. These five are generally considered to be reality, locality, causality, continuity, and determinism.

What these terms mean is as follows. Reality in classical physics is that which can be studied. It is the phenomenal world of the senses. I can see a glass bowl with my eyes, for example, and it is always there. It does not disappear because I am not looking at it. The universe, in this system, is made up of 'real' objects, whether they are being observed or not.

Locality is when something can only act upon another object if there is a way for the one to affect the other by a measurable force. I can only move a glass bowl if I am near enough to it or can use some object to move it, but there is a separation between the two of us. We are not connected in any way, and we remain separately located.

Causality is where everything must have a clear cause and effect, as in if I drop a glass bowl on the floor, the bowl will break due to the impact. If I scrape up the pieces of the bowl and hold them in my hand, they will not re-form into a glass bowl. The breakage also cannot occur prior to the dropping of the bowl.

Continuity is where the glass bowl remains a glass bowl and not, say, a ceramic bowl. It started out as a glass bowl, and it is always a glass bowl, and it does not disappear from view only to reappear later somewhere else as something else. Continuity, then, demands that things are as they are without a break in their existence.

Determinism is a doctrine which says that all events have causes which are external to the will of the individual, so that if the glass bowl fell and broke, it was due to gravity and the hardness of the floor and the initial motion given to it by my hand moving. In other words, even if we can't know everything, we can predict what will happen if we have enough information to put together about a situation.

That is the classical position with regard to reality. It is something dependable and reliable and measurable and consistent. Above all, it is how we appear to interact with the world in our daily lives. It seems to make sense. It would be unsettling, to say the least, to have a glass bowl change suddenly in shape or size or transform into a flower. We like the way things are. It makes us feel comfortable and safe. And, at the back of these five assumptions lies the further assumption that both space and time are fixed; that time flows ever forward (the bowl breaks after it is dropped), and that space doesn't suddenly contract or expand arbitrarily (the bowl and myself are in two distinct and separate places, for example).

We spoke earlier of perception and how it can depend so much on the individual. But if, as intuition suggests, two of the basic platforms of our supposed reality, those of time and space, are wrong, then what does that suggest? As Carl Jung once said, "It is almost an absurd prejudice to suggest that existence be only physical. As a matter of fact, the only form of existence of which we have immediate knowledge is psychic (i.e., in the mind)...we know of matter only in so far as we perceive psychic images mediated by the senses." Or, to re-phrase that, there is nothing outside of perception. That beautiful picture on the wall? It exists in your head where the perception occurs. Where the image is is where it actually is. Without eyesight, that picture would not exist. It would only be an object you could feel. And where is the sense of touch? Where does it exist? Where you perceive it, inside you. Nothing exists unless it is perceived. Which is what Bishop Berkeley said, "To be is to be perceived."

Think about that for just one moment. There is nothing outside of perception. If we do not perceive it, whatever 'it' is, it does not exist. Not that it is hiding out of our sight, beyond the horizon or in the dark, but literally does not exist. We create our world through our perceptions. Logically, and this is where things begin to sound more unsettling, if we only perceive what we perceive, then the universe did not exist until we perceived it. All those stars twinkling away in the night sky? They did not exist until someone looked up to see them, and then they were 'real.'

Such reasoning sounds absurd, because it goes against our five fundamentals of reality. But let us take a step back from such a concept and approach it in another way. And, in so doing, hopefully, we'll also approach the source of our intuition. This approach involves looking at quantum physics as an alternative to classical physics.

Before we begin our deeper dive, we should be reminded of Richard Feynman, the Nobel Laureate, on this subject: "It is my task to convince you not to turn away because you don't understand it. You see my physics students don't understand it…That is because I don't understand it. Nobody does."

Having given ourselves permission to be amazed and confused, let us continue. The essence of what we need to explore is something which, although it might be somewhat familiar to you from popular science articles and books, is basically contrary to how we think normally and, more to the point, has a direct relation to that moment when you suddenly, without warning, just know something to be true.

In what follows, I do not presume to be a physicist, only someone interested enough to try to explain experiments and formulate concepts in ways which a non-scientist (myself) finds more comfortable.

One theme has been predominant in this exploration of intuition (apart from the quandaries of space and time), and that is the importance of the observer. No matter what else might be said about perception, about how we see the world, the plain fact of the matter is that our intuition happens to us and to us alone. It does not matter whether we are in a crowd or not, our perception is all that counts, and we cannot share it as it happens, only afterward is that possible, to a greater or lesser degree.

Therefore, we need to examine this phenomenon of how the observer can shape the world, as it lies at the heart of everything. Once this has been established, we can then move on to the other particulars involved in explaining our intuition, chiefly, the problem with time and locality, or space. The classical model insists that time is a flowing river (although we have seen enough to be able to be comfortable in dismissing that without, as yet, having something to replace it with), and it also insists that we have no connection with anything which is not within our reach (and I include telescopes and microscopes as examples of extending our reach). With these three—perception / observation, time, and locality— we can then begin to put together a better picture of how our intuition works.

In terms of observation, of how we perceive the world, various experiments over the past century have revealed that the classical model of physics does not account for the results obtained. One of the most famous experiments involved light. Isaac Newton had said that light consisted of particles. Others doubted him and set up experiments which showed that light consisted of waves.

Then came the double slit experiment. Here a light source was shone, and the light could either pass through the left or the right slit. Doing so, the expected result would be a band of light behind each slit. What actually happened was a series of bands, as if the light was made up of waves. Waves collide with each other, canceling out or amplifying each other. Particles don't do this. The observed pattern could only have been made by waves.

Refining this further, individual photons of light were shot at the slits and, surprisingly, the same result was obtained after sufficient photons had passed. But how could individual photons, particles if you like, show wave-like properties? That was the conundrum. In further refinements, light which had been polarized—meaning that the photons could only travel in one direction (let's call it horizontally or vertically)—and the slits set up so that each slit would only allow one type of photon polarization to pass through it, the results showed that photons were, indeed, particles, because the pattern which ended up was that of two bars of light. That doesn't sound peculiar, except that you have to ask what happened to the previous result where it was obvious that light was a wave? Was light a wave or a particle?

The only answer which made sense of the results (even though it seemed impossible) was that it was both. It was the same light, but it showed different results or qualities. How could that be? The only difference in the experiments which could account for the change in results was that, in the first, only the end result was observed, but in the second, there was a measurement made of each photon. In the second one, an attempt was made to see which photons did what—travel horizontally or vertically. There was an observation made of that particular aspect of each photon and that alone, apparently, was enough to determine that it was a particle, and not a wave. In the first experiment, with no other observation except the end result, it looked like the photons could choose what they were to be. And that meant, paradoxically and against all common sense, that they passed through both slits before ending up on the recording screen and were then measured (or observed).

To reduce this to its basic principle, the mere act of observing a photon before it hit the screen altered it. In the first, it could be either a wave or a particle, but in the second, because we were looking at particles to see where they went, it became a particle. Looking at the photons changed what they were. You can see them as either a particle or as a wave. What you cannot do is see them as both. The observer is the one who decides which it is to be, and that is a result of the experimental model. The observer determines the reality of the photon by focusing on one aspect of it. You can either know the end result or you can know the path it took. You cannot, it seems, know both at the same time. The end result of the first experiment happened because either wave or particle was possible. The observer wasn't interested in knowing which was happening. The end result of the second experiment was because the observer forced the photon to be a particle, because he was interested in knowing what type—horizontal or vertical—the photon was.

This experiment has become a classic for its clarity in showing the strangeness of quantum mechanics. Richard Feynman called it "a phenomenon which is impossible […] to explain in any classical way, and which has in it the heart of quantum mechanics. In reality, it contains the only mystery [of quantum mechanics]."

The double slit experiment's results were due to what is called superposition. This is the name given to the sort of blurry state of the photons in the first experiment. They could be anything they wanted to be. But, when they were looked at in the second experiment, the superposition 'collapsed' into a particle. The photons no longer had the ability to be whatever they wanted to be (superposition) because they were being looked at (became collapsed).

That experiment and the conclusions derived from it of course are not what we would call normal when compared to our classical model, but a development of that observer effect experiment brought about another unexpected and equally strange discovery: entanglement.

Now, instead of looking at individual photons and thus deciding what they should be, let's suppose that there are a pair of photons which are born together and shoot off in different directions. Such photons are said to be entangled. They could be on opposite sides of the universe, hurtling away from each other. If we do not look at them, they remain in a state of superposition. But, and here is where it again gets unexpected, if I look at one of the twins—let's say I see it as a vertical photon—then the other twin immediately assumes the complementary aspect—in this case, horizontal. The key word is 'immediately.' No matter how far apart, it happens at the same time.

These experiments deal harsh blows to classical physics' insistence upon locality (an object can only be acted upon by something in its neighborhood) and reality (the existence of objects whether or not they are being observed). Time and space, therefore, seem not to exist. Matter and energy (particles and photons), it seems, can transmit information across the universe instantly.

But there is yet another experiment's result which expands upon this blow to classical physics. In this, the basic principle of a double slit experiment is set up, except that in this case, instead of looking at individual photons, entangled photons are being measured. The twin photons A and B are set off around different routes to two different detectors much as in the double-slit experiment. When the second photon (B) arrives at its respective detector, a counter, called a coincidence counter, records the event as both have completed their journeys. In other words, only when the second photon arrives is any measurement made. Run like this, and the result is an interference pattern of a wave. There is no way of knowing which slit a photon took, so they remain 'blurry', or in a state of superposition until they hit the screen. But then if you introduce a polarization filter before the slit for photon A only, a particle pattern is seen with two clear bars, because you are seeing what type of photon it is.

So far, so expected (given the results of the double-slit experiment). But then the next step is to switch off the coincidence counter. Everything else is left in place, including the polarization filters in front of photon A's detection screen. The only difference is now there is no way of knowing which slit a photon took because the counter can't tell us when they have both arrived. With the filters still in place but no way of knowing when a photon arrives, the detector shows a wave pattern.

Somehow, by switching off the counter, the photons altered their function from particle to wave. The counter allowed us to gather information. When that is removed, the photons changed. How did they know of this change? The only answer can be that we stopped observing them, because that was the only change made.

In 2002 a variation of this experiment revealed something very unusual. In this, the distance the two photons had to travel to reach the detection screen could be varied so that photon A, for example, would be traveling a shorter distance than its twin, but still passing through the polarization filter in front of the double slit. That was the only change made to the original setup: the second photon took a longer route. The coincidence counter is turned on so information is being gathered about them both, and photon B, traveling the longer route, will always be hitting its screen after its twin had registered on its own screen. The results do not change.

This means that with the counter on, the detector screen for photon A shows two bars, the pattern for a particle. But that happened *before* photon B had arrived. Recall that previously having the counter off ended with a wave pattern. In this version, the counter is effectively off because it has *not yet* registered a hit from the B photon, and yet the pattern is the same as if the counter had already registered the arrival of photon B. In other words, the final result of two bars (meaning particles were being measured) is obtained because, in some fashion, photon A knows whether or not the information about it *will* be known. It has, in effect, obtained knowledge of the future. Photon A apparently knows that some time in the future, information about photon B will be collected. Photon B will hit the screen later, and the counter will then register its arrival, and therefore information about it will be obtained, and that future information is somehow known by photon A *before* it happens.

Photon A somehow knew the future as it related to photon B. Entanglement means that one photon will react to what happens to the other instantaneously. In this case, one photon reacted to what was going to happen to the other. The second was going to be observed, so the first photon acted accordingly.

In the October 2010 issue of *Scientific American,* Stephen Hawking and Leonard Mlodinow wrote, "There is no way to remove the observer—us —from our perceptions of the world... In classical physics, the past is assumed to exist as a definite series of events, but according to quantum physics the past, like the future, is indefinite and exists only as a spectrum of possibilities."

Let us close this chapter with another quote, this time from Richard Feynman. "I think it is safe to say that no one understands quantum mechanics...Do not keep saying to yourself... 'But how can it be like that?,' because you will go down the drain into a blind alley from which nobody has yet escaped."

It's OK to be confused!

The universe may now seem to be far different from what we normally imagine it to be. But if we are to find a way to understand intuition, then it must be that the new physics of non-locality, of observer influence and the rest is the only satisfactory way of explaining this common experience. It is clear now that the familiar classical model of physics which seeks to explain how the world works is incapable of explaining how the non-physical world of intuition operates. The new physics of quantum reality is the only one which can account for intuition's seemingly inexplicable confounding of space and time.

Therefore, the only conclusion which can fit these new facts is that there is something, some 'reality,' which underlies everything and which connects everything in the universe. It cannot be the reality as determined by the classical model, because that cannot account for how glycerin suddenly became crystalized, nor can it account for the results of the RNGs anticipating future events. What that something might be is consciousness itself, for without it, neither space nor time exist, and yet it can, in some fashion, bring about events which materialize in this, our perception of the universe.

The defining characteristic of consciousness in the eastern model is of insights beyond the phenomenal world. That approach seems to be a better 'fit' with both the examples of quantum physics and of intuition's characteristics. So it is to that underlying field which we turn our attention next in order to examine how intuition and physics might intersect.

11

THE FUNDAMENTAL FIELD

Distance doesn't exist, in fact, and neither does time. Vibrations from love or
music can be felt everywhere, at all times.
Yoko Ono (Artist)

If time and space, those elements which we normally think serve to separate objects and events, are elastic, as they have to be for intuition to operate as it does, then it is reasonable to suggest that there is something else which connects everything together. Backster called it primary perception, but did not speculate as to what form it might take. Yet if entangled photons and remote viewing have similarities, in that they both ignore the classical concepts of time and space, then there is some basic aspect of the universe as yet unaccounted for which allows such a connection and communication to take place.

Talking about individual photons and measuring what they are doing, even when they are heading off in different directions and deciding whether they are waves or particles may not, at first glance, seem to reveal very much about intuition. But how is the universe different because of these discoveries? Perhaps one way to describe it would be to say that, instead of the stars and the trees and the rocks and tables and yesterday's meetings and tomorrow's vacations we know about, there is a vastness of possibilities where everything is waiting and from which everything we know arises. That vastness, that sea, is what we dip into with the bucket we call intuition. Or, perhaps with more accuracy, we get splashed by it every now and then and call it intuition. That sea, it seems, is what connects everything, but in a way which is more immediate and more direct than our classical view of reality allows for. For intuition to work, this underlying connection must lie beyond time and outside space as we usually consider these concepts.

Of course, the real questions remain. What is this sea? What does it consist of? How do we know that it is truly the basis of everything? And, if it is there and operates as we suspect, what specific connections exist to allow us to access it?

Before beginning to answer these questions, it is important to note that there are various interpretations of those experiments' results of the previous chapter. These are those who adhere to the idea that there are many different worlds, each one caused by each measurement, and that this gets rid of the role of the observer. If that is so, then this theory leaves no room for intuition, as there seems no possibility of accessing the future in such a scenario.

Next, there are those who say that the paradoxes observed in the experiments are really caused by limitations in our language and logic, and once those are dealt with, quantum reality will be a lot easier to understand. If this is so—and the problems we have with language and how we experience the world will be examined more closely later on—then a better understanding of quantum reality does not negate quantum physics as being a way to explain classical physic's problem with intuition.

Finally, some would like to suggest that when quantum objects interact with the environment, there is a collapse caused by the interactions, and everything acts like the 'classical' physics universe. If so, then, again, that would not be amenable to explaining the problems of time and space we have uncovered.

The interpretation we are following here is that the central and crucial part of reality is consciousness itself, because it is through consciousness that we have perceptions. It is also through consciousness in some form or another that we experience intuition, or more accurately, experience the phenomena associated with it.

If consciousness is indeed the substrate of the universe, the underlying field permeating everything, then it is possible to suggest that intuition, rather than rational thought or physical perception, is the clearest connection to it and is, therefore, to be more highly regarded and valued than familiar modes of understanding.

Some physicists are not happy about this position, because it echoes so much of Eastern philosophy and how mystics have expressed their understanding, fearing that it detracts from the rational, empirical approach they adhere to. Nevertheless, there are Nobel prize winners and other eminent physicists who do promote this view and have found no serious flaws in arguments supporting it.

It seems to come down to this: what we think we are living in is not the universe we grew up in, where everything was ordered and easily measured and separate from ourselves; instead, it is a new one of perception and timelessness and non-locality. Where to begin?

Probably the best place to begin is with the blank space of the universe. After all, if the universe is born of our perception, and it contains everything we can think of, then it makes sense to look more closely at it and what it might be concealing as we currently perceive it. Despite looking up on a clear night and seeing the sky filled with stars, there is an awful lot of space between them. Some of that space is filled with cosmic dust, and there's a lot of electromagnetic radiation. Say you get rid of the dust and you also get rid of a lot of the radiation (the thermal part of it) by cooling it down, you still have some electromagnetic waves in evidence. The vacuum of space, it seems, is not really a vacuum at all, but it's about as close as we can get to nothing. And yet that nothingness still contains something.

You know from experience that cold makes things frozen, and frozen things don't move. The coldest we can conceive of making things so that nothing moves, or as close to nothing moves as possible, is a frighteningly low temperature. It is generally referred to as zero degrees Kelvin (after the nineteenth-century physicist). Zero degrees Kelvin is -459.67 degrees Fahrenheit, which is -273.15 degrees Celsius. That is three degrees below the temperature for the vacuum of space. That is Absolute Zero or the zero point.

The fact that space does not reach the zero point is due to the remnants of the Big Bang, which is evidenced by the cosmic microwave background. The average temperature of space is about 2.73 kelvins, or -454.76 Fahrenheit, -270.42 Centigrade. The closest anyone has come to cooling anything down to the zero point was measured at 0.0000000001 kelvin.

We need to go back to quantum mechanics for just one moment. Recall that observation or measurement was paramount in the experiments. One of the pioneers of quantum physics, Werner Heisenberg, in 1927 said that you can either know (observe) the position or the momentum of a particle. You can't know both at the same time. This principle has been called, for obvious reasons, the Heisenberg uncertainty principle, or simply the uncertainty principle. (This principle was not arrived at theoretically but through observation.)

Now, as colder temperatures reduce the movement of molecules so that they are at rest, we would then know both their position and their speed, thus violating the uncertainty principle, which is really referring to a fundamental property of all quantum systems rather than an observational effect. Moreover, if there was absolutely no movement, nothing happening at all, then there would be a complete silence or absence of any detectable energy. But that is not the case. There is something happening even at the zero point. Its existence registers as low-level noise in electronic and optical equipment.

The presence of these fluctuating electromagnetic waves that are always present and can't be stopped imply that 'empty' space contains energy which we cannot see but is always there. This idea was expressed by David Bohm, a physicist who once worked with Einstein. He remarked that "Space is not empty. It is full, a plenum as opposed to a vacuum, and is the ground for the existence of everything, including ourselves. The universe is not separate from this cosmic sea of energy." This 'sea' is what has been termed zero point energy.

So it seems that there really is something underlying what we can measure. That means there should be a lot of energy unaccounted for. This vacuum energy is vast. If it is calculated using quantum field theory, then it is infinite!

Richard Feynman and another physicist, John Wheeler, calculated that a cubic centimeter of 'empty' space contained enough energy to boil all the seas. Which sounds wonderful in terms of renewable energy sources, but there is no practical way of accessing that energy. Plus, following the idea of harnessing such energy would take us away from our search for the cause or source of intuition.

The important aspect of zero point energy is that there are some interesting aspects to it which do have a bearing on our investigation. At or very close to the zero point (within a few billionths of a degree), a new type of matter forms. In 1955, John Wheeler, the same one noted previously, called it quantum foam. He saw it as a sea of bubbling energy-matter. The modern names for it are Bose-Einstein condensate or superfluid vacuum, which sound less friendly than quantum foam.

In 1924, an Indian physicist, Satyendra Nath Bose, wrote to Einstein with an idea that at a temperature just a few parts of a degree above absolute zero, particles would stop being individual and act more as a single one. Such a substance would be able to flow with no loss of energy whatsoever. (Think of water droplets down a large window. They start off large but lose energy—water—if they don't meet and mingle with any other droplets and will eventually come to a halt. A droplet does not continue indefinitely without gathering more water.) This effect is the reason for calling a Bose-Einstein condensate a superfluid (in a vacuum).

At such a low temperature the individual atoms, in a sense, lose their individual identities and become enmeshed and tangled with each other. It is a state which is not a gas, a liquid or a solid, but an entirely new one. In essence, such a substance is one single particle spread out everywhere in space and time, and the energy necessary for maintaining that state comes from the zero point field. Such a condensate was first achieved in 1995. It is, if you like, a super-atom made up of overlapping atoms all sharing a single quantum state. Of course, language here is not up to the task of clearly explaining or defining such a state, being able only to use analogy, which is why mathematics is more able to offer a precise explanation of it.

The universe that we observe when we look up at night, the stars, the galaxies and so on, that observable part of it only accounts for a little less than 5% of the mass of the universe. The other 95% is, obviously, not observable. Dark energy and dark matter make up the rest. Dark matter (both mysterious and invisible) is thought to account for 25% of the mass, and dark energy (considered by some to be what the zero point field is, and is that force which repels gravity and is responsible for the acceleration of the expansion of the universe) makes up the other 75%. Therefore, it would seem that there is an underlying force or field which permeates the universe, making up most of everything.

But there still remains the question of how this zero point field might help us understand intuition. We know that time and space are dependent upon the observer. We also know that information in one form or another is the essential part of any intuition. Is there then any way in which these two can be related? Does the zero point field, in effect, provide anything useful apart from its presence everywhere? And can we use it to help us understand how information might arrive in us?

If the zero point field provides energy for the condensate or superfluid, then what is this energy? This quantum foam world seems to be made up of standing waves of energy and, it has been proposed, that there could be minute wormholes in it which could be hyperspatial links to other dimensions.

What those other dimensions might contain is impossible to know directly, but one of the possibilities would be that it is what has been called Pleroma or the Akashic record. Pleroma comes from the Greek for fullness and has been used by both Gnostics and Christians to describe the place where God or Christ dwells and which is, therefore, the place where divinity and divine powers are to be found. Recall that in

Christian theologies, God and the angels knew all. It was the most perfect of knowledge and was often referred to as intuitive knowledge. That's a theological theory.

The Akashic Record is the term given by theosophists toward the end of the nineteenth century to what was considered to be an etheric or more subtle energetic plane of existence than the familiar solid, liquid and gaseous states of being. The word 'akasha' itself is from the Hindu concept of a fifth element. This subtle plane or field contained, so it was said, everything that has happened or will happen, a way of saying that the field was in a state of superposition where it could become anything which, in itself, is another way of describing angelic perfect knowledge.

The zero point field contains electromagnetic waves and virtual particles which appear and disappear at random. Where they go and what they take or bring with them is not known, but these two terms, Pleroma and Akashic records, are two different ways of saying the same thing: that there exists a dimension or state of being which contains energy in some form and, presumably that energy interacts in some way with our universe.

Theosophy, established in the latter part of the nineteenth century in the USA by Helena Blavatsky, a Russian émigré, still has thousands of adherents today. (We met her earlier in the discussion of the pineal gland.) Theosophy was partly responsible for increasing public awareness of Asian religions in the west. Among two of its most prominent members were Annie Besant, a socialist and supporter of Indian and Irish self-rule, and Charles Leadbetter, formerly a priest before joining the theosophical movement.

Both of these individuals claimed to be adept, after intensive training, in one of the siddhi techniques we discussed earlier. This one was the ability to reduce the body to the size of an atom, or to so structure vision that the microscopic world was easily seen. Leadbetter's own explanation of this 'siddhi sight' was that there exists a tube-like structure from the third eye chakra and that by using this tube, one can see the infinitely small. (You will recall that the third eye chakra was often associated with a connection with the universe in some fashion and was also thought to be associated with the pineal gland.)

Over a period of years, Leadbetter and Besant applied their siddhi technique in viewing various chemical elements, dictating what they saw. Their descriptions were translated into drawings to accompany the words they dictated. The results were eventually published in the book *Occult Chemistry* in 1908. It was reprinted in 1919, and a third edition was printed in 1955. They worked at this when they could over a period of 38 years, publishing their last article in 1933. There had been nothing like it before.

They were aware of and interested in the concept of Akashic Records being held in some type of etheric plane where everything was known and from which everything arose. It resonated with what they knew of Eastern mysticism, to which they were both attracted. They were also interested in observing the fundamental building blocks of various elements and compounds as a way of gaining a better understanding of how the etheric aspects of the building blocks of the world (based upon chemicals) were formed. They said that the etheric state consisted of four substates. In Annie Besant's words, "The method by which these four etheric substates were studied consisted in taking what is called by chemists an atom of an element and breaking it up, time after time, until what proved to be the ultimate physical unit was reached."

In essence, Besant and Leadbetter used their siddhi sight to see more and more closely into elements to determine how they were constructed. Bear in mind that these exercises were begun before Ernest Rutherford had succeeded in splitting the atom in 1917. Up until that point, the atom was considered to be the ultimate particle which was the basis of all matter.

To quote from a review of their work published by Andrew Clewell and Stephen M. Phillips in the Winter 2015 edition of *Quest* magazine, "Besant and Leadbeater not only described the inner structure of atoms, they identified four new elements (promethium, technetium, astatine, francium) before scientists discovered them. They described several isotopes (elements with atoms containing extra neutrons) before isotopes were known to science. They discovered that geometrical configurations of atoms corresponded to the position of elements in the Periodic Table of Elements. They discovered that the atomic weights of all natural elements, as determined by science, were proportional to the number of ultimate physical atoms (UPAs) in each atom. UPAs were the smallest discrete subatomic structures that Besant and Leadbeater discerned." (Later, they used the Sanskrit word Anu (both singular and plural) instead of UPA. Anu means, amongst other things, atom or molecule.)

When the pair of clairvoyants looked at hydrogen for example, they did not find single atoms, but 18 smaller Anu in various etheric stages which together composed the chemical atom. They found 290 of these Anu in the oxygen atom and 261 in nitrogen. They were, in other words, looking at the substructure of atoms.

This discovery of theirs, that elements were more complex than anyone at the time thought, is of interest to us. Again, in Annie Besant's words, "In this ultimate state of physical matter two types of units, or Anu, have been observed; they are alike in everything save the direction of their whorls and of the force which pours through them. In the one case force pours in from the "outside," from fourth-dimensional space, the Astral plane, and passing through the Anu, pours into the physical world. In the second, it pours in from the physical world, and out through the Anu into the "outside" again, i.e., vanishes from the physical world. The one is like a spring, from which water bubbles out; the other is like a hole, into which water disappears. We call the Anu from which force comes out *positive* or *male;* those through which it disappears, *negative* or *female."*

It has been suggested that the pair of Anu form what are now termed matter and antimatter states. Their discoveries were given validation in the late 1970's by Stephen Phillips. He came across *Occult Chemistry* while he was a physics graduate student at the University of California. He did not dismiss it, but took a closer look and came to the conclusion that they had in fact anticipated modern physics. In his book, *The Extra-Sensory Perception of Quarks*, he suggests that what the theosophists saw and described were quarks and sub-quarks and that the whorls which Besant saw are the 'strings' of modern string theory.

String theory is a possible way of explaining a complete and fundamental picture of the universe and how it operates. It is certainly controversial and, as yet, unproven. The strings themselves, theoretically at the heart of the idea, are inconceivably small, about a millionth of a billionth of a billionth of a billionth of a centimeter long. Or, to put it more bluntly, far too small to be seen with even the most powerful microscope. However, the theory is that such strings and the possible ways in which they could vibrate could well provide an explanation for how the four fundamental forces of the universe—gravity, electromagnetism, the strong and the weak nuclear forces (the latter two being concerned more at the atomic level)—all operate. Indeed, it is suggested that all such forces are nothing more than different manifestations of these strings. Think of them as strings on a musical instrument. Depending on the length of the string and on how great a tension it is under, it will make a different note. That, of course, is far too simplistic, but the basic concept of vibration and changing outcome is at the heart of the theory.

String theory is by no means proven, and there are arguments over various points of the theory, but the essential element remains: that of everything arising from one basic object or field—an echo of the idea first observed by Leadbetter and Besant over 100 years ago. It is echoed in another theory about the universe, loop gravity, where there is no space or time, merely a coming into and out of existence of various fields.

These various discoveries and theories point to a reinforcement of the central thesis that there is an underlying field in the universe. In modern physics this is the zero point field, which apparently contains a mass of particles flicking in and out of existence (just like the Anu of the theosophists). The particles seem to be able to connect with another dimension (the place from which they appear and disappear), and that dimension has been recognized in various forms and across cultures as being accessible by humans through the chakra system and through siddhi techniques (which might ultimately prove to be two sides of the same coin).

It is usually considered to be a timeless dimension, in that mystics believe it to contain all knowledge past and present and future. This ability to see beyond the present has been reported or commented upon across cultures, and it is always associated with something other than this, our 'normal' universe of the physical senses. The connection between ourselves and the wider universe is echoed in the sayings of the mystics. In amongst these beliefs about the chakras and their connection with the universe, there lies the idea that in such a connection, the individual person is not important and can, in fact, disappear, in that the difference between what I identify as myself and what is not me becomes indistinct.

"Pure consciousness cannot say 'I'," said Sri Ramana Maharshi, who died in 1950. Parmenides, a fifth century BC Greek philosopher, said, "Being is without beginning and indestructible: it is universal, existing alone, immovable and without end: nor ever was it nor will it be, since it now *is*, all together, one, and continuous." The grandson of Confucius, Tsesze, remarked that the 'absolute truth' (or reality) is indestructible, eternal, infinite, and contains all existence. A similar idea was put forward by the English mystic, William Blake who said, "the world of imagination is infinite and eternal" and that what we see in this world, everything which passes away, is only a reflection of what is permanent in the eternal world. Black Elk, of the Sioux Nation, said, "All are really one."

This commonality of thought across cultures and times has long been noted. Marco Pallis, a Greek-British author and mountaineer, summed it up neatly in his book, *Peaks and Lamas*. He said, "This belief in the transcendent Intellect, a faculty capable, and alone capable, of direct contact with the Real, is common to all traditional doctrines, of all ages and countries." But perhaps a French 18th Century philosopher, Louis-Claude de Saint-Martin said it best. "All mystics speak the same language, for they come from the same country."

The hidden universe implied by the existence of the zero point field provides a reason for the words of the mystics. All that is required now is to examine how our bodies might connect to this underlying field of potential which permeates everything. By so doing we will be able to satisfactorily explain the full spectrum of intuitive experiences.

12

YOUR CONNECTION TO THE UNIVERSE

Water is H2O, hydrogen two parts, oxygen one, but there is also a third thing,
that makes it water and nobody knows what it is.
D H Lawrence (Novelist)

By examining the possible ways in which we in our physical bodies can connect with and access the underlying field of the universe, we could then confidently assert that, in conjunction with the other modes of accessing information in supra-sensory ways, we have a viable theory for how intuition works in all the various ways it presents itself. This chapter will look at the ways in which we could make the connection with the underlying field, thus accounting for the so-far-unexplained range of intuitive expression: knowing the future and the past.

The Bose-Einstein condensate, as we saw, is where the energy of the zero point field manifests. That would seem to be a particular problem for us humans, given that such a state of matter appears a few billionths of a degree above absolute zero, or −459.67°F (−273.15°C). However, a German-born British physicist, Herbert Fröhlich, who died in 1991, took an interest in the condensate, believing that such a state was possible in other conditions. In 1968 he predicted that a similar process, albeit at a much higher temperature than absolute zero, could concentrate all the vibrational energy in a biological protein into its lowest frequency vibrational mode. To put that another way, at room (or body) temperature, something very like the Bose-Einstein condensate would appear in living things. Such a condensate would, as in the Bose-Einstein version, consist of a differing form of matter, in that it would form a connection with either something similar to the zero point field or with that field itself. When this prediction was proved to be true via experimentation in 2015, such a state was named the Fröhlich condensate in his honor.

Such a condensate could well be the way in which biological organisms, as opposed to elementary particles, interact with the field first identified as the zero point. In the original zero point field, matter appeared and disappeared and formed the basics of the material world. In Fröhlich's version, presumably the same processes occur, but only with regard to biological effects. Given that this new condensate has been detected experimentally, there still remains the problems of how to interact with such a field.

It is well-known that we are made up mostly of water, amounting to about 60%, according to the USGS. That figure hides the fact that the brain and heart are 73% water, the lungs 83%, the skin 64%, muscles and kidneys 79% and even bones are 31% water, and that our cells depend upon water for their biological processes.

Water is an intimate part of us and all around us and seems so familiar that we have tended to overlook some of its more interesting and unexpected properties. Dr. Jack Kruse, an American neurosurgeon, says that "Water allows the quantum dance to happen in all life, not just us." And that is because water is not only a liquid, but has also been found to be capable of forming a new kind of solid. This solid is known as a quasicrystal, which is to say, a crystal which is ordered, in that it has a shape, but is not periodic, in that one crystal cannot be matched exactly, or overlain exactly with another, such as a square can. Even so, such crystals can completely fill all available space without repeating the pattern of tiling.

The existence of quasicrystals was first discovered in the early 1980's, and the Nobel Prize for Chemistry was awarded in 2011 to their discoverer, Daniel Schechtman of Israel. The Nobel Committee noted that this discovery "led to a paradigm shift in chemistry." Since then, hundreds of quasicrystals have been reported and confirmed. In the case of water, such a quasicrystal is shaped as an icosahedron. The icosahedron was the fourth of the five Platonic solids (the others in order being the tetrahedron, the cube, the octahedron, and the dodecahedron). Interestingly enough, Plato associated the icosahedron with water and the subsequent dodecahedron with the universe. Although tenuous and circumstantial, it is of interest to us, as we are contemplating how we humans can be connected with the zero point field which underlies the universe.

To take this a stage further, these last two solids, the icosahedron and the dodecahedron, are the only ones associated with the golden ratio in their construction. This is a never-ending number beginning with 1.6180339. It cannot be described as a round number (just as in quantum physics, the uncertainty principle means that we cannot be precise in our determination of a particle), but is approximated to 1.618. It has been noted, written about and explored since the time of Pythagoras. The golden ratio is considered to be most aesthetically pleasing and has been found in much renaissance art (including da Vinci's) as well as in the proportions of many models and artists who are generally considered to be beautiful.

To see it more simply, the Fibonnacci sequence consists of a series of numbers; 1, 1, 2, 3, 5, 8, 13, 21, 34, 55, 89, 144, 233 etc. The ratio of a number in the sequence to the previous number approaches the golden ratio the further along the sequence you travel. This golden ratio is most frequently found in nature. The positioning of flower petals, the shape of shells and tree branches, even hurricanes and spiral galaxies exhibit this pattern or relationship. So do DNA molecules. In 2010, it was reported that the golden ratio was to be observed in the magnetic resonance of spins in cobalt niobite crystals: the golden ratio at the atomic scale.

With these various examples there does seem to be, at least at one conceptual level, that of numbers, a connection between the human and the cosmic universe, an echo of the Pythagoreans and of Galileo who said that the universe is a grand book written in the language of mathematics. Numbers and their relationships do seem to be a way of explaining the universe: mathematics is the only satisfactory way of explaining and understanding quantum physics, for example.

Water, despite being so familiar, has been found to be a remarkable substance. For example, it exhibits quantum properties such as coherence and self-organization. Quantum coherence in this instance is best illustrated by the movements of large flocks of birds. They turn and move as if they are one organism (they act coherently), even though there is no obvious controlling mechanism.

Similar coherence in the human body, if proved, would imply that there is a mechanism to explain the complex coordination of the processes and activities necessary for proper function. In the human body, water maintains its structure through tiny electromagnetic fields. It is theorized that the electrical charges in water molecules form a dipole (a separation of the positive and negative charges), and that small domains of water will occur at room temperature and take on quantum characteristics.

A quantum domain—a coherent domain, that is—will be able, according to the theory, to hold frequencies of an electromagnetic nature without loss of information. And you will recall that electromagnetic fields are measurable from the heart and brain, and that they are the exact same type of fields as used by cell phones, therefore able to hold and transmit similar types of information.

It is possible that such a structure of water could be responsible for the transmission of information around the body and within cells. Given those ideas, it is permissible to think that there would be a wide range of information being made available, some of which could be acquired from other structures in the body as well as from the surrounding environment. This assumes that a Fröhlich condensate exists within us and allows access to the same field that the zero point field seems to connect with. Given what we have learned so far, that is not unreasonable.

However, to more fully explore the possibilities within our bodies and how they might interact with the sea of consciousness (and therefore deepen our understanding of intuition), we need to look at two other interesting aspects of the human body: microtubules and biophotons.

Microtubules, as their name implies, are microscopic tubes which exist in all cells and were discovered by accident in the 1960's. They are found in every cell in plants and animals. They are, in effect, the skeletal structure of the cells, as well as being the transport system within them responsible for carrying whatever is needed to wherever it is needed. They have a positive and a negative charge. The positive ends generally point outwards and the negative ends generally point to the cell's center. They are extremely versatile and flexible and are formed and broken down constantly in response to the demands of the cell. More importantly, for us, they are also present in the brain.

In 1989, Roger Penrose, the British mathematician, in his book, *The Emperor's New Mind,* suggested that consciousness, that difficult concept we looked at earlier, could be explained by quantum effects in the brain. He expanded upon this idea in 1994 with an American physician, Stuart Hameroff. Hameroff had been speculating about the role of microtubules in thought and consciousness for some time before this collaboration. An anesthesiologist by profession, he believed that microtubules could also be of great relevance in explaining what happens to patients undergoing surgery: brain functions continue and neurons keep firing, but consciousness does not exist. Why?

To Hammeroff, microtubules had to be part of the answer, if not the whole answer. Microtubules, Penrose and Hameroff argued, could be capable of vibrating. They said that such vibrations would explain EEG readings. For an electroencephalograph reading to take place, electrodes are attached to the scalp to pick up electrical impulses. Brain waves were speculated about at the end of the nineteenth century, and the first human brain waves were recorded in 1924. Since then, there has been greater sensitivity in the machines, and various frequencies have been identified such as alpha, beta, theta, gamma, and delta.

However, although such machines record the synchronized activity of thousands or millions of neurons, nobody really knows what is causing the brain waves or how they originate. Penrose and Hameroff claimed that such vibrations were responsible for forming a quantum superposition in the brain. This superposition, you will recall, is that quantum state where any outcome is still possible, because there has been no measurement or observation.

Their theory is called Orchestrated Objective Reduction (Orch-OR). In the brain are billions of neurons that connect and which pass signals across the very tiny gaps between them. Traditional ideas of consciousness assert that these inter-neuron connections give rise to thought. Orch-OR, on the other hand, claims that it is the quantum interactions inside the microtubules inside the neurons which gives rise to consciousness. That might sound like nit-picking on a microscopic scale, but the difference is larger than at first apparent.

As we have learned, in quantum mechanics, observation is key. Observation collapses the wave function superposition (the potential) into a specific state. Something either is or isn't when observation occurs. Orch-OR, however, states that instead of the observation causing consciousness by collapsing the wave function, which is what you would expect, it is the collapse of the wave function itself which creates consciousness. Out of all the possible events which could happen, they propose, it is only when the wave collapses that consciousness arises, and it is not the other way round. When a wave function collapses, then 'reality' occurs. And all this happens *inside* the neurons rather than *between* neurons.

The 'Orchestrated' part of the name is due to the orchestration of the microtubules which, acting in concert, would form a quantum superposition. The collapse of this into 'reality' is the 'Objective Reduction' part. Obviously, we are talking here of the western view of consciousness, in that it is something which happens within the organism (rather than being due to control of the mind). But this explanation of consciousness and how it arises also brings in the earlier ideas of superposition and something analogous to interacting with a field beyond the brain.

Such a field has been shown to exist in the Bose-Einstein condensate.

Most critics have said that such a thing as outlined by Penrose and Hameroff was impossible due to the warm, wet and 'noisy' nature of the brain. However, the coherent state of water as outlined above would suggest that such a thing is possible, as would the concept of the Fröhlich condensate. Added to that, experiments have proven that quantum mechanics explain the way migratory birds navigate and how plants photosynthesize sunlight. Indeed, warm quantum coherence has been shown to exist in brain microtubules.

Biological quantum effects seem to be possible. If that is the case, then it is also certainly possible that part of those quantum effects could be interacting with the field which underlies everything: the Pleroma of the Gnostics or the Akashic Record of the theosophists. It seems reasonable to suggest that having a means of accessing such a field not limited by time or space within a biological organism would go some considerable way to understanding some of the intuitive insights which at first seem difficult to explain.

It is interesting that this approach to understanding consciousness also appears to bridge the gap between what western and eastern concepts of consciousness might consist of. The Orch-OR thesis takes physical aspects of the brain, neurons, and microtubules, and by positing a quantum mechanism, brings in the possibility of interaction with the zero point field, the cosmic sea of energy which Bohm referred to as the ground for the existence of everything and which appears to be what eastern definitions of consciousness interact with.

If microtubules offer at least some measure of progress toward our answer, then biophotons also add some further ideas. Biophotons are the smallest 'bits' of light in a biological system, just as photons are the smallest 'bits' of light outside such systems.

Every human emits weak light in the form of photons, with the light itself ranging from the near ultraviolet to the near infra-red range. Which means at their extreme range, they are just outside of what is usually considered to be the visible range of frequencies. The light emitted is about 1,000 times less intense than the visible light we normally see, and a very sensitive detector is required to examine them, enabling single photons to be recorded.

It's important that this emission is not confused with the light emitted by, say, fireflies, or the glow which some sea creatures can emit. Such phenomena are termed either bioluminescence or chemiluminescence. Biophotons are not usually emitted from us in a coherent, orderly fashion, but vary according to the time of day and the health of the individual. That is not to say that they are not coherent within us. They arise from activity in the mitochondria of the cells. The mitochondria are usually referred to as the 'powerhouses' of the cell, because together they produce about 90% of the chemical energy needs of the cell.

Biophotons were first discovered in 1923. A Russian scientist, Gurwitsch, observed optical radiation in onion roots and called it mitogenic radiation. There was little development or understanding of this radiation until 1974 when a German biophysicist, Fritz-Albert Popp, proved the existence of biophotons as well as demonstrating that they were present in our DNA and that they were coherent, in the same way as a laser consists of coherent light (i.e., not spreading out or diffusing).

Dr. Popp argued that this biophotonic light, which is also very weak in intensity, was a vital component in maintaining health. Perfect communication at the biophotonic level equaled health, whereas when such communication broke down, ill-health was the result. In other words, biophotons were acting as a coordinating source of information in some form.

This is because light carries information. At the most basic level, that of its frequency, it carries information about its color. But, as optical fiber technology has shown, light can carry a great deal more information than that. From Dr. Popp's findings about biophotons orchestrating molecules, the only conclusion must be that there is information being transmitted. The question then becomes, what information, and how is it transmitted?

To answer the last part of the question first, think of a group of people drumming together in a busy place where there are lots of other people passing by or looking on, some of them talking loudly, others listening.

Each drummer has his or her own drum and beats upon it as he or she wishes. The resulting sound is confused and has no beat. It is incoherent. But, if all the drummers drummed using the same rhythm, the sound would be coherent. It would, in a sense, be a binary sound—an on-and-off sound—silence, then drum beat. Using that on-off idea, it would be possible to make a code and send messages. Anyone not 'on the beat' would disturb the coherence. One drummer wouldn't make too much of a difference, but the more drummers who miss the beat, the more incoherent the message would be. The more drummers are with the beat, the louder the message is, and the easier it would be to hear it over the many onlookers making their own noise.

The same principle, it is supposed, occurs in biophotons. A Russian scientist, Sergey Mayburov, studied eggs from fish and frogs and found that the patterns of biophotons emitted came in short, irregular bursts, which would be how information would be sent most successfully over a noisy channel, (think of the drummers and the noisy onlookers). It has been estimated that a biophoton could carry more than four megabytes of information. Further, it has also been estimated that our brains with their billions of neurons could convey more than a billion biophotons per second. That is a huge amount of information.

There has to be a vast amount of information being processed in our bodies, because if there was no synchronization between the cells, we would not be here. It has been estimated that a single cell in our body has anywhere between hundreds of thousands and several millions of chemical reactions *each second*, depending on what the cell is being asked to do. Let's take an average and suggest that the number be 500,000 reactions each second. That is in one cell. Our bodies are composed of several trillion cells, each one averaging 500,000 chemical reactions, meaning billions of reactions are happening each second. Such vast figures, as well as the complexity involved, are as hard to grasp as the concepts revealed by quantum physics. Both are staggering and confusing. And yet here we are, and it's happening to you and me right now, all the time.

Given that there has to be a continual and precise organization of this vast complexity, biophotons certainly appear to be major players in the necessary coordination. However, there is one other aspect to consider, and that is that in order for such orchestration to take place across trillions of cells, there should be, it is presumed, some sort of over-arching coordinating field such that all of the relevant biophotons with their own specific information send their data clearly and at the right time. The existence of a biophotonic field has been suggested as fulfilling this role. This field, it is argued, contains the blueprint or template of our bodies. Such a field has been proven, it has been said, by experiments whereby a leaf from a plant has been cut and, using cameras able to capture and record biophotons, the outline of the whole leaf has been seen. This outline slowly fades over time. In other words, the template of the leaf was still being carried by biophotons even though there were no receptors where the missing piece had been. This idea of a controlling field of information was first postulated by Harold Burr of Yale in the 1930's and later in the decade the photography of Semyon and Valentina Kirlian made this visible (although they only made their results public in the 1950's).

The speed of transmission of information around the body has always seemed to be faster than could be accounted for by purely chemical reactions sent along neurons. Biophotons, by their nature, are able to convey information at the speed of light, but it is unlikely that such transformation is solely down to light flashing around inside the body in a haphazard fashion. In order to control the flow, it appears that biophotons use the microtubules we looked at earlier.

The connection between the two is, for our purposes, important. While the amount of information exchange happening on a regular if mind-boggling basis in our bodies is fascinating, it does not contribute to further extending our understanding of intuition. However, the connection between neuron structures and biophotons may well be what we are looking for.

Apart from their role in coordinating chemical reactions within and between cells, it has been suggested that biophotons may also act as an information carrier in the brain. In order to travel quickly, biophotons in the brain would need waveguides, pathways along which they could move. Microtubules have been suggested as being able to guide light without loss and free of the 'noise' created by the warm environment (think of the non-drummers, the noisy onlookers, in the earlier analogy).

Apart from microtubules, other structures called myelinated axons have also been proposed. Axons are the fibers which carry the neurons' signals. Myelinated axons are covered in a fatty substance, myelin, which acts as an electrical insulator. A team investigating the hypothesis concluded that such axons could convey between 46% to 96% of the light they received and that more than a billion biophotons per second could be transported in such a fashion. They concluded that, "This mechanism appears to be sufficient to facilitate transmission of a large number of bits of information, or even allow the creation of a large amount of quantum entanglement." Entanglement you will recall is the name given to the immediate transmission of information between particles or groups of particles.

It appears, then, that there are two distinct ways in which we as humans could be interacting with the zero point field or its warm-body equivalent. A room temperature condensate exists inside us. There is no reason to think that the zero point field is only accessible at temperatures approaching absolute zero, particularly if such a field is believed to underlie everything. Such a field would, it has been argued by metaphysicians in differing cultures, contain everything in potential, the past as well as the future.

Microtubules in neurons, acting in synchrony, have been proposed as one possible quantum state which would explain consciousness. Such synchrony might also be capable of not only bringing consciousness about, but could also be able to access the zero point field itself. In addition, biophotons have been shown to be capable of carrying large amounts of information around the body and have been theoretically shown to be capable of quantum effects inside the brain and could be using either microtubules or myelinated axons as transport systems. If the former, then the synchronization of the microtubules into a superposition could well result in interaction with the zero point field. As for the latter, as one paper has summarized it, "if optical communication involving axons is harnessed by the brain, this would reveal a remarkable, hitherto unknown new aspect of the brain's functioning."

No matter which point of view is considered, the key point is that there are massively complex arrays of information moving around inside us, but we are uncertain what such information might consist of. If either, or both, of these processes do eventually prove to be functions which have definitive quantum effects, then it would seem that they could very well be the end point of our exploration of the processes involved in intuition.

If we consider the varieties of ways in which intuitions arrive, as well as the many different types of information contained, with specific reference to those which transcend time and space, there is nothing inherently ludicrous in supposing that all such types of information could be contained within the quantum coherence of water within us, within the biophotons or the actions of the microtubules. Indeed, different types of intuitive information might be due to different combinations of these possibilities. And remember, the key elements of intuition have been shown to be those found in quantum physics, specifically non-locality, where time and space do not exist.

The amount of information which has been pieced together about how our bodies work has grown enormously and continues to grow at a frantic pace. The numbers quoted earlier about the chemical reactions within cells is almost inconceivable, and there is a temptation to assume that the major processes at work are now mapped out. Yet Dr. Jack Kruse, the neurosurgeon, has said that we probably only know about 5% of all there is to know about our bodies. And that is a sobering thought.

This view is borne out by the multinational pharmaceutical company, Hoffman-LaRoche. They are responsible, among other things, for providing, free of charge, a huge and vastly complex mapping of the biochemical pathways and the cellular processes in our bodies. The maps are truly mind-boggling in the scope and detail they offer. This mapping has been successively updated with additional detail over four decades. They make it quite clear that our biochemical knowledge doubles every five years, suggesting that there is a very great deal more to come in our understanding of ourselves. And that increasing complexity is only with regard to one aspect of our bodies: the biochemical. All other aspects, as well as the interactions between them, must be considered to be equally complex and equally unknown so far. In other words, we are barely up to our ankles, and we are examining the water around our feet while there is a whole unknown ocean ahead of us.

Given that there is no such thing yet as a definite, all-inclusive and accepted theory on even the most common aspects of our bodies (for proof of which, read the conflicting theories about diet and how they are supposed to work and the grounds for each one's supposed superiority), it would be both foolish and exhibiting extreme hubris to declare that we have found the true cause and origin of our intuition.

If we know so little of the physical body despite many years of detailed research, it is safe to assume that we know even less of the subtle, energetic aspects of our bodies. Of course, an alternative opinion might be that with the coming of the scientific paradigm we have lost or forgotten much of what we once knew. Whatever the truth might be, at the present time we are woefully ignorant of the non-physical aspect of ourselves.

There is no single, definitive proof that some elements in the brain's structures act in such a way as to draw energy from the zero point field, and neither is there certainty that the zero point field is the field of potential from which ourselves and the universe somehow condenses. But there are sufficient pointers to at least acknowledge that it is probable that such connections at a quantum level do exist inside of us, and that those connections can, at least theoretically, provide us with an answer as to what intuition really consists of: an unavoidable interaction with something beyond our physical world of the senses which provides a glimpse of a reality vastly different from that which we are accustomed to imagine.

Before we go on to piece all the evidence together and form a more complete picture, it is necessary that we take some time to explore an inherent problem of intuition, which is, how the language we use to refer to it does not help make it readily understandable to each other.

How can I tell you exactly *how* my intuition felt, what it was like, what precisely I knew as a result of it, when all the ways I have of speaking about it at my disposal are vague? Intuition is difficult to speak about, and this makes it equally difficult for it to be accepted as a valid and important part of our lives. The language we use, as we will see next, explains much of how intuition itself is viewed.

13

THE FAILURE OF LANGUAGE

Drawing on my fine command of the English language, I said nothing.
Robert Benchley (Comedian)

In order to look more carefully at intuition as a human phenomenon and to be able to place it beside the spiritual and scientific exploration of it, we need to draw back a little and adopt a somewhat different viewpoint. Conan Doyle's Sherlock Holmes, in *A Case Of Identity*, speaking to Dr. Watson, says, "Life is infinitely stranger than anything which the mind of man could invent. We would not dare to conceive the things which are really mere commonplaces of existence." Intuition is, as I hope has been shown, a remarkable and exceptional thing, and yet it is a 'mere commonplace of existence,' accepted by everyone, usually without question. If there is a sense of wonderment, it does not usually last and is forgotten quickly as daily life takes over again. Why is that?

Perhaps one of the difficulties of appreciating our intuition is that it is so hard to talk about with any degree of accuracy. Language is imprecise and vague when attempting to describe it, and that imprecision makes it difficult for listeners to comprehend the experience of the narrator.

If it cannot be explained clearly, then intuition automatically becomes less important in a society such as ours which appreciates and values precision. If I cannot point with language to a readily agreed upon and easily discernible action or occurrence, then the gap between what I experience and what I can say about it grows so that there is a real difficulty for the listener to bridge that gap and truly grasp the entirety of my intuitive insight. When I had the insight of European history, it was engulfing and holistic and it felt impossible, indeed was impossible, to have spoken about or described it other than in the most simple of terms which could never begin to encapsulate what I had experienced.

Most people when speaking of their intuition will use terms such as 'had a feeling,' or 'a gut reaction,' or more simply that they just 'knew' that it was so. It is worth asking if our language is a barrier to our ability to share our intuitions. Could it be that if we had a different language, then we would be able to transmit that 'knowingness' to another person and allow them to undergo the same awareness we had? In other words, would a different language make intuition more accessible and understandable, make it a more complete and commonly understandable part of our lives?

Consider how we can speak of that most obvious of physical aspects, our breathing. We can gasp, gulp, wheeze, breathe shallowly or rapidly, slowly and deeply, even hold our breath. Each is a way of letting the listener understand not only how the breathing happened, but also allowing him to gain a perspective on the emotional state of the person doing the breathing in most cases. Yet we are severely limited when it comes to describing our intuition. For example, our language deals in tenses—past, present, and future—which tie us to a restrictive temporal order which we know now does not actually exist. We can know the past and the future and experience it in the present, yet there is no easy way of using language to fully share such an experience.

The philosopher Jean-Jacques Rousseau in his 1755 *Discourse on the Origin of Inequality* and his 1781 *Essay on the Origin of Language* suggested that language, at first, was more 'musical' and had emotional power as opposed to rational persuasion. Oliver Sacks, commenting on this in his *Seeing Voices*, said that such language would give everything its true and natural name. It would have been a language so concrete, he believed, so precise, so exact, that the precise essence, the 'it-ness' of everything was captured. There would have been no evasion or deception, because the language could not have allowed it. It would have had no logic or grammar, no metaphor or abstraction of thought. Such a language sounds too good to be true.

To be able to say exactly what you wish to say without there being any chance of being misunderstood is something some, but not all, people would embrace. Politicians, for example, certainly wouldn't! If you have ever tried, unsuccessfully, to describe an experience, any personal experience, to someone else, then the wish for such a language becomes readily apparent. It is certain that lovers would wish for such a language, so that the object of their love would truly understand exactly how they felt. Instead, we are left with poetry, metaphor, and cliché. Franz Kafka said, "Language, then, is just a poor translation of feelings and intentions."

Of course, language, the means by which we transfer ideas amongst ourselves, has always intrigued people, particularly philosophers. At the end of the nineteenth century, Nietzsche, for example, believed that all words were merely metaphors and that "we possess nothing but metaphors for things—metaphors which correspond in no way to the original entities."

Wittgenstein, in the last century, was particularly interested in what language could and could not do. He began by trying to strip language back to its barest logical form in order to better see and understand the logic of the world. If language could not be meaningful, then it was better to say nothing. Thus, he ended his *Tractatus Logico Philosophicus* (his first major work, published originally in 1921) by saying, "That whereof we cannot speak, thereof we must remain silent." In other words, if the world, as he then thought, consisted of facts or states of affairs, language could be used only to describe it. It would have been impossible, therefore, to speak about metaphysical subjects. Later on, however, he revised his ideas to say that language could be far more flexible. "In most cases," he said in his *Philosophical Investigations*, published posthumously in 1953, "the meaning of a word is its use." By this he meant that how you used words and the context in which you used them was important. "If we spoke a different language," he said, we would perceive a different world. And, as we have seen, there is a very different world at the subatomic level which defies easy description. Maybe, if we were able to use language differently, we would be able to understand more clearly what is happening and, beyond that, have the ability to convey with great clarity and ease such things as the intuitive 'knowings' we experience.

The same idea holds true, in a smaller sphere, for quantum mechanics. You will recall that one of the possible interpretations of the exotic peculiarities of quantum mechanics was that we lack the proper language to be able to deal with it and make it understandable. That idea of language channeling how we perceive the world was taken up by physicist David Bohm in his 1980 book, *Wholeness and the Implicate Order*. Bohm (whom we met earlier talking about space not being empty and that what it contained was the ground for the existence of everything), is considered to have been one of the most significant theoretical physicists of the twentieth century. How we commonly use language, he said, makes it clear that it is linear: the cat sat on the mat, for example. Things happen sequentially in our language. They cannot, linguistically, occur all at once. Our present language lacks the ability to convey emotions easily, as we have seen. It is also ambiguous. Often it is not clear what is being spoken about. For example, do you actually have anger or are you angry? And how can you make instantly clear which is which to your listener while still speaking of the cause or focus of the anger? For Bohm, the problem was easily encapsulated by the phrase, 'It is raining.' He would ask where the 'it' is that is doing the raining. 'It' should be the rainer doing the raining, but such a thing does not exist. It would make more sense, he suggested, to say, 'rain is going on.' This was because he felt it was more important to focus on the processes going on around you than the objects undergoing the processes: the cat and the mat, for instance. The objects would be of less importance and would only have relevance once the process involving them had been made clear.

The reason he took this view of language was because of how he thought of the world as it is perceived. His idea of a language which was better suited to movement and awareness of what was happening, he called a rheomode, based on the Greek word for movement. Processes occur and events happen, and thus the world exists around us in a dynamic and unfolding fashion, instead of a series of plodding objects, each of which is static and where there is no sense of dynamism. Language, in other words, locks everything in place.

For Bohm, the world as perceived by us is the explicate world. Anything at all, even an electron, is a manifestation of the underlying implicate or enfolded order. This underlying, enfolded or implicate order was, he said, where, "space and time are no longer the dominant factors determining the relationships of dependence or independence of different elements." It was, he believed, a more fundamental order of reality.

In essence, he was referring to the zero point field, where everything was in potential or superposed. He believed that there was an inherent tendency in mankind to think fragmentally and not see that there is a wholeness or completeness beyond the various competing ideas. In this wholeness, or flow, mind and matter are the same and not separate substances. Our language was the result of this fragmentation. More explicitly and importantly for our purposes, he also said, "relativity and quantum theory agree, in that they both imply the need to look on the world as an undivided whole, in which all parts of the universe, including the observer and his instruments, merge and unite in one totality."

Here, then, is a physicist willing and able to state what much of what we have been exploring so far has pointed to: there is something which is hard to define, yet which underlies everything, and out of which everything arises, and there is no such thing as a separation between ourselves and the world we inhabit, and space and time are not the dominant factors. Ravelli's research in quantum gravity (where time, you will recall, is not a necessary variable for describing the world) also points to the fact that our world is one of events rather than of things: how things change with respect to each other, echoing Bohm's rheomode concept.

Bohm knew that our language is inadequate to express how we interact with the world. His theory of the implicate order was hinted at in the 15th Century by a German philosopher and theologian, Nicholas of Cusa. In his *On Learned Ignorance*, he wrote, "You know how the divine Simplicity enfolds all things. Mind is the image of this enfolding Simplicity." He wrote using the terms enfolding and unfolding in much the same way that Bohm used them, as ways of explaining reality manifesting in the world.

Those who experiment with language and attempt to force it into new modes of expression are never easy to read or to understand. Published in 1939, *Finnegans Wake*, for example, is a work of experimental fiction by James Joyce which took 17 years to write, and there is still no consensus of agreement as to what, exactly, is going on in it. The language used, it is generally believed, is supposed to recreate the experiences of sleeping and dreaming. (However, it is true to say that there is still no definitive and critically agreed-upon plot synopsis.) Sleeping and dreaming are activities which everyone experiences, and yet this book, which seems to be exploring what goes on there, is largely unread because of the difficulty of gaining any understanding. It is probably amongst the best known and least-read works of fiction for this reason.

For those who have heard of it but not read it, the opening few lines provide ample illustration of the language used and the challenges it offers to the reader:

"riverrun, past Eve and Adams, from swerve of shore to bend of bay, brings us by a commodius vicus of recirculation back to Howth, Castle and Environs.

Sir Tristram, violer d'amores, fr'over the short sea, had passencore rearrived from North Armorica on this side the scraggy isthmus of Europe Minor to wielderfight his penisolate war; nor had topsawyer's rocks by the stream Oconee exaggerated themselse to Laurens County's giorgios while they went doublin their mumper all the time..."

It continues for about 600 pages.

Language is a significant barrier not only to conveying an intuition, but also to explaining how it was perceived. For example, one time when I was teaching, I was having lunch with some colleagues. There was some general chatter as usual at such times, and I was happy to sit and eat without having to provide much input, my mind wandering over the afternoon lecture without any real degree of concentration on the conversation. One woman was speaking about how her leg hurt, and that she had injured a knee playing netball when she was a schoolgirl, and that it was probably that which was responsible for the present leg pain. She hadn't mentioned which leg or which knee, but without thinking at all, I told her it was her left knee and that it had been the anterior cruciate ligament which she had damaged badly. All conversation stopped as she looked at me, jaw dropped in amazement. "How do you know that?"

I stammered and had no idea how to tell her that I had suddenly seen her knee as if it had been illustrated in a medical textbook. The area of damage was quite obvious at first glance. I merely had to describe it. But how I obtained that picture, I could not say. I had not asked to be shown it, nor had I been giving any special attention to the conversation. It had arrived without force, without anything approaching interest on my behalf and yet, there it was. In some ways it was very similar to Alec Guinness' warning to James Dean. He opened his mouth and the words came out; the exact same thing happened to me.

I felt very embarrassed, and the only way I could describe it to her was by saying that I had seen it. My embarrassment was due to an inadequacy of language, together with the feeling I subsequently had of inadvertently intruding into something quite personal to her. My words did not really help her understand it. I could not tell her how I had seen it, or in what detail I had seen it, only that it had suddenly appeared to my inner eye in great detail. Subsequent mealtimes were spent at different tables.

If there had been a clear way of describing to her my intuition, a way which automatically assumed that everything is connected at some level, and that information is always freely flowing between everyone, and that the language had the syntax to say that swiftly and elegantly, then there would have been no need for embarrassment or much explanation. It would have been a fact without need for wonderment.

Of course, if such a language had existed, then the conversation at the table would have been about entirely different subjects, subjects which I cannot conceive of. The information about everyone would have been available to everyone meaning no privacy as we currently conceive of it. It is this limitation of language which is also revealed in the way mystics have tried to share their visions and understandings. A different world or reality exists outside of our senses, and to translate that so that we can grasp it fully is beyond the ability of the language we have available in this reality of the physical senses.

It is also intriguing to speculate how a culture and language are intertwined, and how such an interconnection affects how we are able to speak of intuition and therefore, how it is viewed. In this western culture, we have difficulty in conveying intuitions, of speaking of experiences which lie outside the usual range of our everyday senses. We have no such problems in speaking of the empirical, scientific worldview where everything is observed, measured and annotated.

The fact that there is such a difference between the two world-views— the intuitive and the rational—speaks very clearly as to which is considered the most 'important' or most 'useful.' Attempts to explain the personal and the intimate experience of intuition in all its forms can lead to disregard, derision or, at worst, ostracism. People who wish to speak clearly and with confidence about intuition are considered odd, peculiar, strange, or eccentric. Because they emphasize their non-rational experience at the expense of the rational, measurable ones, their rational judgments and analyses are not always well-regarded, in that their ideas are valued less, because they cannot communicate in ways in which their listeners can readily understand.

Language therefore indicates where the power lies in a culture. Those who control language control thought. If scientific terms are used for what are considered un-scientific ideas, those speakers are condemned for their misappropriation or willful misunderstanding of concepts created and guarded by the prevailing powers. This was neatly summed up by George Orwell in his *1984:* "If you control the language, you control the argument." Thus we see scientists deriding 'New Agers' (itself becoming a pejorative term) who try to use ideas of quantum mechanics as being able to explain something they can only apprehend at a personal level, when such a term does not help any such description. It happens to be the one which, because of the astonishing and incredible associations the word 'quantum' signifies, is most nearly apposite to explain the personal awareness at the heart of the communication.

This division between the rational and the intuitive, particularly with regard to the dominance of science and scientific thinking, has been well expressed by Raoul Francé, an Austro-Hungarian scientist who is now considered to be the founder of modern bionics (biologically inspired engineering). He died in 1943, having written 60 books and popular science articles. He was considered an unconventional thinker who gave up narrow academic research for more wide-ranging philosophical writing. In one of his books, *Germs of Mind in Plants*, he wrote about the effect he felt Linnaeus had on the world.

Linnaeus, who died in 1778, is known primarily for his work in classifying the natural world, especially in using a classification system which has changed little since his time. His system consisted of a hierarchy of domain, kingdom, phylum, class, order, family, genus and finally species, the latter, after his work, having only two words to describe it. It is the quintessence of scientific organization and cataloging, and it was against this ordering of the natural world which Francé railed. In *Germs of Mind in Plants*, he wrote, "We have become separated from nature…Wherever he (Linnaeus) went, the laughing brook died, the glory of flowers withered, the grace and joy of the meadows was transformed into withered corpses… whose crushed and discolored bodies were described in a thousand minute Latin terms… The blooming meadows and the storied woods disappeared during the botanical hour into a dusty herbarium, into a dreary catalog of Greek and Latin labels. It became the hour for the practice of tiresome dialectic, filled with discussions about the number of stamens, the shape of leaves, all of which we learned only to forget. When this was completed, we stood disenchanted and estranged from nature."

What science has provided for us, Francé argued, it did so by removing us from what it studied. And it replaced the way we think about it by using its own carefully structured language. That means that information —of the world and all it contains—is only accessible to us using that same structured linguistic channel. Oddly enough, this impersonal removal of the scientist from the object of investigation came about because it was felt, from around the late seventeenth and early eighteenth centuries, that the best way of understanding life was to break it down into its smallest units and, by studying them, gain insight into the complexity of it all.

Science, therefore, in order to gain greater knowledge of the world, retreated from the holistic and encompassing view into ever narrower domains of research and was unable to perceive greater horizons. And, in scientific, empirical terms, if something cannot be described accurately, it has no value, because it cannot be studied.

In an essay titled, *The Power Of Language; A Philosophical-Sociological Reflection*, the authors, Professor Dr. Johannes Weiß and Dr. Thomas Schwietring of Kassel University, write, "Its language (science) is the real lingua franca of the developing world society. Its authority is fundamentally egalitarian and democratic; for it and with respect to it, nothing counts but "the non-violent force of the better argument."" A little later, they directly address the problem of having such power. "But the deeper problem consists in the fact that scientific language, as helpful and indispensable as it is for rationally revealing and taking hold of the world, tends at the same time to an enormous narrowing of man's perception of reality. Not only recently but as long as there has been science, people have observed and criticized the extent to which our experience of the world and of ourselves is stunted when it is restricted to what can be expressed in scientific language." Again we are drawn back to Bergson's observation that we restrict what we allow ourselves to perceive.

Despite the dominating nature of scientific language and its determination to catalog the world in precise words devoid of emotion, there is, it seems, an undeniable and deep-seated need in us to attempt to express in some fashion that which spoken language finds difficult or impossible to express. Of course, it is worth considering that if language was not as it is now, but something different, giving us a different world, would there still be the same drive to express the creative aspect, or would that be an unnecessary or unthinkable objective? In other words, how much of our creative need is driven by the inability of language to convey all that we sense? Music, for example, has the ability to transform our emotions quickly as we listen to it. A novel can produce a more complex emotional response over a longer time period. Poetry often compresses language to convey deeper or multiple meanings and images than ordinary writing customarily reveals.

An excellent example of this desire to express the inexpressible at the same time as taking opposition to the new and increasing rationalization and industrialization of its time is to be found most popularly in the works of the Romantic poets. As the eighteenth century was coming to an end, society was undergoing the transformation of the Industrial Revolution, as well as dealing with the events of the French Revolution, which was rational, intellectual, and unfeeling in its persecutions and executions. Against this background, the Romantic poetry of such as Shelley, Coleridge, Blake, Wordsworth, and Keats can also be seen to be a reaction to the dry intellectualism of the preceding neoclassical period of poetry. Their poetry was focused in Nature and in imagination and on emotion. They sought to find harmony between humans and the natural world when the world they observed seemed to be drawing further apart from nature. Wordsworth described the basis of their poetry thus: "I have said before that poetry is the spontaneous overflow of powerful feelings: it takes its origin in emotion recollected in tranquility: the emotion is contemplated till, by a species of reaction, the tranquility gradually disappears, and an emotion, kindred to that which was before the subject of contemplation, is gradually produced, and does itself actually exist in the mind." Saying that feelings and emotions become real in the mind is as good a way of expressing one aspect of intuition as any other.

Finally, if, as we have seen, intuition allows us to access information in a direct fashion, avoiding all the accepted scientific channels, then it is also a way of being aware of one's own power. The information received via intuition is not mediated in any fashion by any other person or organization and becomes the recipient's own truth. If such a truth does not agree with the prevailing power structure (as was the case with the theosophists' understanding of the atom), it remains personal and lacks the ability to expand deeper into the culture, because the channels of dissemination open to science, for example, are closed to those of intuition. Intuition, then, because of its lack of ability to use language effectively, can only be intimate and personal. Instead of permeating the culture in which it has risen, it becomes a way of expressing one's own personal power and personal experience of engaging in a harmony with the surrounding world, however fleetingly.

We are left, it seems, with only the ability to be vague and indeterminate about our intuitive experiences. The full force of them lies beyond our linguistic reach. They must, because of that limitation, remain as personal apprehensions, the truth of them to others being evident only in the limited way we can express the impact they have within us.

If intuition had access to a better language, then, as Wittgenstein said, the world we live in, the culture we experience, would be different. Perhaps we should leave the last word on this subject to Nietzsche. Speaking of language in the evolution of culture, he makes it clear how language set up a separate world and that mankind falsely "really thought in language he possessed knowledge of the world."

It could be argued that an intuitive experience really is a personal possession of knowledge of the world beyond our physical senses. But the modern, technological emphasis upon proof and measurement, on impartiality and 'reality' precludes our word of intuitive experiences being taken with great seriousness, for the necessary words are not available to us. Intuition, it seems, lies still on the fringes of what is normal, despite everyone experiencing it. And that commonality of experience is what we must return to in the next chapter.

14

HOW INTUITION WORKS

PUTTING THE PIECES TOGETHER

We are victims of the post-Enlightenment view that the world functions like a sophisticated machine, to be understood like a textbook engineering problem and run by wonks. In other words, like a home appliance, not like the human body.
Nassim Nicholas Taleb (Scientist)

———

Before we put together a picture from the evidence gained so far to explain how intuition might function, we must accept that some of what we think of as being intuitive experiences might in fact be due to the natural sensitivity of our bodies. Our physical senses are capable of extremes which we might not normally acknowledge, the operation of which might tempt us to confuse what they bring to us as intuition. If we take a quick look at some of the possibilities and appreciate just what such extremes of our physical senses are capable of, we can then proceed to collect and collate what we have discovered so far and offer a theory as to how intuition might be said to work.

We have seen that our bodies are remarkably sensitive to many different influences, even solar winds. Frequencies beyond our normal range of hearing can adversely affect us. For example, an air-conditioning plant on the roof of a building opposite the office of an engineer made him always feel nauseous when working there. He discovered that the distance between the plant and his office was exactly right to allow a resonance to occur of seven cycles per second, and it was that resonance which created the nausea.

Sounds between 10 and 20 cycles per second (again, below the usual limit of hearing) can produce symptoms of recklessness, euphoria, and loss of balance. If those experiences were always associated with a specific location, then the temptation would be to assume that there was some past history of the place, and we would attribute such feelings with an intuitive 'hit' when, in fact, it was a physical phenomenon caused by machinery.

There are people who can hear bats as they fly nearby or hear a dog whistle being blown. Others see auras around people. Most people, however, don't exercise such abilities, which is why, when we hear about others performing actions we would regard as impossible, we are astonished or, at the very least, entertained. A 22 year-old girl, Lauren Kornacki, lifted a BMW from her father after it slipped off the jacks as he was working on it. Another woman (and many such stories involve women, it seems), Angela Cavallo, lifted a Chevrolet Impala off her son and held it up long enough for people to both replace the jacks from which it had slipped and to pull her son, Tony, from beneath it. While such feats are physical, they illustrate the same principle, which is that our bodies have physical abilities which we are not usually aware of.

It is worth repeating that we are extremely sensitive individuals. There are many examples of people exhibiting abilities beyond the usual, accepted range. For example, when white men first arrived in Samoa, they discovered that there were blind men who were able to 'see' objects by holding their hands over them, and they were able to describe them in detail. It is a degree of sensitivity which has been exhibited by many people since then. Rosa Kuleshova in Russia, for example, could read the fine print of a newspaper with her right hand or even her elbow, a facility termed 'skin vision' or 'bio-introscopy.'

In France in the latter half of the nineteenth century, two scientists discovered a boy who could, it seemed, guess correctly the number of any page of a book chosen at random by someone else. What they discovered was that the boy's eyesight was so good that he could read the page numbers from the cornea of the person sitting opposite holding the book open. The image was back to front and only one-tenth of one millimeter high, but it was enough for him to see it. Such instances may be called abnormal, but they are not unnatural. The sensitivity of the human body is phenomenal, and such sensitivity should not be ruled out as providing information not usually considered accessible via our five physical senses.

We should also not rule out the occasional expression in ourselves of what have been termed siddhi abilities. Leadbetter and Besant's viewing of the Anu was a deliberate and focused use of one type of this ability, and Radin has said that such things can happen without similar focus.

We must also consider that our brain, the chief organ of perception, can present or interpret the world to us in any number of surprising ways: as lack of colors, reduced or no sense of touch at all, giving us no fine control over our movements or our speech, causing us to lose consciousness when lights are flickered into our eyes and so on and on. It can cause us to hear voices, see what isn't there, have savant-like abilities and even block all external stimuli as we lose consciousness. So, why is it that we persist in our daily attitude that what we see is all that is really there, and that what we can measure is the proof of anything?

The fact that our brains can do all those things and present the world around us in many different ways is fascinating enough. But intuition trumps whatever the brain can do. If the brain can amaze us, why are we not jumping up and down in excitement at having intuition, which does so much more, no matter how vague its form? Why do we not talk about it more? The previous chapter looked at the problems language has with intuition, but even if it is hard to describe exactly, then we can at least share that we have intuitions. But often we don't.

Part of the problem is due to doubting ourselves. Often our first reaction to an intuition is wondering whether it can be trusted or not, if it might be wrong. People want the certainty that science seeks to provide and prefer rational thought to rapid insight. It seems more comfortable that way. But, even if intuition is something almost private and very personal, it exists, and belief and confidence in it can be acquired through its persistence.

In a 2016 survey, it was found that half of Americans trusted their gut feelings to tell them what was true or false (admittedly a skewed and reduced idea of the scope of intuition). Despite this caveat, research has shown that more people believe in psi experiences (a general term for intuition in all its forms) than don't, and that level of education is not an indicator of belief.

From the various findings, Dean Radin has said that a person who would be very likely to report psychic or intuitive experiences would be, "…a left-handed female who is thirty-something or younger, physically highly sensitive, suffers from chronic anxiety, is somewhat introverted, makes decisions based more on feelings than logic, practices one or more of the creative arts, engages in some form of mental discipline like meditation, is open to unconventional claims and is interested more in possibilities than in facts."

That might not sound you like at all. The above personality is simply the one who is more likely to *report* having an intuitive experience. Yet, as we have seen, intuition is available to all in the same way that our physical senses are.

If it is a common experience, then it is a faculty experienced in different ways and for possibly different reasons. Many people will never experience anything like Toynbee's visions, others will only ever have feelings about other people, whilst still others will get a nudge to do something, like Conrad Hilton. It comes, as we have seen, in many forms, and not everyone is equally susceptible to all of those forms. The reasons for this are not yet known.

These various forms of intuition mean that there is no one simple explanation to encompass them all. Just as our physical senses rely upon different channels to provide us with their information, so it is with our intuition. From what we have seen so far, we can say that there are various probable causes or channels. The terms clairsentience, claircognizance, clairvoyance and so on help point out this fact, although the totality of an intuitive experience and the way it is perceived is not quite the same as the way our physical senses process information.

The analogy of there being a similarity between the physical and the non-physical channels is not a complete one. We do not, for example, have a whole body certainty when we see something. The closest we get to that is when a specific taste or smell can transport us back, via memory, to specific times. Marcel Proust's narrator eating a madeleine and recalling his childhood is probably the best-known example in his most famous work, *À la Recherche du Temps Perdu (In Search of Lost Time)*.

Therefore, although differing terms for intuition exist, their use and therefore their importance lies in the fact that they point out that intuition can and does present itself to us in various ways, using various processes and channels within and around our physical bodies, and that intuition is merely a general term for various specific modes of accessing information not available to the physical senses.

It is important to stress that whereas we can speak of all intuitions as being some form of information, we cannot also say with certainty that the information is accessed or understood in the same way. This leads to making generalizations about certain types of intuition. Such generalizations allow for a way to form theories or arrive at conclusions by taking into account the different ways in which intuition works. Such generalizations cannot account for the personal differences of intuitive perceptions, so that where one person might only have a gut feeling, for example, about a person they are meeting, another might have the same feeling about the history of a place. In all that follows, this distinction between the general and the specific should be born in mind.

Firstly, one of the most common expressions of intuition is in the form of gut feelings. The gut or enteric nervous system contains huge numbers of microbes, many of which are non-human in origin. Backster showed the existence of what he called 'primary perception' in non-human cells. Also, Radin's research showed that there are indeed measurable gut reactions to emotional changes. In addition, the brain and the gut are connected by the vagus nerve, which transmits messages in both directions, with the majority going from gut to brain.

There is every reason to suppose that what we term gut feelings are the result of our microbial inhabitants reacting to the world around us. Such a reaction is also an important reminder that we are inextricably and inevitably intertwined with our environment, not only due to what we eat, but also at an energetic level. This deep connection with the world is one of the major aspects of intuition which will be examined in the next chapter.

Gut feelings tend to be about a person or place or action in present time. But then there are those intuitions which are associated with understandings or insights about people in present time, but which do not necessarily cause a gut feeling, but produce more of an understanding or awareness. Such intuitions might well result in trust, but they can also result in acquiring intuitive information about the individual. This second source of intuition lies in the invisible energy fields emanating from and surrounding us. The large, measurable fields which emanate from the brain and the heart have the potential to carry huge amounts of information, allowing us to assess or 'know' a person when we first meet them. Such a thing would explain how Richard Branson can make up his mind so quickly at a first meeting. Perhaps he, and others like him, have honed that ability to 'tune in' to another's electromagnetic field and, without realizing what they are doing, gather all that they need to know with apparent ease. It could also explain Anna's understanding of her client's issues and the way it helped her to identify a milk allergy, similar experiences which are anecdotally shared amongst many therapists who offer a more holistic approach to healing. Such therapies often occur in quieter surroundings than an allopathic interview, and the intention is usually to dig beyond the presenting symptoms to find underlying causes. In other words, there is an intention to be open to as much information as possible, allowing such information-rich moments to occur.

Such examples also speak to the possibility that some people are able to selectively access the large amount of information available within the fields surrounding each of us, seeking out only that which is of interest to them at that moment. At a basic level it would operate in such a way that, when meeting a person for the first time, we instinctively feel well-disposed or antagonistic to them to varying degrees. Honing that ability to 'read' the field of the person would allow us, presumably, to clarify that first impression. Such a reaction suggests that it probably started out as a survival mechanism for assessing the safety or danger inherent in the environment or when meeting strangers. Think of the Neanderthal link in this regard.

And let us not overlook the idea that, because we are all on this Earth together, we are naturally and inextricably linked, not only via our biota, but also via the Earth's magnetic fields or flux lines which, in turn, are affected by the sun. Our hearts beat to the same rhythm, creating a resonant energy field which automatically connects with the Earth, and therefore connects us with everyone else. How such a field might operate on our minds, let alone our hearts, is not yet known. It is a new area of study, but the existence of this connection is real enough. What sort of information transfer might be possible is not known, nor how often it might occur, but intuition could most certainly be influenced by it, as it certainly constitutes a different channel of information from the usual physical ones.

Although the energy fields which have been measured could certainly be capable of carrying information within them, there is no reason to suppose that the subtle energetic aspects of the human body, typified by the chakras, should not also contain complex information which could be downloaded into the body and made available in some fashion. Indeed, different cultural beliefs of the non-physical aspect of the body all point to a connection with the wider universe in some fashion, presumably allowing access to information normally unavailable to the physical senses. Although there is presently no explanation as to how the chakra system might access such information, it is possible to think that a connection with the zero point field might exist using different—and as yet unknown—channels.

Thirdly, there is the idea that the past is somehow imprinted in the fabric of the environment in some fashion. A vinyl record, for example, has one groove on each side which reveals nothing until a needle traverses it.

Similarly, without a particular light source, a DVD is only shiny plastic. It is conceivable that there is also some aspect within us which is able to allow us to 'read' the history within the structures around us. It might also explain the psychometric ability which many people show. Holding an object allows us to connect or interact with it in some fashion, and part or all of the recording is revealed to us, either in great detail or only as a quick snippet or feeling.

The Bold Street phenomenon could also be explained in this way, as a recording held in some fashion so that individuals with certain, if as yet unknown, capabilities or proclivities can access it. Perhaps the variety or complexity of information is due to differing abilities of the person or a difference in some energetic structure of the object, or maybe the difference is in allowing ourselves to believe such a thing is possible.

It is worth pointing out that there are more reports of psychometry, or token-object reading, which result in strong negative emotions than there are of emotions or situations concerned with the lighter, more positive emotions such as love and general happiness. Does this imply that only emotions or events involving anger, murder or intense fear or hatred are able to be recorded or recalled using this method, or that they are the easiest to 'read'? Does love for another not become so easily encoded in the environment as sadness? Or are the softer emotions less easy to comprehend, so that only a general feeling of well-being is sensed?

The fact that token-object reading is the most common method for gaining insight into cases of murder makes such emotions more closely associated with the method. The results of studying emotional effects upon the environment would tend to support such a hypothesis. The research into soil changes related to strong emotions may also provide more detail in the future on how the past is recorded more generally in the environment. Whatever the real reason, it is important that we do not always assume that psychometry is inevitably associated with the darker side of humanity.

A fourth source of intuition is indicated by the sleep experiments suggesting that the older brain structures, which incidentally contain the pineal, are instrumental in allowing complex imagery and understandings to occur very rapidly. Stan Gooch thought that the Neanderthal brain, a significant part of the older brain, was where intuition came from, and such flashes of understanding have certainly been reported. The stage just prior to falling asleep or to waking up is when such things occur and does certainly appear to have a link with intuition as it is normally conceived. Similar states can also be approached when very tired but relaxed. It is close to that state attained by some mystics in order to still the mind and see beyond 'normal' reality.

A fifth intuitive source is probably due to some form of excitement of the pineal gland. Being in the vicinity of a quartz-rich structure which is under stress in some form might allow perturbations within the gland which could give rise to visions. Dr. Rawls' experiments certainly showed that something was happening with perceptions of space when his pineal was stimulated, but it seemed to be without focus or purpose. But he was stimulating it artificially within his ordinary workplace, and what arose seemed to have little or no connection with his surroundings. Such stimulation within or near buildings or megalithic structures, however, seem to be able to produce glimpses of the past of those areas. Similar stimulation might also be occurring due to interaction with the Earth's magnetic field or when the sun's flux enters our atmosphere, as it does so regularly.

Apart from the magnetic stimulation, in general cultural and spiritual understandings around the world there is a consistent belief that the pineal or some other part of the brain is where there is a link between ourselves and the wider universe. Further, and this is repeated in various ways for various intuitive channels, there is also a belief that there is some form of interchange of energy, a flow of information in an invisible form, and that our bodies are always in contact with both the immediate world around us as well as the universe at large.

We have seen that space and time as traditionally taught in the classical model of physics are fluid concepts with regard to intuition. If we accept that the past could, in some fashion, be recorded, there is still the problem with accessing the future. Yet precognition exists. The heart, it seems, is good at perceiving up to at least six seconds ahead. Time and space are concepts rather than absolutes, and quantum mechanics provides sufficient evidence to show that they are not central to any aspect of the world, but merely appear to be that way to us. An integral part of this quantum world includes the zero point field where everything is in potential, and from which everything arises, and which, if the Pleroma concept and the theosophic idea of Akashic records have any validity, is where the past and the future are equally accessible.

This field of potential could be considered as a field of consciousness, as its contents are accessible only when attention is brought to bear upon it, so that a form of superposition occurs and information cascades down into us in some fashion. It would seem that the brain is probably involved in accessing that information somehow, and there are various theories about particular structures within the brain—microtubules and biophotons—which would allow us to do exactly that. There is certainly sufficient bandwidth associated with these structures to allow the transmission and reception of large amounts of data. This emphasizes again that both the past and the future are available to us, even though the precise mechanisms are not yet understood. Therefore, we also have a probable explanation for Toynbee's and Goddard's visions of the past and the future.

Yet there remain two aspects of intuition which are not yet completely susceptible to explanations: a knowing of what to do and its counterpart, that of unwitting actions to avoid problems.

The 'knowingness' is something which many of us have probably experienced in some fashion. Knowing which way to go in a strange town, or what best to do in order to help someone else in difficulty. Such things are occasionally reported, but have been well expressed by George Washington Carver's attitude toward the plant kingdom: a simple knowingness as to what to do to achieve his ends.

Similarly, compulsion also seems to be a part of some intuitions. Such compulsion must be due to a sensing which lies below the usual intuitive channels. It should be considered to be different from that of a correlation to a physical feeling or sensation, although there is still an element of future time involved. Of course, the reason for a compulsion being evident is another question which we will look at more closely in the following chapter. Sometimes the compulsion is subtle, as in the case of the choir members all not going to choir practice. Usually, however, the compulsion is more obvious. Often in such cases there seems to be a compulsion to say something, as when I spoke up about my colleague's old injury and Alec Guinness asked James Dean not to drive his car. But there are also physical compulsions, as illustrated by Kirk's remorseless searching for a language program, not knowing that was what he was doing until he found it. Both the 'knowingness' and the unconscious actions are aspects of a broader view of intuition which will be dealt with in the following chapter.

It should by now be abundantly clear that intuition is not to be easily explained with one theory, whether that be God or quantum mechanics. Feelings are obviously different from visions, which are different from a silent compulsion at work.

What is important to realize is that each may be caused chiefly by a different set of energetic fields within and around you or the people you are with or the place you are at. Of course, it might be the case that intuition is not to be defined by differing types of fields, as if fields were the only method of communication. It is plausible to suggest, from what we have discovered, that intuition may have many forms of communication (other languages?) different from fields. What those might consist of is impossible to say.

If we recall how little is known of the physical body, then it would be extremely presumptuous to insist that we now have provided the definitive explanation as to how intuition operates. We can only give suggestions and offer possibilities and make assumptions. In essence, we are using neolithic tools and perceptions to explore complex and technical machinery made up of materials we can only guess the composition of.

If there are various theories as to how intuition might work, and how different intuitions might rely upon different sources, there are still some large, unanswered questions. For example, why do not all people have the same clarity of intuition, or experience it in the same forms? Some people will go through life only ever having vague feelings of foreboding about the future, whilst others will have occasional, brilliantly clear, if short, visions of another time or place. What are the differences which allow such discrepancies? Are such discrepancies an inevitable result of the intuitive function, so that some people are incapable of accessing some types of intuition?

Although it has been emphasized that there are various intuitive channels available in the same way that there are different physical channels of perception, it does not follow that such channels must be equally uniform in the way that the physical senses are broadly uniform. They could have widely varying capabilities. To use the analogy of eyesight for the moment, eyesight works very poorly in the dark. Lack of visual perception in such cases does not imply that the person is physically, permanently blind, only temporarily so due to exterior conditions. In the same way, intuitive channels may allow a flood of information only at certain times due to certain circumstances presently unknown. The lack of intuition at any one time does not mean that there is no intuition, only that it is temporarily inhibited, perhaps by exterior circumstances, perhaps by internal ones.

Also, if intuition is an entirely natural aspect of being human, and the commonality across cultures and times points to that being so, then why do we not use or access it more? Most of the stories about intuition seem to indicate that, for the person involved, it was not their normal mode of being. Surprise and wonderment are often seen in their reports. There are some people who use their intuition every day in small ways and to great benefit, but that does not appear to be how the average person accesses it. In which case, the question then becomes one of how can we access it more regularly and with greater effectiveness so that it becomes an integral part of our lives?

That latter point is hugely important. However, before we look at it in more detail, there is yet another question which we need to consider. What is intuition for? Why do we have it, and what is its purpose? The most dramatic examples of intuition tend to be those where a life or lives were saved. But that cannot be its only purpose; otherwise, there would be a far greater number of people reporting how their intuition saved them from death in any number of ways. People die from accidents every day, and many of those accidents, one supposes, could be avoided, by either performing or not performing a given action, going to a certain place at a certain time, for example. Why did Alec Guinness have to warn James Dean? Why didn't James Dean have any precognition himself? Or perhaps he did, but chose to ignore it. But, still we come back to why was it Alec Guinness, who had arrived for the first time in the country earlier that day, and not some other person, a friend perhaps? The connections are not obvious, and the reasons not at all clear.

In the experiments where the electromagnetic field of the heart perceived the future up to six seconds ahead, it is doubtful that the subjects of the experiment sensed anything different. There were just the physically unremarked reactions noticed and recorded by machines. After all, if it is true for the subjects of those experiments, it is true for all of us and, for myself, I cannot say I always have a conscious 'knowing' of up to six seconds ahead of something good or bad about to happen. At least, not as a rule. There have certainly been times when that has been the case, and also times when it has not.

Could this inverted intuition imply, therefore, that there is another sense, a field or channel as yet unidentified, which feels the future but does not give feedback to us in physical terms, but only in ways which we can later understand? Might it be able to divert our attention away from the impending problem by giving us something else to think about or do? Each of the choir members, for example, had mundane issues holding them back from going to the church. The empty planes of 9/11 and the trains which later crashed would also seem to be examples of such a thing. In which case, of course, there is an entirely new line of questioning involved, and that is concerned with what might be considered to be involved in guiding the choices we make in our lives? If there is such a deep sense of a future problem, is there a reorganization of our lives such that we are moved away from the danger? How could that work? Is it a different form of consciousness, and where would it be found? Could it, in the case of big disasters, have something to do with the mass mind registered by the RNGs, and only some humans are picking up on what a larger group are sensing? We simply do not know enough yet to have any certainty of the answers.

Of course, there is also the question that the 'lucky' survivors, those who presumably listened to their intuition, all had something in common. What that something might be, however, is difficult to say, as we have no idea who they are. But, again, this is an aspect to be considered in the next chapter.

Intuition is not solely about saving lives. That is obvious. It is about information which spans the spectrum from the mundane to the life-saving, from visions of the past or future, to sudden understandings or awarenesses of a subject which has been occupying the recipient's mind.

The state of mind does not seem to matter too much, either. Certainly a relaxed mental attitude brought about by tiredness or by approaching sleep does seem to help in some cases. But often, there is nothing to prepare for a sudden intuition in the middle of some other activity. My 'seeing' the fight in the cathedral came when I was occupied and looking around the place. I certainly wasn't being still and reflective. The same for the story of the vision of the Drem airfield which occurred when the pilot was focused on trying to find a bearing to help him navigate in low visibility and difficult conditions; it was hardly a time for meditation and relaxation. It would seem that it is not necessary for the mind to be disciplined in order to have intuitions, although there might be a correlation with a close focus of the mind. I was focused on the cathedral, Goddard on surviving. Both of us received something unexpected.

Those who do follow mental disciplines, such as yogic masters, seem to be able to perceive more than those who do not, for it is from such people that the common approaches to spiritual connections with the universe arise. Even so, the tale of Emmanuel Swedenborg shows that ordinary people can do extraordinary things without preparation, although the adjective 'ordinary' might no longer be useful with regard to what people can do.

The frequency with which the pineal gland is mentioned in relation to the non-physical aspects of the body does seem to suggest that there is something important about it in the context of intuition at least. Given its apparent importance, is it then fair to take up Stan Gooch's suggestion that intuition is something which the Neanderthals bequeathed us via their brains? If so, would that then make intuition something which is inherently a part of our makeup, and that it harks back to a time when there was a different sort of relationship between our human ancestors and the surrounding world?

If that is true, then perhaps the fact that not everyone listens to it or acknowledges that it exists as a useful tool is due to our more rational and analytic approach driving it into the deeper aspects of our mind, so that it is only able to break into our consciousness occasionally and with varying degrees of intensity. What one person might sense as a clenching in the stomach, another might perceive as full vision or as nothing at all, yet both might be responding as Neanderthals.

The mystics from all cultures agree that an open and uninterrupted connection with what is beyond us and around us is possible. Could it be that the exercises they follow are methods of suppressing the modern analytical brain in order to uncover the Neanderthal brain instead? Here, quantum mechanics, biophotons and microtubules all play their parts in such a connection, much as they did, one supposes, in the Neanderthal body and brain.

Perhaps as our modern brains have developed, we have altered the ways in which we allow intuition to work. Where once it may have been used primarily as a way of navigating the world, of appreciating a connection with people, plants and animals, our analytical minds have allowed it to surface now and then to help us gain insights into rational problems on top of the original purpose of the intuitive connection as perceived by the Neanderthals.

None of that can be proven, and yet there remains the problem of a stuttering intuition which fires at random moments about odd things as well as for some, but not all, life-threatening events. The RNG machines around the world, as well as the experiments conducted by McCraty show that we as a race have an ability to foretell the future. That is part of what being human involves, it seems. There is no reason to suppose that our ancestors of 50,000 to 100,000 years ago were so very different from us in that regard. The Neanderthal brain case was larger than ours, which does not make them more intelligent (as we currently measure it, using tests devised by our brains to measure our brains), but it does indicate that that brainpower was available to be used, but perhaps in different ways from ours.

For a long time it was supposed that Neanderthals could not speak, but that theory is no longer tenable given the discovery of Neanderthal hyoid bones. Maybe their language was like Rousseau's hypothetical primal language, and they used it in entirely different ways to us; perhaps it was a reflection of the way they interacted with and understood the world. If intuition is an inherited trait from our ancestors (and even if it isn't), there still remains the question of why it is only fitful in appearance?

As to its purpose, perhaps the best that can be said for it is that it acts as a guidance system in our lives. It pushes us to do or not do things, or to go or not go to places, to understand and gain greater insights to issues troubling us. This aspect of intuition, as being an integral part of our lives, is the final one to be examined in the next chapter.

It remains to be emphasized that we are incredible beings. We can shape space and time. We can access any information we choose from the past and the future. We are connected with both the world around us and with the wider universe.

A 19th Century English poet, Francis Thompson, in his *The Mistress of Vision* once wrote:

> *All things by immortal power,*
>
> *Near and far*
>
> *Hiddenly*
>
> *To each other linked are,*
>
> *That thou canst not stir a flower*

Without troubling a star.

It has been amply demonstrated that we cannot avoid this connection, but it is still not something we have in the forefront of our daily consciousness.

Another aspect of our abilities with regard to how we interact with and experience the world was proposed by Abraham Maslow. An American psychologist, Maslow put together a psychology of human needs. At the bottom were the basic needs such as food and water, safety and so on. At the top of his pyramid was self-actualization, which was about achieving your full potential. Individuals who were self-actualized, according to Maslow, had peak experiences. In his words, these were, "rare, exciting, oceanic, deeply moving, exhilarating, elevating experiences that generate an advanced form of perceiving reality, and are even mystic and magical in their effect upon the experimenter."

Self-actualization included being creative and following your creative streak. He believed that there were few self-actualized people, but peak experiences involving such moments as he outlined could happen to anyone and could be had in simple moments as well as intense events.

His point was that those who had peak experiences tend to have them more often, as they were more likely to seek further peak experiences. This view has been confirmed. There is something called latent inhibition. This allows us to carry out multiple tasks without being swamped by overload. For example, if we looked at every chair we came across as something new and wonderful, we would be overwhelmed by the sensations. However, we are aware enough of chairs in general not to be too concerned with each and every one. We can discern the difference between familiar and non-familiar chairs, and that is helpful. That is what latent inhibition is. But creative people, it has been found, have a lower latent inhibition, meaning that they are more open to new stimuli all the time. Low latent inhibition has been linked with creativity and with higher IQ scores. Also, creative people report more psychic (i.e., supernormal or peak) experiences than others. Maybe they are seeing more in the world than others whose inability or unwillingness to perceive beyond what they are used to inhibits them.

A certain level of inhibition is useful, as is demonstrated by the story of Pieter van der Hurk (better known as Peter Hurkos), who was a house painter until 1943 when he fell from his ladder. Recovering from his injuries, he discovered that he had gained clairvoyant abilities such that he was able, while having extended conversations with anyone, to "see visions of the various phases of his life and the lives of his family and friends." The one thing he was unable to do was to go back to being a house painter, because he could no longer concentrate on anything. He had virtually no latent inhibition, which made his life very difficult until he decided to make use of his abilities on the stage. He spent the latter part of his life in the US, where he demonstrated his ability using psychometry. He also worked with various police forces as well as consulting with every US President from Eisenhower to Reagan.

As he aged and suffered the first of two heart attacks, Maslow changed his ideas somewhat and spoke of what he termed a plateau experience, which was one which could be entered more easily than a peak experience. He described it as "the simultaneous perception of the sacred and the ordinary, or the miraculous and the ordinary… There is nothing excepted and nothing special, but one lives in a world of miracles all the time. There is a paradox because it is miraculous and yet it doesn't produce an autonomic (involuntary) burst." And that is as good a description of our response to our intuition as is likely to be said. We live with something miraculous but see it as ordinary. The only difference is that the "awe, mystery, surprise" which he noted last only for brief moments and then are quickly forgotten until the next time.

Colin Wilson believed strongly in what he called Faculty X in man. Faculty X, according to him, was the direct opposite of feeling "accidental, mediocre, mortal." In the preface to his book *The Occult*, he described it in the following terms: "Man's consciousness is as powerful as a microscope. It can grasp and analyze experience in a way no animal can achieve. But microscopic vision is narrow vision. We need to develop another kind of consciousness that is the equivalent of the telescope." Colin Wilson believed there are seven basic levels of consciousness available to us. Level 1 he called dream consciousness, something we all experience as we sleep. Level 2 was basic waking consciousness, the sort of awareness which is behind our habits. We can get out of bed or sit in a chair as we let our bodies take over without our consciousness being involved overly much. Level 3 was what he referred to as "greyness and boredom," that is, how we can go through a day without really becoming involved in it and without being moved by it or noticing much detail. It is the level of consciousness we have when we follow routines. Level 4 is normal everyday consciousness, the sort of awareness where we chat with others, do tasks, perform our normal activities and so on. Level 5, for Wilson, was what he termed "spring morning consciousness." This can best be described as that feeling you get when you go outside and realize for the first time that year that summer is on its way, because there is something undefinable in the air. It is experienced in that moment when you feel lighter or happier and the world becomes a little more real or has a sharper focus for you. Level 6 he termed "magic consciousness" or pure delight. You can see that in a child's face at Christmas, but it seems to become less common as we age. And finally, level 7 was the level Wilson believed where Faculty X existed. It was "when the mind seems so energized—or deeply relaxed—that other times and places are as real as the present."

He argued that most of us remain at level 4. But intuition, it would seem, can occasionally push us up to level 7, where Faculty X takes over. It is an interesting idea, and I feel there is a certain amount of truth to it. We do remain bored or wrapped up in our everyday lives, which is why when the unusual happens—great delight, or great dreams—we remark upon them.

Wilson said, "Man is literally a god; a god suffering from laziness, amnesia, and nightmares." While that might sound like so much hyperbole, there is, again, some truth in it. As Dr. Johnson of dictionary and stone-kicking fame once remarked, "When a man knows he is to be hanged in a fortnight, it concentrates his mind wonderfully." By which he meant that everything around him suddenly becomes more vividly real and has a far greater significance than could have been imagined, because he knows he is about to lose it forever. There is an immersion in life when it is threatened to be taken away from us.

If we have been lucky, we have had such exceptional experiences ourselves for brief moments, but without the threat of imminent death. Suddenly, we see the world with fresh eyes, and everything is vibrant and has meaning for us. It is an intense moment of realization. Our perceptions seem to undergo a change. Bergson suggested that our brains filter out much of what is possible to be perceived, and Wilson's point that our reliance on our analytical and rational powers suppresses our perceptions acts to bolster that idea.

The ideas of Maslow and Wilson, together with Bergson's comment, all point to the same thing: that we tend to live in a world which is restricted and narrowed by our physical senses, because it is what we have become used to. Maslow's peak experiences and Wilson's Faculty X are not the norms in terms of experience, but they are something to which we should be aspiring, because they are how we break free from the daily grind of our everyday world and can realize our true potential.

What neither Maslow nor Wilson said was that we already have that ability in our intuition. It is our intuition which has the ability to cut through the filters of life, where we do little more than get through the days, and it brings us information from beyond our senses. Intuition of itself does not promote peak experiences, except in the rare cases of sudden understanding, but it is a gateway to a much wider world which, if we acknowledge it, will give us access to a deeper level of appreciation of life—Maslow's 'plateau experience'—where we live in the world of miracles all the time.

Just as one person might be drawn to playing the piano and makes it seem easy, and another is a gymnast and a third becomes an astronomer, if we stand them side by side, we cannot see what makes those preferences and allows them to be expressed. There is something inside them which finds expression in different interests, hobbies, abilities, and desires. In much the same way, we do not know why one person gets precise feelings or sensations about an event whilst another 'sees' it clairvoyantly or a third understands a deeper connection between two similar events.

The variety of ways in which we can naturally access information beyond the reach of our five senses leads inevitably to the last aspect to be considered. This has been hinted at in this chapter, but it needs a more careful examination. The question which needs answering above all others is this: if intuition is so obviously bound up inextricably with our physical existence, what purpose does it serve, and can it be considered to be a constant companion rather than an occasional visitor?

15

INTUITION: A NEW PARADIGM

"The more you trust your intuition, the more empowered you become, the stronger you become, and the happier you become."
Gisele Bündchen (Model)

The previous chapter set out the arguments for intuition to consist of information accessed by a variety of channels or modes, making a simplistic single explanation no longer acceptable. The variety of channels through which intuitive information arrives act in much the same way as our physical senses operate, and therefore the supra-sensory apparatus within us should be thought of as somewhat analogous and effectively complementary to the better-known five physical senses, although the differences in the form of awareness between the physical and the non-physical senses should always be born in mind. If we keep to this analogy, we can attempt an explanation of how intuition may be seen in a wider context than just some occasional moments. We can then begin to answer the larger question concerning the role of intuition in our lives.

Our five physical senses exist and have evolved to navigate us through this world. They give us feedback on our surroundings and act as survival mechanisms. We are connected to this physical world through them. The fewer senses we have, the greater restrictions we experience, or the greater the obstacles are placed in our way to acquiring a complete comprehension of our surroundings. In other words, we become less efficient and effective as individual beings. In terms strictly of survival, a blind person, or one who is deaf, is more at risk.

This analogy of feedback and survival is also, I believe, the role of intuition. But it is not solely associated with the remarkable stories we saw in the first chapter. Those are just the outliers. Intuition is, I believe, much more than those occasional bursts of insight. Intuition, as we have seen, comes in various formats. If someone chooses to ignore their intuition, or to only listen to it when it is at its strongest, they are acting as if they have poor eyesight and are, analogously, at a huge disadvantage compared to a person with good eyesight. The only difference here is that poor eyesight can be helped only so much, while not attending to intuition is something which can be changed completely. And, just as poor eyesight handicaps a person in the physical world, so not using intuition, even though it is always available, handicaps a person in both the physical and the non-physical worlds. Restricting yourself and preventing insights, hunches, and compulsions from being perceived or influencing you is limiting the information available to you.

Because of this analogy of the intuitive channels mirroring to some extent the physical ones, I would like to propose an additional idea about intuition. Much earlier, I offered a definition of intuition which was sufficiently encompassing as to include all the varieties which are available to us.

To remind you, it was as follows:

> *Intuition is the perception of or reaction to information in any form which either bypasses the rational and logical mind, giving immediate insight or knowledge not directly associated with or mediated by the usual five senses, or is associated with a different time or place, but is presented as being 'here and now' to the recipient.*

I want now to take that definition and look at an underlying pattern about intuition in general by placing it in a wider context, a context which will, I hope, open up a new way of looking not just at intuition as it occurs at random moments, but of looking at our lives in totality. It will also, I believe, fully and completely answer the question posed at the end of the previous chapter, that of the purpose of intuition in our lives.

Even if we cannot say with absolute certainty where each intuition originates, there is enough evidence to suggest that, no matter how we experience it, as visions or only as a gut feeling about something, there is always the basic faculty at work in our lives, whether we wish to acknowledge it or not. The perception and awareness of intuition can be improved, most simply by becoming aware of its existence. And the fact that it can be trained to be something larger and more obviously a part of our lives gives credence to the existence of a base level, if you will, of some natural force at work within us.

Take, for example, the story of Jim Corbett, a big game hunter in the 1920's and 1930's who wrote about the man-eating tigers and leopards in India he set out to kill. Here was a man who had spent his life in the jungle and was at home there. In one of his books, *Jungle Lore*, he describes how he unconsciously avoided a tiger. Walking home one day, he realized from the color of dust on his feet that he had, without realizing it, crossed to the other side of the road as he neared a culvert. Going back the next day to see if he was correct, he noticed the marks of a tiger which had been lying there beneath the bridge. As he put it, "My subconscious being was not prepared to take this risk (of being attacked) and jungle sensitiveness came to my assistance and guided me away from potential danger." While few us need to be wary of being attacked by wild animals, there are numerous stories from reliable sources which show that people avoid danger in various ways without knowing how: avoiding collisions at traffic lights, avoiding a mugger or robber, and so on. And, beyond those stories must lie myriads of others where there is no danger being avoided, but simply a nudge here or there which takes you in one direction rather than another, and which as a consequence makes your life better, happier, safer or healthier.

I would suggest that the people who missed trains involved in accidents, the passengers who did not fly on 9/11, and the choir members who avoided an explosion all exhibited aspects of the same type of intuition which Jim Corbett called 'jungle sensitiveness.' The fact that the people involved had no clear message to avoid situations is pointing to something which has been there in the background throughout most of this examination of intuition. It has never taken the center stage, but is implicit in virtually every aspect or example.

Quantum physics has shown that non-locality—the opposite of our traditional view that space and time separate everything—exists. Further, the mystics speak of how everything is connected in some fashion, a view supported by the ideas of the various systems of chakras and energetic bodies found across cultures. "All things are connected like the blood that unites us. We do not weave the web of life, we are merely a strand in it. Whatever we do to the web, we do to ourselves," said Chief Seattle of the Suquamish tribe.

To illustrate this point further, Margaret Wertheim, a science writer who also looks at the cultural history of physics, writing in *Seeing Further,* tells of how we have forgotten that words like 'cosmos' and 'cosmology' have changed their meaning. Both now refer to the physical, material domain when, in medieval times, they referred to multiple levels of being. She continues, "Contrary to accounts given in many popular science books, medieval cosmology was underpinned by a rigorous logic that attempted to encompass the totality of humans as physical, psychological and spiritual beings. Medieval scholars read the world in an iconic rather than a literalist sense; nature was a rebus in which everything visible to the eye represented multiple layers of meaning within a grand cosmic order. The physical world was the starting point for investigations that ultimately sought to comprehend a spiritual reality beyond the material plane and what is so beautiful here is that the metaphysical duality of body and soul was mirrored in the architecture of the cosmos." There is not just a metaphysical idea behind this, but a historical viewpoint and an understanding which we have lost. Wertheim adds, "…we tell ourselves that older cosmologies are childish tales and that we moderns supposedly have outgrown these stories and faced reality 'squarely' to work out where we 'truly' are." Our western culture, it seems, once had a more encompassing and inclusive view of the relationship between ourselves and the world.

Microbiologists speak of how we are walking rain forests, and how the food we eat affects the various microbiomes inside us. William Tiller, Emeritus Professor of Materials Science and Engineering at Stanford University in his book *Science and Human Transformation* speaks of how we create fields of varying frequencies around and within us automatically as part of our existence, something which the experiments of Rollin McCraty also supports. We are both transmitters and receivers of these human fields, as well as those fields from other organisms. We are at the center of what we perceive, and thus we are not and cannot be disconnected from the world around us. We are, as Chief Seattle said, but one slim strand of consciousness within a web of infinite complexity which is constantly being woven and re-shaped every moment of every day.

I want to propose an analogy with what we have discovered so far and apply it to intuition. In quantum physics, it appears that beneath everything lies some sort of potential out of which arrives the world we perceive with our senses, even though we cannot perceive the field from which it comes. Mountains, elephants, ants and grass, lemons and microscopes and everything else arise in some fashion from the potential around us.

In much the same way, our intuition shows itself to be sometimes complex and sometimes almost rudimentary. If we think in terms of communication, then some forms of intuition are highly complex with sight and sound, involving more of the supra-sensory channels, whereas other forms are much simpler, involving only some sort of vague feeling. If there is a field from which our perceived world arises, then I suggest that there is a similar field out of which our intuitions arise. The evidence for such a field is, I believe, to be found in those instances where there was no premonition, no forewarning, or only the vaguest of nudges of unease to do something differently: take a different route, stop instead of moving, hurry instead of pausing. I liken this to the ground state of intuition, analogous to the zero point field, whose existence can be sensed in the small but measurable fluctuations in electronic equipment when all else has been accounted for. In the same way that the zero point field appears to be permeating and connecting everything, so I believe that there is a similar state which connects us all to everything and which thereby 'sees' connections and implications. Just as we are incapable of moving outside of the effects of the zero point field, so we cannot escape the web within which we and everything else exists.

What this means is that, because of this interconnectedness at the physical and energetic levels, everything which happens to us and around us is of importance. Remember that my definition of intuition referred to the perception of or reaction to information outside the five physical senses. As we live our daily lives, we experience the physical world through those senses. What I propose is that our life which is sensed but is beyond our physical senses is also intuition writ large. Our physical senses provide us with the very basics of what we need to live. They help us navigate through the world. But that wonderful experience of consciousness above and beyond our senses brings to us that which we need to make our lives richer and fuller, deeper and more meaningful. That undercurrent of consciousness creates those moments, those intuitions or phenomena, which our senses are then able to perceive, but it does so by virtue of the nature of the web of life itself. As we live, we pull on strands of that web, and those tugs and movements are felt and come back to us as intuitions.

It is for these reasons that intuition, I believe, is always at work every moment of every day. It cannot be otherwise, given its nature. This ever-present aspect of it is important to remember, just as it is important to remember that we cannot escape it. That is an impossibility. We are too closely and intimately part of the world beyond our physical body. It is therefore up to us to notice what intuition continually provides. John Lennon once said that life is what happens to you while you are busy making other plans. I would suggest that intuition (information) is what comes to you when you are busy living your life.

This does not always mean that inevitably there are visions given to you or that you will always have gut feelings about the future. But it does mean that you are always being given opportunities to notice what is happening to and around you, connected as you are to the past and the future, the here and now and the far distant. This connection is the 'ground state' of intuition which explains Jim Corbett's experience and all the other stories where people unwittingly avoided disaster of one kind or another. It also explains that 'knowing' of what to do and how to act as shown by Carver's understanding of plants. It is the primary perception of Backster, ever-present and always providing feedback to us.

If we were to have to settle on one purpose of intuition, to explain why it is in our lives, I do not think that it is to preserve our lives at all. That is a welcome side effect if and when it happens. Our physical senses might be thought to have started out with that aim in mind, but they do much more than that now. Intuition is, I believe, designed similarly to enrich our lives by ensuring that we have opportunities to live more closely connected with the world around us than our present, busy, logical, analytical, data-driven lives would seem to allow us. Such a closed, heads-down-and-charge approach to life limits our vision; it makes it, as Colin Wilson said, microscopic, focusing on the small and the particular rather than the grand and the expansive, which is always present if not always acknowledged.

Consider for a moment the fact that we are intimately connected with the world around us, both the immediate environment and the larger universe beyond. The immediate world connection is easier to accept perhaps, the wider connection less so. Nevertheless, such connections are axiomatic as a result of our existence, as I hope has been proven. What that implies, however, is that such a connection is not and cannot be only one way, from us outward to the world. In order to receive impressions and information from our intuitive senses there must, obviously, be a two-way connection. We accept that we can access physical information coming to us readily enough. However, what comes to us is not limited solely to some understanding of the people, objects or places we come into contact with. To assume that is all is to deny any intuition which involves the future or the past or any intuition which is not about what we are involved in at the present moment.

What is vital to accept is that, just as we are always pumping out information about ourselves without realizing it—such that others can form immediate impressions about us, for example—so the universe at large is constantly providing a huge and endless stream of information, and we are always in that stream. Some of it we intercept as an intuitive hit and mark it as special because of the unusual nature of it. But, the rest of that ceaseless flow is still available to us each and every day through the people, places, objects, and events which come into our sphere of perception. We do not necessarily always recognize them or understand them, yet they contain information for us. Certainly our physical senses take note of a helpful person or event, but it is the arrival of the event, the offering of information in that particular form at that particular time which is what, in my opinion, constitutes intuition in the broadest sense of the word. Just as someone like Richard Branson can tune his intuition to 'read' a person quickly to help him in his work, so each one of us can learn to 'read' the events around us and benefit from that information in our lives.

Intuition is the force at work behind all our experiences, providing us with opportunities to understand that connection, to accept it and to embrace it. Such an approach to life is the opposite of the scientific reductionist approach to understanding (know more and more about less and less and lose sight of the grander picture of life itself and its inherent and wonderful and necessary complexity).

Time and again we are given evidence, anecdotes, and examples of our connection with everything. Time and again throughout this book there have been references to the bigger picture of us and how we are part of everything and not separate in any way—through what we eat, how we sense and react to others, how landscapes and buildings influence us.

Intuition is simply a natural aspect of us all which provides a way, composed of various channels, for accepting and accessing that connection. It is not something granted to only a special few, because it is an intrinsic aspect of being alive. It is always active, always there, if only we allow ourselves to be conscious of it.

Accessing intuition, or allowing it to happen to us, may depend on our emotional state and our beliefs, as well as our environment at any given time. It might be that we are able to have amazing intuitions, but for only a short period of time. We may only get that one vision of the future or the past in great detail, and for the rest of the time we only get vague nudges and hunches. The how and the why of expressing or experiencing intuition may be uncovered someday. But if you ever feel deprived by not having a glorious technicolor 3D experience, you can always console yourself that you can be aware of the day-to-day intuitions which are always there for you. Intuition's presence is known through the people it brings to you, the sights and the sounds you perceive, the help offered when you need it most. Intuition is evident in the experiences continually being brought to you. All you have to do is accept that intuition is there and learn to see it for what it is: proof of your connection with the world beyond you, beyond your everyday normality.

With what we have learned about how intuition works and what we are capable of, our current attitude toward intuition may seem muted, understated or just plain ignorant, but the fact of its existence is impossible to ignore. Once we accept that intuition in this form does exist, and that it continually makes itself known in various ways, then we have to admit that it opens up the doorway to a new view of the world and our relationship with everything in it.

Intuition is always providing us with information which, if we allow it, will provide help, encouragement, and guidance in our lives. By denying it or relegating it to a secondary role, we are restricting our ability to fully immerse ourselves within the world in the same way as someone walking along with earphones on listening to music is willfully blocking out one whole spectrum of the surrounding environment.

To listen to our intuition regularly is a choice which extends our perceptions beyond the immediate and the physical. If we are willing to accept such a challenge and choose to both accept it and what it provides for us, then it also demands of us a way of widening the doorway to our intuition, of taking a macroscopic view.

We live in a closed, tense environment, overwhelmed with information from all sides: auditory, visual, electromagnetic. We think and analyze and use our intellect constantly to find our way through this blizzard.

What is needed is a way of looking beyond the physical and mental clothing we have become accustomed to, beyond the merely rational and the analytical, and find ways to free ourselves from their restrictions.

We need to see life as something more than what happens to us randomly every day. We need to make a conscious choice to understand that we are part of something much larger than ourselves, much grander, much more magnificent and above all, infinitely more meaningful. It is akin to living in a forest of tall trees with various pathways meandering through it. You follow a new path one day. Walking it, the path leads to the edge of a cliff and there before you is a view of mountains and valleys, depths and heights, of the sky and rivers, flowers and animals, all filled with colors you never realized existed until that epiphany. And from that moment on, you cannot think of the forest in the same way again, and no matter how deep you move inside it, you will always know that there is something more, something grander beyond it. Accepting what intuition implies is akin to this realization.

How do we do this? How do we gain that new perspective? There are many ways. Simple meditation is one of the most well-known because it has been used so often over time. Slowing down and taking our time to immerse ourselves in everyday nature which presents itself to us is another. Losing oneself, for example, in appreciation of a flower, in the complexity of color, the scent, the structure, the very 'it-ness' of it, as Oliver Sacks said, opens us up to what is truly around and within us. That apprehension of the totality of what is around us is what Dr. Johnson meant by fear focusing the mind; everything is seen more clearly and fully. The second part of this book will provide far more detail and help with regard to recognizing and understanding your natural connection with the world.

Essentially, we have to find time to get out of the small rooms we live in, the rooms of habit and work and 'normality,' the microscopic vision, and the inherent boredom and tiredness and emptiness they bring and realize there is something far richer awaiting us outside of them. We have but to see it all. And intuition is an integral part of that seeing.

Intuition, any intuition—a gut feeling about a place or a sense of something good or bad ahead; meeting a stranger at a party you weren't sure you'd go to who can help you achieve a dream of yours; finding the perfect book you have been looking for in a yard sale you were passing by; simply knowing that a different shop has exactly what you want at a better price—all such things are signs we are given to realize that there are new and exciting horizons awaiting us. All that is necessary is for us to grasp the idea and begin to condition ourselves to see beyond what our narrow physical perceptions limit us to and to know, truly know, that there is much, much more awaiting us.

Because of the variety of ways we are intimately interconnected with the universe, intuition cannot fail but be something which is always operating at many different levels, in much the same way that we can watch a tennis match and also see the stadium and the people and feel the hardness of the seat and the warmth of the sun as we smell and taste the strawberries and cream we are eating. If only one of our senses is working, we get an entirely different perception of the event, similarly with only two or three senses. With fewer physical senses operating, our understanding of the event, the tennis match, becomes restricted, and what we perceive will be very different from the understanding gained when all senses are working perfectly.

In the same way, I contend intuition is always there, sometimes stronger and sometimes weaker, but always there, and what we perceive with it is dependent upon which channels of communication are open to us at any moment.

It is also greatly dependent upon how much we let ourselves accept what our intuitive senses bring to us. The 'picture' we get with our intuitive senses will vary accordingly in just the same way as in the above example of the different physical senses' apprehension of the tennis match. As an aside, we may think that what we obtain with intuition is always like that: varying in information density and only occasionally happening. But that is not true, as the perception of intuition can be heightened through various practices.

From all of this, it should become obvious that I believe the central concern of intuition is always that of linking us with the world around us, and using that connection to inform us of dangers, of opportunities, of bringing us what is needed or being focused on. We are both transmitters and receivers of information. To think that we are only received by other people and not by the plants, the animals and the whole universe beyond is so unlikely as to not be worth consideration. How could we otherwise explain our premonitions, if we are not in touch with the universe, and it is not in touch with us?

That there is a reciprocity is most obviously evidenced by the many stories of people with supposedly 'green fingers' who are able, somehow, to make plants grow with ease where others struggle. Patrick MacManaway, a consultant and teacher working with domestic, commercial and agricultural landscapes around the world, describes a very simple experiment anyone can do which shows the connection which exists between humans and plants (and thus between humans and the universe). Bring two trays of sprouting seeds into the kitchen, give 'loving attention' to one tray only, but feed and tend them both equally and the one which has been cared for will have seedlings which "tend to look better, grow more, and have deeper root structure, often up to a 30 % increase in plant mass after just a week or ten days, depending on the species." This approach is nothing more than sending a feeling (as opposed to receiving it).

It is the role of intuition to respond to who and what we are, what we are transmitting even when nobody else is there, just as seedlings will respond to us. If we persist in our human-centric vision of the universe, we are automatically restricting ourselves in what we can perceive. Such a vision is patently false. Something which medieval minds knew for certain is something we have forgotten. The universe may appear to be remote and uncaring, but it is not, and intuition is the way it shows that it both listens to us and responds.

Intuition is, therefore, our greatest gift, transcending as it does time and space, giving us access to untold amounts of information beyond the reach of our senses and reminding us, if we let it, that we consist of far more than we allow ourselves to think.

We are, therefore, far more than we perceive. Intuition is constant, always operating, always responding to us, and always providing information. It never stops. Just as someone walking along with headphones on is willfully blocking out one aspect of the world around them, so it is with us if we choose to ignore what is always coming to us, if we choose not to accept intuition's gifts; we are depriving ourselves of one whole spectrum of existence, living plainer and duller lives as a result.

It seems appropriate therefore to end with a quote from one of the great physicists of the twentieth century, Werner Heisenberg, the originator of the uncertainty principle. It serves as a summary of all that we have learned about ourselves, the world, and our intuition. He said, "Whoever dedicates his life to searching out particular connections of nature will spontaneously be confronted with the question how they fit harmoniously into the whole."

PART II

HARNESSING YOUR INTUITIVE ABILITY

1

EVERYONE IS INTUITIVE

Nothing exists for its own sake, but for a harmony greater than itself which includes it.
Wendell Berry (Poet)

As we have seen, intuition is not only an entirely natural aspect of what it is to be human, but it is also something which, by its very nature, is ever-present and unavoidable. The connection with the world around and beyond us is inevitable. We both transmit and receive information all the time. Just as our physical senses bring information to us through the various channels of sight, sound, touch, taste, and smell, so our intuitive senses bring us information in various ways through channels such as gut feelings, clairvoyance of the past and future, premonitions, emotions, and the like. We also transmit information about our past and about our emotions which can be picked up by those around us, humans and animals as well as plants. It also seems likely that we leave some sort of impression upon the environment in some cases which can be picked up or tuned into later on. Both our environment and ourselves are in a constant state of interaction, a dynamic exchange happening every moment of every day. And it is in that dynamic state that intuition lies, endlessly bringing and sending information beyond the physical senses.

The examples scattered throughout the first part were used to show the variety of intuitions available to us all. What you need to remember is that although you might yearn for an IMAX style intuitive 'hit' full of color and sound and special effects, the fact remains that you always have intuition available to you in different forms. The IMAX style may only happen once in your lifetime, or never at all. But the continual sending and receiving, the ground state of intuition if you will, is a constant, and you are always connected with it. That means that instead of intense visions, you might experience nudges, gut feelings, whispers, and those are, in the end, just as valuable as the high-definition action sequences you can hear about from others.

Think of it this way: the IMAX format of intuition could be compared with, say, superb eyesight in the physical world. But if you don't have the other formats such as feelings and premonitions or flashes of understanding, it would be the same as you only being able to see well, but being deaf or unable to smell or taste. To keep to that analogy, you probably do have one dominant sense in the physical world (perhaps you have excellent hearing), and that is very likely to be true in the world of intuition; one form will be stronger than the others, but that does not make the others redundant.

It's also important to realize that being intuitive as it is generally thought of, that is, having a series of detailed or comprehensive intuitive hits, does not necessarily last. It might be that you have a period of a year or two when your capacity for gaining information in this way seems to be set on high, and that you keep getting hits of one kind or another. However, after a while, that might slow down and even halt for an indeterminate period, and you go back to the baseline of nudges, hunches, and feelings. One reason for this increased awareness might be due to the emotional state you are in during that period.

Speaking of my own experiences, I had a lot of sudden insights—some of which I have shared—which took various forms of subtle visions, 'knowings,' and awarenesses that happened, on reflection, to coincide with a period of increasing emotional turmoil. When my life became simpler, smoother, with fewer emotional highs and lows, so I reverted back to the ground state. After a while, however, I noticed that my capacity to allow more complex intuition rose once more. This time, I was studying metaphysics in more detail, working to expand my ideas and beliefs, becoming more and more interested in approaches to life which were less conventional. That brought about another richer period of intuitions. Some time after that, when I became more comfortable in my new approach to life, so I found that I was more and more able to call upon intuitions when I needed them.

My point is that whatever your state of receptivity to intuition is right now, it is likely to change over time. The exact causes and the precise amount of change can't be predicted. In relating my own experiences, I have only been able to guess at possible causes. I might be highly inaccurate as to the reasons I changed in my receptivity, but the fact remains that I did experience a variety of intuitions over time, with peaks of more complex, more detailed information and periods when it was very much less than that.

If you have a stressful life which you feel precludes you from having deep insights, then you might find that when the pressure is off, such as on vacation, that's when you get stronger intuitions. There seems to be no definitive mode of being which will automatically connect you with complex intuitions. Some people with stressful jobs and lives are able to access their intuition more readily—often in only one small sphere of their lives, such as Richard Branson's ability to size up people—because they have come to rely upon it, and therefore they give it room to express. It is entirely personal, so don't think that something is wrong if you seem to be living a lifestyle which you think should allow intuition in more freely. It might be that you need to recognize it more (something we'll be looking at) or that some other change needs to happen before it flourishes. No matter what your circumstances, rest assured that you are already daily experiencing intuition in your life.

Part One of this book sought to explain how intuition works using mainly scientific research to explain it. But, as we saw in the chapter on language, there are restrictions as to how useful the scientific approach can be, in that it misses out or is unable to deal with the personal and subjective aspects of life. And intuition is, above all, very personal and very subjective. In Part Two, although there will be some emphasis on proven (i.e., scientific) ways of strengthening your awareness of your intuition, the majority of this section will be emphasizing the personal and the subjective aspects of intuition.

We are going to be looking at how you can improve your intuition, from recognizing your particular intuitive strength to the physical, mental, spiritual, and emotional ways you can improve that recognition. You might be someone who never really trusts their intuition fully. In which case, what follows will help you to become more reliant upon it. If you currently have the receptivity to allow highly complex information in via intuition in the shape of detailed visions or absolute certainty arriving in other ways, then the subsequent chapters will also serve to help maintain that ability for longer. The science of Part One feeds into the personal in this, Part Two.

The key fact to have before you, when reading this book and when living your life, is that intuition is always occurring around you and for you. You are always being brought information to enrich your life. You don't need to strengthen your intuition. All that is necessary is to become more aware of it.

2

INTUITION AND YOU

He who lives in harmony with himself, lives in harmony with the universe.
Marcus Aurelius (Roman Emperor and soldier)

Before beginning to look more closely at recognizing your own intuition, it is important to take the time to understand more clearly what our connection with everything actually means and how it reveals itself. To begin with, the world in which you are immersed is not only touched by your existence, but it is also connecting in its own way to you. There is feedback at work. The connection and feedback is two-way. The information in the fields emanating from you interconnects with those fields arising from the physical and non-physical aspects of reality. Each influences the other.

As you progress from day to day, events occur, objects appear, people speak to you, and each of these, in its own way, provides proof of your connection in the form of feedback to you. You are sending out information into the world constantly through your very existence via the fields generated automatically by your body, brain, and heart, not to mention your non-visible energetic aspect. Similarly, information is coming to you via your gut, your mind, from the information naturally stored in the environment, as well as from your interaction with the zero point field.

There is a natural meshing of what is you and what is not-you, and there is an inevitable interchange because of that meshing. It is from that meshing that the ground state of intuition, of information arriving from the supra-sensory world, is presented to you. It is, if you like, the basic state of being in the world. It is the ground state from which everything else arises. What follows will illustrate this ground state of intuition, in that it shows how the world around you can bring to your attention the things you need to see.

To fully appreciate how your intuition is always active, or that you are always in that field of intuition, consider the following. Once, my grandmother was very, very ill. My mother spent as much time as she could with her, as well as working with my dad in his butcher's shop. I often drove her between the two places, a distance of about 20 miles. One day, after leaving my grandmother and heading toward the shop, I suddenly 'knew' that she had died. I looked at my watch and noted the time, but didn't say anything to Mum, because although I knew, I couldn't tell her how I knew, and it made no sense to upset her more. We arrived at the shop about ten minutes later, and the phone rang almost immediately. I knew it was going to be my grandfather breaking the news. He said she had died about ten minutes before.

I never had that feeling about anyone again, not even when my grandfather died. It happened with my grandmother, and I was aware of it, and that was the end of it. There was a general connection with the world, and there was specific feedback in the form of knowing when she died. And that is one of the frustrating and interesting aspects of intuition generally. It comes and goes, sometimes being very clear, sometimes less so. Maybe there had been something brought to my awareness when my grandfather died, but I was too busy or too distracted to notice. Maybe, because I was driving and not entirely focused on another type of activity, I was able to be aware of the information more easily. I believe that now I would be more aware of some small message (or perhaps I simply hope that would be the case). But it has not always been true.

Take another example. Perhaps you have been planning a trip to the cinema and you wanted to purchase tickets online for two days ahead to avoid the queue. The only trouble is, you can't manage it. For one reason or another, the sale won't go through, then the website freezes and it simply doesn't work. You give up in disgust and decide you'll try again tomorrow. However, before then, one of your great friends who lives miles and miles away and whose schedule is such that you and she don't get to spend much time together in person or online, emails you to say she's available for a get-together on the very day and time you wanted to go to the cinema. Are you available? Now you certainly are. A couple of hours before, you weren't. Your general connection allowed the meeting to take place.

Native Americans believe that there are messages for them in what they see. Animals have meaning for them. For example, suppose that a person has spent some time reminiscing about an old friend. Happening to look up, he sees a vulture close by. Now, according to some tribes, that would be associated with death or danger. Paying attention to the sign (which is merely a form of information), to the intuition presented to him, he contacts the friend and discovers he needs help now, as he is very ill. Being aware of what is brought before them, Native Americans can become aware of messages they need to hear or things they need to understand. They pay attention to the world. That is the source of all intuition. We will be looking at this particular aspect later on.

Such events might be termed synchronicities. Synchronicity was a term first used by the Swiss psychiatrist and psychoanalyst, Carl Jung. He used it to express a concept where two or more physical or psychical phenomena are connected without any obvious cause. It originated with his working with a patient who was too rational about anything to allow any subconscious awareness to take place. One night the patient dreamt of a golden scarab. In the next session an insect hit against Jung's cabinet window. Upon capturing it he found it to be a golden scarab, which was rare in that climate. Working upon the associations of the dream and the insect allowed progress to be made. There was no obvious causation between the scarab in real life and the dream of the scarab, yet the two occurred and were meaningful as a result. Another way of expressing it is to say that synchronicity is when outer events correspond or become relevant to our inner feelings or thoughts or perceptions. Or, better still, it is another example of the ground state of intuition at work, of connection and feedback, of information continually being presented to you.

All such instances are examples of intuition at work, the recognition of information helpful to you in one way or another. We are always living in the ground state of intuition, the basic field from which all our knowledge comes. All that is necessary is to recognize it when it appears. And that is what we will begin to do in the next section.

3

RECOGNIZING YOUR INTUITION

I dislike the word 'self-help.' Self-awareness, yes, but not self-help.
Deepak Chopra (Author)

In 1975, Daniel Simons of the University of Illinois and Christopher Chabris of Harvard asked about 200 people, split into groups, to watch a video of two teams of people passing a basketball around, one in white, the other in black tee-shirts. The subjects were asked to either count the number of passes made by one of the teams or to count the number of bounce passes versus aerial passes. At some point, a person dressed in a gorilla suit walked through the scene. At the end, the subjects were asked if they had noticed anything out of the ordinary in what had taken place. On average, over half of the viewers did not report seeing the gorilla. In fact, in one group, only 8% reported seeing it. This is not an isolated incident, but a real-world phenomenon usually termed inattentional blindness. There have been many experiments carried out to confirm this phenomenon, such as one where over 50% of people landing a plane in a simulator failed to observe other planes or trucks positioned on the runway. In other words, if you don't expect to see something, even if it is in plain sight, you have a good chance of never seeing it.

In exactly the same way, intuition can only be recognized if you are aware of it happening. A deaf person cannot hear the doorbell. It doesn't mean it did not ring. Unless there is a way to become aware (for a deaf person, it could be a bright light flashing when the doorbell is pressed), the opportunity, the information, is missed. Awareness, then, is the pre-eminent point to remember. And it is not only awareness of something outside of you, like the Native American noticing the vulture. Far more important is the awareness of yourself: your reactions, emotions, and sensations.

Self-awareness, the condition of being able to look inside and notice and give weight to your internal state of being, is vital. All too often, we tend to look outside of ourselves and become immersed in details of the external world and respond to it in terms of happiness or fear, anger or joy. But there are nuances when it comes to listening to your intuition. There are subtleties of feelings which can be overlooked or ignored, because they are not as strong as those we are accustomed to in our daily, externally-focused lives.

Yet without that self-awareness, that willingness to accept less-strong feelings, we may become like the deaf person, but without a strong light to announce someone is at the door; we will not accept our intuition. We run into the danger of becoming blind to ourselves in the same way that viewers were blind to a gorilla on a basketball court, because we are not used to listening to ourselves or to noticing what is happening around us. We are not expecting anything to occur, and so we do not notice it.

In the subsequent sections, the general theme is that of self-awareness: of learning or accepting the ways in which your intuition reaches you, or how it expresses itself in your life. It's important to be clear as to the meaning of self-awareness as proposed here as opposed to its use in psychology or philosophy. Usually those disciplines are using the term to mean an awareness of the self as distinct from other people, or it is used to mean a general awareness of how we act with regard to our internal values (have I acted badly, for example).

For the purposes of this book, self-awareness means focusing your awareness on yourself and what is going on inside you that only you can be aware of. Nobody who looks at you would be able to know these things. They are only accessible to you, and only because you are choosing to examine them. You can only achieve this self-awareness if you are honest with yourself. Self-honesty, the ability to look at the good and the bad, the highs and the lows, the small feelings as well as the large emotions, is vital for an understanding of yourself and your intuition.

Having said that, however, the very first thing of all, the basis of everything which follows, is contained within the following two sentences. Everyone is intuitive. Intuition is always happening in your life.

Read those two facts and allow yourself to accept that they are true. You might not feel that they are true for you, or you may feel that they are only occasionally true. That doesn't matter. Just know that you are a natural intuitive, because, for all the reasons given in the first part, you cannot be any other way.

The first part of this book emphasized that we are all connected with everything and everyone else on this planet. That connection for you might be strongest via the electromagnetic fields of other people or of the planet. It might be that such a connection is made obvious because of the food you eat, because you are so careful about the selection and preparation of meals. Taking it inside you forms that connection on a very physical plane. It might be that for you the connection is more a spiritual aspect of your life, so that you set out to experience it as a way of developing more meaning in your life.

However you understand that connection, it is helpful to see it as not being limited in any way to one particular sphere of your life. The evidence is clear that, whether we like it or not, we cannot escape all manner of types of connections with our environment: electromagnetic fields, quantum mechanical effects and the zero point field, the biosphere; they are always forming complex webs within, around and amongst us. As John Donne said, "No man is an island, entire of itself; every man is a piece of the continent, a part of the main."

If the connection is always there for everyone, then the way we each experience it will be different. That is central to the concept of self-awareness. I have already spoken of how your intuition might vary over time and with circumstance, but there is also the differing natural ability, it seems, as well as the differing strengths we each have. How I might perceive an intuition could be very different from how you experience it.

For example, Maggie, my wife, is far more auditory then I am. As she puts it, she can hear the truth (or falsehood) in what people say. To her it's just something she knows when listening. Similarly, her intuitions, apart from the ground state ones which we'll look at later, come in the form of words or sounds which help her gain greater insight into a situation. Myself, I am far more visual. I can—now—glance at a place and get a feel about it and how it would affect me. It might look darker or lighter, or have a shifting pattern to it, each indicative of its effect. And, when I have an intuition, it is usually in the form of something I see with my inner eye. We each have our strengths. But without acknowledging those strengths, or wishing for 'better' or more impressive ones (like 'seeing' the past or future), we limit ourselves.

There are different ways of gaining information, of course. For example, many people will simply 'know' what to do in a stressful situation, whether that's dealing with an awkward person or choosing the right gift for a person who is both picky and important in your life. It is a gut feeling, a certainty. It could be based in the gut, or it could be a feeling in your back or some other bodily sensation which gives you certainty. Others will be able to touch something and gain information from it, sometimes detailed, sometimes no more than a vague idea, hard to put into words. Some people will be far better at a subtle form of communication than others—those who find it easy to 'speak' with animals, for example. There is some form of communication going on which is not verbal, but it does involve a two-way communication, if not a full conversation. But you might be able to be with an animal and 'know' what it is trying to communicate or what it needs most at that moment. It could be that your intuition is best expressed in your garden where your talent for knowing what to plant where and how best to support the subsequent growth results in a display which is envied by others.

The point is, you are going to find that you are stronger in one area than in others. It does not mean that if you are auditory you will be incapable of feeling anything. It merely means that you will find you are better able to get more complex information in one form than in others.

Think about yourself and how you have 'known' something, but you knew it didn't come to you via any of your five senses. It could be that you walked into a room where there had lately been an argument, and you could still sense it in some fashion. Maybe that 'knowing' was a feeling in the pit of your stomach, or a sense of fear for no obvious reason, or maybe you got goosebumps, or the room felt 'sticky' somehow. Perhaps you have had a feeling about an object, a piece of furniture, for instance, and when you held it or simply touched it, you felt or saw a flash of something: an event like a wedding or another celebration of some kind. Perhaps you can look at someone, even if they're across a room, and you just know they can be trusted or not. If you take the time, you will find that there have been many occasions when your intuition kicked in. It could be that you don't have one particular strength and you don't have 'hits' involving just one channel of communication, but you can see and sense equally well. Good for you!

The examples given in Part One were mostly at the extreme ends of what intuition can be like. You might consider those the norm simply because there are a large number of them. However, that is far from the truth. The examples are there to illustrate the various types of intuition available to all, not to show you how small and limited your intuition is when compared with them. So you don't get to see 2,000-year-old battles, but you could easily get to see a sudden and brief flash of something from the past, as I did in the cathedral. Maybe you don't get to absolutely know something bad is going to happen, but you do get to effortlessly avoid an accident on your way to work one morning (as you later discover). Or perhaps you don't get visions by holding an object in your hand, but you do get the feeling when you walk into an antiques shop that it feels like it is crowded with memories and people, and you can't stay there long because of the pressure in your head.

My point is that if you actively seek out the dramatic and the incredible, you will overlook and ignore the everyday and the useful. You have to let yourself be open to intuition, however it wishes to present itself to you. And for that, you need to be aware of yourself, how you react, what you respond to, how you know you are responding to something non-physical.

EXERCISES

SELF-AWARENESS (HONESTY about yourself) is key in these exercises. In what follows, try to be somewhere you won't be disturbed, and then start by thinking back over times when you think you might have had an intuitive experience. As you do, keep an eye open for how you react to some of the memories. Do you want to shy away from them? Do you realize that you tend to get feelings in specific places in your body, or do you get particular emotions as you revisit your earlier intuitions?

All of what you experience is important in helping you to understand where you are now. Everything is connected, which means the past is still present in your body, in your memory, in your actions and reactions. You are not a lone, isolated figure, but are part of the flow of your life and the flows of everything, every object, every place you have come into contact with. Therefore, everything you experience and think about is helping you to understand more about yourself and your connection with the world beyond your senses, the world from which intuition arises.

Bearing those ideas in mind, take your time as you visit each exercise. Above all, listen to yourself. Don't be afraid to make more detailed responses to the questions. Self-awareness is all about self-honesty, and a journal is an excellent way of achieving that state.

One advantage that journaling has over writing lists and making short notes is that it forces you to slow down in your thinking to keep pace with your writing. As you slow down, you also realize that there are other memories or emotions which come to mind, more than you originally thought, and those 'additional' ones are just as valuable, sometimes even more valuable than the original ones you began with. In other words, a journal will probably take you to places, times, people, and events you would not normally have visited.

Although the following has been divided into different exercises, you may well find that they tend to blend one into another as you review and understand your own strengths and weaknesses. The reason for the division into exercises is to ensure that you do not miss out any single aspect of your intuition. Give each one as much attention as you can.

Exercise 1: Learning Your Own Strengths

THE FIRST THING you need to do is identify how best your intuition expresses itself to you.

When you have an intuitive 'hit', how do you know that's what it is? Think back and make a list of the 'hits' you have had. By each one, note how you recognized it for what it was. Was it visual? auditory? sensing? If it was a sensation, did it occur in one part of your body? Was it a combination of things? It might also help to recollect if you were doing anything specific at the time? Resting? Walking? Or was it an intuition which shouldered its way into your awareness with no regard to what you were doing? If you are normally a visual person, are your intuitions more to do with seeing than feeling? If you are more focused on your bodily sensations in everyday life, do you get feelings when you get intuitions?

Look at your list and see if there is a pattern. Try to recall as many instances as you can, going back as far as you need to. It is unlikely that you will complete this in one session. It is far more likely that you will come back to it again and again as you recall old experiences. That's fine.

It's not a test, only a way of getting you to focus on yourself and your memories.

Exercise 2: Does Your Intuition Have A Focus?

Go BACK to your list and examine it this time for any similarities in what the intuitions were about.

Do you only get intuitions about a small range of things? For example, you might be really good at sizing up people (like Richard Branson) but hopeless at finding your way in a new town or even a new carpark. Or you could find it easy to know where to turn to get a good parking space in a mall but be dreadful at making mouth-watering dishes from scratch using whatever is to hand without having to think about it.

Neither example is better or worse than any other, but it helps to understand how your intuition works for you.

Be honest with yourself about your abilities. Note where you feel more confident and where you feel more at sea.

Exercise 3: Bodily Sensations

You NEED to be aware of your body and how it reacts, not just in terms of your natural intuitive strength—auditory, visual, touch, general sensing, and so on. You might also have noticed that there are different reactions which your body makes at such times.

Perhaps you recall a feeling in the pit of your stomach that made you realize something important was going to happen, but you could not tell *when* it would happen. Perhaps you felt the hairs on the back of your neck prickle, or even a sensation that your back was extra sensitive for a moment. Maybe your legs felt weak momentarily, or your heart rate increased for a short while.

You will probably have been aware of a feeling of certainty about something: a place to go, a direction to take, an understanding. If that has ever happened to you, then you would be advised to recall that sensation of certainty and decide what was it about it which made you so certain. Was it the suddenness of it, or the place you were aware of it in your head? Did it feel like the certainty was in the front or the rear of your head? Did you 'blur out' the world for a moment when it happened, so that everything you had was focused on that intuition?

There are also those feelings you get after making a good decision, especially if it is a hard one. Such decisions point to the future. When you have made a 'good' decision, you might well get a sense of lightness or of contentment which confirms your choice or action.

The trick is learning which of the bodily reactions you notice are associated with an intuition. You might get a feeling in the pit of your stomach because of a bad meal which happened to coincide with an intuition. Not everything you experience in your body is an intuition. You have to learn the difference for you. You have to learn what your body is telling you.

So often we take our intuition for granted and do not spend much time understanding how our bodies might be adding more information to the original intuition. Go back to your list and see if you can associate bodily sensations with certain types of intuition.

They do not have to be strong and overwhelming. Usually, they are subtle and gentle. It might be that you only experience a sense of nervousness at such times, a very general thing. But if it only appears in that form at times of intuition, then it is a definite indicator you can rely upon.

Exercise 4: Synchronicities

SYNCHRONICITIES ARE those events which occur outside of you, yet which seem to have a meaning for you. Recall how the scarab appearing helped Jung's patient.

Take the time now to examine your life carefully for such synchronicities. Have you experienced such coincidences? Did they help you in some way by encouraging you to continue with something or by providing you with an insight you would otherwise have missed? Have you been engaged in some activity and found that, without really trying, things just 'turned out' for you? The right people or the right tool appeared at the right time in the right way?

Alternatively, did the opposite happen? Were you trying to achieve something, but unexpected obstacles kept appearing? What was the end result? Did such difficulties mean that you were able to experience something else, something unexpected or even something which you thought would have been impossible?

Exercise 5: Things That Don't Fit The Above Lists

Be honest if you have deliberately ignored an intuition. It happens. But why that one, or why at that time?

Perhaps you get premonitions without understanding them, like Sonya and her earthquake and air disaster. Maybe you've never wanted to admit that you are capable of such things, because the thought of 'being responsible' for knowing about them is simply too daunting a prospect. Perhaps you were raised to believe firmly in the value of intellect, analysis, and reason and to put aside anything else as a way of navigating through life.

Make a note of those times when you ignored an intuition or didn't detect it or react to it for whatever reason, but you knew what it was later. Those instances will also help you understand how your intuition works best for you.

Whatever your specific circumstances, learn what they are. Understand your strengths and also your weaknesses. If you want to improve how your intuitive awareness works, you have to start from a place of knowing what it's like right now. Therefore, the more detail you can provide for yourself in these exercises, the better your starting position. But don't worry if you can't think of any examples or only one or two. Just know and accept that intuition is always at work for you. We are going to learn how to make your awareness of it stronger and more reliable.

Exercise 6: You And Your Intuition

Having reviewed and considered how much or how little intuition has played a part in your life, you need now to consider how you feel about your intuition. Turn your self-awareness toward your attitude to intuition in general and recall that self-awareness involves self-honesty.

Do you have blocks to accepting your intuition, or in accepting that it is always helpful to you? Could it be that some of those blocks are there because you have spent more time being rational and logical, or that you have been in an environment where such mental attitudes were more highly valued than the irrational, illogical aspects of intuition?

Could it be that there is some part of you that is concerned that you might be powerfully intuitive? What do you fear might happen to you if that were the case? Do you fear that family and friends might turn from you, or become scared of you in some fashion? Have you, in other words, deliberately tried to curb your access to intuitive information; have you deliberately avoided circumstances where it might occur or even ignored the information gained by it?

Alternatively, have you wanted to be intuitive, or more intuitive than you currently are? Has reading about the examples in the first part made you envious of what others can do, but you can't seem to be able to emulate? Do you feel that you have been blocked from accessing your intuition in some fashion? In which case, what have you tried to do to remove any such perceived blocks? How successful were those attempts? And now that you have read this book, do you begin to believe that intuition is never blocked, only your appreciation or acceptance of it?

In other words, to accept information from your intuitive senses, you have to acknowledge that it is always available. In addition, you have to be willing to allow yourself to access it, and you have to accept that access is not restricted to one narrow channel of, say, work-related intuitive 'hits,' but is there throughout your life, every day.

Note

THIS IDEA of self-awareness is not only applicable to reviewing the past. It is vital that you maintain that same level of awareness in your everyday life as well. Consider these exercises as just the beginning, or a warm-up if you prefer, as to how you should be listening to yourself every day.

Consider also that if you have been having fewer and fewer intuitions as time goes by, it could be because there has been a change in your diet, your mental attitude, your emotional life in general or some other aspect of how you live which has meant that you are less receptive than you were. The later section on the physical and mental improvements you can make may well prove to be beneficial to you in this regard.

4

STRENGTHENING YOUR INTUITIVE BODY

Nature holds the key to our aesthetic, intellectual, cognitive and even spiritual
satisfaction
E.O. Wilson (Scientist)

Now that you have had the opportunity to gain a clearer picture of how your intuition manifests best for you and how you regard and react to it in general, let us begin to examine the ways in which awareness of its omnipresence can be made even clearer.

As all intuitions end up in the body as feelings, insights and so on, no matter their origin, it makes sense to ensure that your body is in optimal condition to allow yourself to be aware of them as easily as possible. Of course, such an approach will also prove beneficial to your health in general.

What follows in this chapter will assist you in being ready and able to benefit from the intuitive connection as it manifests. However, in order to take advantage of that, you will need to combine the ideas in this chapter with those in the following chapters on the mental and energetic aspects of improving your awareness.

Most writers on intuition will focus on the mental side of things as if they were the only important ones. But few will talk of the physical aspects which will also prove to be beneficial. In what follows, the key principle is to acknowledge that the body should be treated as a whole, both the energetic and the physical aspects.

Generally speaking, that runs counter to the current attitude toward health, which follows the scientific trend in focusing on small parts and dealing with them, but not tending to appreciate the body as a whole. Such an approach is seen in the prescribing of medicine to deal with a specific issue, which it does, but at the expense of creating other health issues which then require further drug treatment. By seeing and dealing with only one issue in isolation, associated problems are ignored until they become large enough to demand focused attention upon them. Compartmentalizing the body in this way forces a blinkered approach to any dealings with it. The balance of the body is overlooked or downplayed. The best way of being, of living, of being healthy, is to work toward achieving harmony in all aspects of the body and to treat it as it is: a deeply complex organism where everything has a connection to everything else.

The exercises and suggestions offered are provided to bring about balance within you, the mental and emotional balance no less than the physical and energetic. After all, the closer we are in balance with ourselves, the easier it becomes to be in resonance with the world, and such a resonance allows the transfer of information via a variety of channels.

Reconnect

Firstly, there is the consideration of where we are and how we live. Throughout, there has been an emphasis on the connection which exists between our bodies and the wider universe. As Dr. Sachin Patel, a

Functional Medicine practitioner put it, "We are living earth. We are animated earth. There isn't a single molecule in our body that isn't made up from the planet that we live on and the food that we eat, the water we drink, the air that we breathe. So whether we like it or not, we are nature, and one of the things that we've done, the biggest mistakes that we've done is we have tried to basically separate ourselves from nature… and because of that, we will do things to our bodies and to our environments that basically violate the laws of nature because we see ourselves separate from it."

Increasing urbanization is making it more difficult to connect with nature in a very direct way—feeling grass and soil beneath our feet and the wind against our skin, experiencing a diversity of plant life, smelling natural scents. Most of us do not have daily opportunities to have a natural landscape as our place of work. It is something we plan to visit and enjoy on vacations or at weekends. Generally, it is not a normal part of our lives.

One of the major problems we have with our lifestyle is that we tend to think that we can get everything we need from our technology. We can be entertained by it, and it will help us keep track of our heartbeat, our blood pressure, play the music and movies we like, and so on. However good it might be at those things, it is not what we really need.

One of the best—and simplest—things we can all do is get outside. There's no need even to have fancy equipment or do amazing feats of running or jogging. Even if we cannot live and work in somewhere like Yellowstone or some other national park or be always surrounded by superb and uplifting scenery, getting outside is something anyone can do, anywhere.

Once outside, all that is necessary then is to walk. We are walking machines. We are structurally designed to be able to walk easily and, as we do so, we are doing wonderful things for our bodies. Lymph gets pumped around, joints get exercised carefully, lungs get flushed out, our hearts pump a little more vigorously, we can engage more with our surroundings with our eyes, our sense of smell, our hearing.

It is also a phenomenally good way of exercising our minds, because walking is monotonous. That's why children are not usually great fans of simply 'going for a walk.' We place one foot in front of the other, and that's it. There is no need to think about it, because we have evolved to make walking something which requires no thought. But it is because it is such a boring exercise that it provides the opportunity to avoid that same boredom. With the body thus occupied, the mind is freed. Creativity bubbles up. Thoughts can flow more easily.

I have found that whenever I am stuck on some point in my writing, going for a walk reveals the solution to me. Walking thus, allowing the mind freedom, approaches the hypnagogic state and the bubbling up of intuition noted by Mavromatis. Philosophers such as Kierkegaard, Nietzsche, Thoreau, and Rousseau all expounded on the benefits of walking. Immanuel Kant walked the same route every day at the same time for decades. Indeed, it has been said that the first anyone knew of his death was when he wasn't seen walking. Kierkegaard wrote that, "… if one just keeps on walking, everything will be all right".

Added to that, there is the benefit of being in the sunlight. Recall that the sun is what our bodies react to in our diurnal rhythms. It is hugely important, in that its light regulates us in many different ways. But, for our present point of view, it is also something which is vital to be out in. I'm not talking about sunbathing, especially in the hottest part of the day. I'm speaking more of the mornings when the sun is beginning to climb.

Our skin responds to sunlight by trapping energy from it, and it has been found that water is also capable of storing energy from sunlight in much the same way as a battery can. In other words, sunlight is an incredibly useful form of radiation to be bathed in. Neurosurgeon Jack Kruse urges us to use UV light (naturally available from the sun) in order to properly regulate our cells in their general working.

Biophotons, those smallest 'bits' of light we naturally generate, have been found to be affected by the gravitational forces of the sun and moon. Staying indoors with all our energies and activities focused on or regulated by technology is far from helpful in terms of optimal health. It also means that with our artificial lights and our computer screens, we are rarely in synch with the natural world.

The more we do stay inside, the more our bodies have to try to cope with and understand what season we are in and what time of day it is. Getting outside is a very simple way of reconnecting with our surroundings, making us aware of it in a way which is impossible to ignore.

There is a tendency toward blandness in our world. Everywhere we go, we see the same types of fast food places, the same supermarkets, the same adverts, the same books and magazines; the differences in locations are becoming blurred. But that is only true with regards to our buildings and technologies. If we venture beyond them and travel across country, then we begin to see true variations: plains, lakes, mountains, deserts, forests, along with different plants, trees, animals, and weather patterns. That's where the world reveals itself.

Take the decision to reconnect with the world. Even something as simple as parking further away from the store on purpose and taking your time to walk toward it can be a small but significant start. Walk between shops where possible, take detours when you walk the dog, go and visit places such as ancient monuments or the nearest park, the beach or the backyard, anywhere which is outside.

Even if you only begin by doing something like this once a month, it's better than nothing. What you have to remind yourself of is the irrevocable fact that you are a part of the whole world, that you have a place in it, and that you are always interacting with it. Go outside and enjoy being a part of it all.

The benefits of being in nature, particularly in forests, has been known since the 1980's in Japan. Here the term 'forest bathing' has been used to describe the activity of going outside (especially in forests) and simply walking or resting there. Studies have shown that there are significant physiological and psychological benefits from doing this. And, if you cannot get outside, even having murals or pictures of nature in your environment can deliver some of the same benefits. (Of course, having this as a therapy merely points out how far removed we are in today's society from the natural world and its circadian rhythms.)

Avoid Or Reduce Disruptive Energies

AS WE HAVE SEEN, our hearts and brains emit strong electromagnetic (em) fields. Such fields will contain information concerning us, and, as we have seen, certainly form one channel of intuitive information. It makes sense therefore to avoid situations where other, conflicting em frequencies can interfere with such natural fields.

The increasing prevalence and intrusion of stronger and stronger man-made (non-native) em fields in our environment pose an ongoing and increasing health risk in general, apart from any effects they may be having on blocking or reducing our ability to gain intuitive insights. All the equipment around us, in our homes and workplaces, as well as scattered around the country, are producing frequencies which impair us at a physical level as well as limiting our intuitive abilities. Cell phones, computers, electric fields of all sorts are part of this damaging spectrum of frequencies.

Consider that the field from your heart, for example, is exactly the same type as that put out by a cell phone. What information you might transmit or be able to receive from that field is in grave danger of being scrambled and confused by the stronger, similar field of your phone and those of others nearby.

It is important, therefore, that you reduce or restrict your exposure to as many of these fields as possible. This is a large subject and deserves a volume on its own, but suffice it to say that such frequencies generated by technology are unnatural and have been shown to have damaging physical effects. How you choose to remediate your exposure will depend on many factors, but it should be clearly understood that such exposure is dangerous as well as disruptive to your intuitive abilities.

Improve Your Gut

So much for the health benefits of being out in nature and lessening non-natural interference. But with regard to your intuition there are other considerations as well, first amongst which is the importance of what you eat. Cary Fowler, an American agriculturalist, explains it clearly, "Whether we consciously realize it or not, the biodiversity with which we are most familiar, and the biodiversity with which we have most intimate historical, cultural and biological connections, is that associated with food plants."

The gut has been called the second brain. It is also where you get butterflies in your stomach and where you have gut feelings. It would seem useful, then, to consider the ways in which you can help yourself be better equipped to be more sensitive to intuitive hits which arrive via your gut.

A healthy gut means a healthy gut microbiome. One of the best ways of ensuring the health of your gut, making it optimal for intuition (not to mention better digestion), is to provide it with healthy foods. Eating organic food is not just a fad; it is very much better for you. The capacity of foods to store biophotons is a measure of the quality of the food we eat. Measurement is made by shining a light onto the product and then recording the delayed luminescence which results. The coherence of such emission, as well as the length and speed of the emission all speak to how much of the sun's energy is stored within it. Such measurements, for example, can detect the difference between tomatoes picked early as opposed to those ripened naturally. If food lacks any such biophotons, or very, very few, then it has less nutritional capacity for you and offers fewer beneficial microbes to help populate your gut. Eating naturally, eating organically, and avoiding junk food with little nutritional value keeps the gut in better condition, making it more susceptible to receiving intuitions via Becker's 'primary perception.'

A healthy gut mirobiome, as we have seen, has many different bacteria which, in turn, means that you should have as varied a diet as possible. Optimally you should strive to eat seasonally-available foods, especially those which are locally-sourced and therefore better adapted to your environment, so that your gut gets as wide a spectrum of bacteria as possible. Not only is that healthy and an aid to good and effective digestion, it is also important in the necessary communication between your gut and your brain, so that you do actually perceive the gut's reactions.

Hydrate

IF FOOD IS IMPORTANT, then so is water. You will recall how much of your body is composed of water. Additionally, it was pointed out that water in the cells was vital for some of the processes taking place there. This means that you need to ensure that you are always well-hydrated. Beer, coffee, or soda do not count as water. Water which allows for the 'quantum dance of life' is a necessity for the proper function of your body. And the quality of water, water which is fluoride-free, is as important as the fact that it is drunk regularly and often.

Restore Your Pineal Gland

WE HAVE SEEN that one gland in particular seems to be central to several ideas about how intuition works. The pineal gland, if it is to work effectively, needs to be in good condition. You will recall that the pineal gland is responsible, amongst other things, for the production of melatonin, which means that it regulates your daily and seasonal rhythms. However, this gland often becomes less and less effective as we age. One of the biggest problems is what is intriguingly referred to as brain sand.

Brain sand is actually the result of increasing calcification which occurs in the pineal. As the gland hardens, it is less able to produce melatonin, and this affects your sleep negatively. One of the worst offenders for calcifying the pineal is fluoride. With the spread of fluoride, especially in city water, more and more children under the age of 17 are being found with their pineal gland beginning to be calcified. Early malfunction of the pineal also results in a lack of control over the onset of puberty. A healthy gland delays puberty, an unhealthy one allows it to occur much earlier. Another contributor to brain sand is calcium. Calcium supplements, where there is insufficient vitamin D and K2 (sadly the norm nowadays), cause calcium to be deposited in tissues (as opposed to bones), including the pineal.

In order to help your pineal, firstly you should eliminate fluoride by using fluoride-free toothpaste and by filtering the water you drink. Eat calcium-rich foods and get plenty of vitamin D (and guess what is a natural source of vitamin D? Sunlight!), as well as the vitamins K2 and A in proper proportions (probably by taking supplements, as modern diets are sadly lacking in these vitamins). That will eliminate the need for calcium supplements. Amongst the top calcium-rich foods are kale, broccoli, spinach, quinoa, chia, and sesame seeds. But you need to use the organic varieties, as otherwise there is a very good chance that the vegetables will have been sprayed with one or more chemicals which will contain fluoride. And if you like wine, you should go organic there as well, as grapes are often sprayed with fluoride-containing pesticides, as well as having other chemicals added at various stages of processing.

If you have been using fluoride, you will have calcification. It's a simple fact. Getting your pineal back to a normal state is really getting back to a proper balance in your body, a way of being in harmony with the world around you so that you can react to the sun appropriately. And if you are not in harmony with the sun, the most important regulator we have in our lives, then you are, in a very real sense, disconnected from nature.

To decalcify the pineal, there are several steps you can take. Which you decide to use will depend on, amongst other things, availability as well as price. Taste might also have an influence.

These are in no particular order, so choose based on your own criteria.

- Tamarind fruit is excellent at removing fluoride. It's entirely natural and good to eat, but can be expensive and not always easy to find. Tamarind paste sold in jars can be found online and in food stores that feature Asian condiments and sauces.

- Iodine, usually in the form of seaweed or kelp, is good at removing sodium fluoride. Or you could eat foods rich in iodine, such as organic cheese and yogurt, or organic potatoes.
- Vitamins K1 and K2 are also helpful. K1 is present in many leafy green vegetables. K2 can be obtained by taking cod liver oil or eating foods such as organ meats and organic, pasture-raised eggs and dairy products, amongst other things. (See the Resource section for suggestions.)
- Turmeric is also helpful in this regard, as well as providing other health benefits.
- Boric Acid (which is a form of the trace mineral boron) is also good. It can be found in some foods (e.g. avocados, beets, walnuts and many others) or can be taken as borax in very small quantities in pure water.

You could also help yourself by taking a cleanse or using a sauna to help detoxify yourself.

It is highly beneficial to your pineal if you can help it recognize the normal hours of sunlight and darkness. To do this, you need to sleep in complete darkness (and that means no artificial lights at all) and not use electric lights or any laptop, phone or handheld device after the sun has gone down, as well as to use an effective blue light filter when using these devices during the day. In essence, you need to retrain your pineal to go back to normal and not use artificial light—which contains too much blue light at the wrong time of day, which tricks the pineal into not knowing when it is night and when it is day—so that it can perform its functions properly.

If you take the time to help repair your pineal gland, you will also have gone some way to helping your entire body by looking after it with healthier foods.

Summary

1. Reconnect with the world by going outside. Walking is highly beneficial.
2. Avoid or eliminate as much as possible your exposure to manmade em fields around you.
3. Improve the health of your gut by eating organic, locally-sourced foods wherever possible.
4. Restore the function of the pineal by eliminating fluoride, decalcifying it and avoiding artificial light at night, especially from electric lights, computers, laptops, tablets, and phones, to help reset the diurnal rhythms of your body.

NEXT, we will look at what are the mental attitudes you can use to help encourage your intuitive awareness to blossom.

5

KNOWING YOUR INTUITIVE MIND

Soon silence will have passed into legend. Man has turned his back on silence.
Jean Arp (Sculptor)

Having looked at physical aspects as they relate to improving receptivity to intuition, it is now time to turn to the mental ones. The first and most important thing to do (if you haven't done so already), is to accept that intuition in some form is accessible to you at every moment. That doesn't mean that you will be bombarded with intuitive 'hits' throughout the day, making normal life impossible. What it does mean is that you are both willing and able to allow such 'hits' to be recognized. If you rely greatly on your rational and analytical mind to the point where you think that aspect of your intellect is the most important, or indeed the only, thing which counts, then you will have a hard time accepting that information can come to you in any way other than via your mental processes.

Secondly, if you have worked your way through to this section, you should already be aware of your strengths in terms of intuition. If necessary, go back and revisit the section where you explored your memories of intuition and remind yourself of how you reacted. Recognizing how your mind reacts or feels at such times puts you in a much better position to become more aware of it when it happens again, and that recognition of it will allow you to be more fully receptive to the intuition, because you are more prepared for it.

Thirdly, another mental exercise you can do to help allow your intuition to reveal itself more clearly to you is to notice how many things you think are your thoughts and ideas, but which actually belong to someone else. Look at the exercise below for further information on this aspect.

Finally, there is a need to slow down. Modern life is fast-paced, full of information in a multitude of forms, and it is up to you to switch off from it. Ingrid Bergman said, "You must train your intuition—you must trust the small voice inside you," and Oprah Winfrey has said, "I've trusted the still, small voice of my intuition my entire life." The sage Paramahansa Yogananda said, "Intuition is soul guidance, appearing naturally in man during those instants when his mind is calm."

These quotes serve to emphasize that intuition most often comes quietly, without a great fanfare. They also serve to say that such quietness can be overwhelmed by the 'noise' of everyday life. It should become obvious from all that was said in Part One and from your own experiences that an intuitive 'hit' happens best when you are not rushing around madly, but are able to take the time to enjoy just being alive. That is not to say that people who rush do not get intuitive 'hits,' but it does imply that they will miss all but the loudest and most insistent 'hits' in their lives. Which would be a shame, as we have determined that intuition is always present, always operating and always available to provide information to assist you in so many ways in your life.

The single best way of slowing down, even if you have a hectic job or lifestyle, is to take some time for yourself and meditate. Sometimes that word 'meditate' can conjure up all sorts of terrifying scenarios of taking huge amounts of time and effort to achieve… well… anything, or having to have a special room or place set aside purely for that activity, or even having to be in nature so it becomes more 'effective.'

The truth is that it can—and should—be much, much easier than you think. The purpose of meditation is to slow your mind down. That's the basis of it. And, to slow your mind down, you have to learn to exercise control over it. If you recall the siddhi powers were a result of disciplining the mind to focus on one thing alone, then by setting out to meditate you are doing exactly the same thing, albeit on a much smaller scale.

There are other benefits of meditation which build upon discoveries made in Part One. Deep meditation is usually brought about by rhythmic breathing to the point where there is a resonance occurring in the deeply relaxed body, which has been found to measure about 7Hz. The resonant frequency of the Earth, the Schumann resonance, is also at about 7Hz. This resonant range is termed the Theta state of the brain and is the one most associated with dreaming sleep, daydreaming or imagining, which, you will remember, sounds very much like Mavromatis' hypnagogic state. In essence, a meditator in a very relaxed state is in resonance with the Earth, and a transfer of energy can occur, which could, of course, include information passing between the two fields, human and global (which could contain some information about the local aspects as well).

Another mental aspect associated with allowing intuition to become more prominent in your life includes how well or how freely you are able to express yourself in a creative fashion. If you recall Maslow's theory about peak experiences, he said that those who achieve peak experiences are able to repeat them more frequently. In other words, by doing it once, you are able to do it more often. That can apply to meditation to an extent, but he also said that self-actualization, or achieving your full potential, involved being creative and following your creative streak. However, in order to be creative, you need to be able to express yourself, and you cannot do that if you cannot look at yourself inquisitively.

Looking at yourself and what you want and how you feel about what you want is also part of the whole self-awareness approach to life. If you have always wanted to be a writer but never felt any encouragement, how does that make you feel? And if you are expressing your creativity in some fashion, are you satisfied that you are giving it sufficient time or effort?

How to express your creativity is another large subject. It is enough now to realize that, even if you do not feel creative or have never allowed yourself to express your creativity, it is never too late to begin. Julia Cameron's book *The Artist's Way* is probably the most widely known introduction to unleashing your creativity. And creativity is a way of approaching those peak experiences, those times when the commonplace world thins and you are closer to the invisible world of information which surrounds you.

Exercise 1: Accept Intuition Is Always There For You

IF THERE IS STILL some doubt about the availability of intuition for you, it might be due to you having relied for a long time on your rational and analytical mind, leaving little opportunity for your intuition to be heard. Another reason might be that you are unhappy about your life, and that if you believed that intuition really worked, then your life would be different.

In either case, you need to reassure yourself that intuition does indeed work for everyone. The simplest way of doing this is to search the internet for stories of intuition at work, where you can read testimony after testimony from people in all walks of life about how they recognized and followed their intuition in different ways for different reasons. As you do so, you will begin to see that you have also experienced similar events in your life. You are not alone.

Exercise 2: Your Mental Reaction To Intuition

MANY PEOPLE HAVE BODILY sensations about intuitions, and you should have charted and understood how your body reacts in a previous chapter. Others, however, have a mental certainty or, at least, a mental change when they have an intuition. It can range from a feeling of irritation, a nervousness, or an awareness that everything feels calmer within you—all tensions go, and you can relax mentally. It could be that you are aware that a specific area of your brain is where you get a sensation. It might be toward the rear of your head, or toward one side.

Also, the way you think about intuition is important to understand. If you have been brought up to believe implicitly in your intuitive ability, your mental picture of how you relate to your intuition will be entirely different from that of someone who does not really trust it or tries hard to understand it but finds difficulty in allowing it to happen. Although this has been touched on before, it's worthwhile taking some time to focus on your mental approach to intuition as a subject, rather than as an experience.

However you mentally react to intuition, you should make a note of it, adding your descriptions to the list (or journal) you started in the previous chapter.

Exercise 3: Which Thoughts Are Your Own?

THIS MAY SOUND STRANGE. Obviously the thoughts you think are your own. But that is not the point here. What we are looking at now is how much influence has been given to others to shape the way you think. There might be some areas of your life where you have quietly accepted (and probably not even realized it was happening) how others think.

In earlier times, it could have been how parents thought their daughters should be married by a certain age, or which profession they chose for their sons. In today's world, it could be how your friends have influenced you to think about certain types of music, or behavior, or foods or drink. It could be about how your family believes you should behave or vote or what you should read or watch.

Sometimes it might be hard to know which are your own thoughts and preferences and which are those of others you have adopted as your own. Knowing the difference between these two is important, because without an awareness of the difference, you might well be influenced to interpret or understand an intuition incorrectly, assuming it came from your own mind rather than from an opinion which is not yours.

For example, you might have ideas about what you should feel like as you get older. Are those really your ideas, or things you've read or heard of, or that someone has said to you? Similarly, you might think that how you react to certain situations, to things like political parties or the government are your own reactions. But what shaped them? And when? Simply looking at yourself and wondering why you think the way you do, why you act the way you do, even if you never get definite answers, will be of service to you.

In other words, one of the most important things you can do for yourself is to understand yourself more clearly, become more self-aware. Intuition is about listening to yourself. But if you don't even know why you think or feel or react the way you do, then you are not going to be as susceptible to listening to strange thoughts or impulses if they don't match how you normally are. The greater the amount of self-awareness, the easier it will be to allow any sort of possible intuition to be known.

Exercise 4: Meditation

MEDITATION IS HUGELY beneficial in your quest to improve your intuition. The purpose of meditation is to quiet the mind so that, when you have finished and are ready to get back into your normal stream of life, you can spend a moment or two thinking about a situation, an event, a person or whatever else you feel is drawing your attention and simply listen to what your intuition tells you. It might be that your intuition speaks to you with a feeling or a word or a sight, and because you have been telling the rational mind to take a back seat, your intuition can be heard more clearly.

Meditation is simply about controlling what your mind does. You can do it with your eyes open or shut, walking or standing still, looking at nature or a brick wall. All that matters is you control what you are thinking about, and what you are thinking about should not be any random thought which comes into your head. All you do is look at one thing at a time or think about one thing at a time. That's it!

Put like that, it doesn't sound too difficult, does it?

The more you do this, the easier it becomes to quiet the mind and listen to yourself. How you meditate will be up to you. Most people will think of sitting cross-legged on the floor with eyes shut, possibly with some humming going on or gentle background sounds. That does not have to be the case. What follows are some ideas for you to try out for yourself.

Pick a type of meditation from below to begin with and a time and a place where you will find it easiest to do. Some people find that getting out of bed ten minutes earlier and sitting on the floor by the bed, or supported by it, works well for them. You might find that before or after lunch works best, or that an unused corner of a room works well. Maybe you can get out into your garden and sit there. Perhaps you always take your dog for a walk, in which case, use that time for your meditation as much as you can.

You don't have to devote hours and hours to it. Any start is good. As time goes by, you'll probably find adjustments you can make. Your aim is to get to a point where stilling the mind to do one thing comes to be a comfortable part of your day in some fashion.

Sitting meditations

Sit comfortably in a chair. Close your eyes and think about a color, such as blue. See blue in all its forms: the sky, the sea, clothing, carpets and so on. Whenever you find yourself not thinking about the color, simply stop and get back to it.

Sitting comfortably but not slouched or slumped (because your body will complain about being uncomfortable if you do), look out of the window at nature. Look at the sky, the clouds, the trees, the birds, whatever is there. When you find yourself thinking about something else, gently bring your attention back to what's in front of you. In good weather, do this outside.

Alternatively, focus only on your breathing, the in and the out breath. Nothing else, only your breathing. Try counting the breaths. As soon as you find your mind going off on its own, restart your counting. This is about as simple as it gets.

Walking meditation

If you have the opportunity to get outside and walk, then walk. Walking regularly has many physical benefits, as we have seen, but it is the focused mental aspect which concerns us here. For our purposes, we want the monotony of walking to be uppermost. The simple activity is all.

Allow yourself to walk with care. Walk gently, without rushing, and while you are walking, observe what is going on around you. Don't judge it, don't do anything except observe it. A dog walks across ahead of you? Observe the color and the way it looks around. You pass a tree? Observe the bark and the colors and shapes of the leaves. That's it. Walk and look. That's also meditation.

When you find yourself thinking about what's for lunch or something else, gently bring your attention back to looking around yourself, to observing that your legs are moving and your feet are taking you on a walk, that there are clouds overhead, and there are flowers nearby.

––––––––––––

Summary

1. If necessary, become comfortable with the idea that intuition is always there, always working for you. Read and recognize the many ways it shows itself.
2. Become familiar with what it feels like in your head or your mind when you have an intuition.

3. Take the time to examine which are your own beliefs and which you have 'picked up' from others.

4. Meditate in whichever fashion you find easiest to fit into your day. Take it slow, but be determined to quieten your mind more and more for that part of the day.

6

YOU ARE NOT JUST YOUR PHYSICAL BODY

The universe is not indifferent to our existence—it depends upon it
Stephen Hawking (Physicist)

One of the main ways in which we connect with the universe around us is via the energetic body. As we have seen, various cultures speak of energy centers associated with the body. It makes sense, therefore, to ensure that your body is as energetically receptive as possible—that your energy centers are operating as efficiently as can be—as well as to help understand the energetic associations which manifest as part of the natural intuitive process.

As the most well-known system is that of the Hindu chakra system, we shall look in the exercises in more detail at how to help the chakras of that system be optimal in their performance. However, the general principles will also be of relevance to the other systems mentioned. We will also look at ways to interpret intuitive signs, signs which are the result of your connection with the world beyond your physical body.

Although the idea and descriptions of the energetic aspect of the body have been shared for centuries (particularly in the East), such knowledge has not taken root in the West and become a natural part of how we think of ourselves. The concepts have only arrived relatively recently, and consequently the idea of the health of the energetic body has few adherents here. Nevertheless, because of the importance given to this type of connection with the world beyond us, it makes great sense to attend to our non-physical and subtle aspects, just as we attend to our physical bodies.

In the majority of the energetic systems reviewed earlier, the connection with the universe beyond the body was to be found in the higher chakras, particularly in the crown of the head. We have already seen that the pineal gland, the principal gland associated with energy centers at the third eye (between the brows) and the crown, can be made healthy. The immediate temptation is to put great emphasis upon the chakras in the head. However, to do so would be to create an imbalance in the energetic system whereby the lower chakras are ignored. And recall how the allopathic system focuses on one issue at a time, always chasing to try to correct imbalances it causes. It is the harmony of the body in toto which is of paramount importance, and that holds true for the energetic systems as well as the physical.

The lower chakras are where the energetic balance between your own body and its connection with the physical world occur. If only the upper chakras are concentrated upon, then, by default, the natural connection with the earth, with the physicality and practicality of that connection, is neglected. In its place there is an over-emphasis upon 'higher consciousness,' a desire to avoid engagement with the realities of the world. This is responsible for the attitude toward people called (usually disparagingly) New Agers, who are judged for being 'otherworldly' in their lifestyles and beliefs. Some of these New Agers will accept such judgment gladly, as it convinces them that their attitude and their approach is the correct one, believing that physical existence is somehow inferior to spiritual awareness. Plainly, this is an unbalanced approach to life. The reason for saying this is that, throughout, we have been stressing our natural relationship with the world and that we live in harmony with it. Therefore to place emphasis upon the upper chakras and their relationship with the wider universe is to do so at the expense of the lower chakras which are our energetic connections with the here and now, our immediate surroundings. It is clear that all the chakras need to be in balance so that we are in proper harmony with all levels of our connections.

As an aside, it might help to consider the chakras in terms of Maslow's hierarchy of needs. The lower parts of his hierarchy were concerned with the physical needs of the body, leading to the topmost being concerned with self-actualization which included "elevating experiences that generate an advanced form of perceiving reality." In much the same way, the hierarchy of the chakras echoes Maslow—the lower chakras being concerned with the physical, the highest ones concerning themselves with the non-physical and the world beyond the senses. For Maslow, to attain the peak experiences, it was necessary that the lower needs should be addressed. And so it is with the chakras; maintaining the lower chakras is necessary to give stability to the insights provided by the higher ones.

Whether or not you subscribe wholeheartedly to the idea that there is a non-physical aspect of yourself always in communication with the universe, you still might have a belief or understanding that you can and do receive messages in various forms from someplace else: the universe, the world, God, the angels, or however else you might call it. An earlier example was given of the appearance of a vulture when thinking of an old friend, or that of the scarab beetle for Jung and his patient. You might feel that the world does something similar for you; it gives you messages, brings you people you need to meet, helps you by finding a book you really need to read, and so on. Jung called such moments synchronicities, but you might prefer to call them messages, nudges, or help. Most people can recall one or two such moments in their lives when something outside of them, something not directly related to what they were engaged in, arrived in their awareness and was a direct help with a situation.

In both cases, chakras and synchronicities, there is nothing in the physical body, nothing about the physical body, which can be seen to act as a connection extending beyond ourselves, outwards in all directions, and yet there is something which does exist and does act as that connection. In the case of synchronicities the connection is physically real, but it is less so in the case of the chakras.

Exercise 1: The Chakras

EXAMINE your beliefs about life in the following way. Do you tend to see life here on Earth as something to be scared about or to be constantly fearful of in various ways? If so, do you also like the idea of an afterlife which is so much better than here?

Alternatively, do you delight more in the physical aspects of life on Earth —those things which affect the body directly and bring physical pleasure? Do you give much thought to the idea that there is a non-physical connection with something beyond your body, and that it has an equal importance in your life?

It might be that you are somewhere between these two, but still find yourself spending more time on either the physical or the non-physical without being completely given to one extreme or the other. Be honest with yourself as you consider this question, as putting emphasis on one more than the other leads inevitably to a lop-sided view of the universe.

Broadly speaking, the lower chakras are involved with you, your body, and how safe and supported you are in the world, moving toward considering how you connect with the world beyond your physical sense as you go through the upper chakras. Depending on what your self-assessment revealed, you should consider helping to develop whichever are the 'weaker' or less emphasized chakras in order to attain a better balance.

There are numerous books on working with the chakras, some of them focusing more on color, others more on sound, many of them with specific meditations or actions you can take. Some helpful ones are listed in the Resources section. You will, if you approach them with an open mind, find that they offer valuable assistance in improving your physical and emotional aspects through their emphasis upon balancing the non-physical aspects. Such work will, of course, be of benefit to you in having better access to your intuition.

Exercise 2: How The Universe Communicates

SYNCHRONICITIES ARE one way you can recognize the universe is communicating with you. Having spent some time wishing that you could start a kitchen garden, but not knowing the first thing about soils, composting, which varieties of plants and so on, it all seems too big, then you notice a small sign announcing a course for beginner gardeners happening nearby. Or you wish you could watch some of those old movies you used to enjoy with your parents, when you notice a box set of them in a bargain bin of your local store.

Those are obvious examples. However, there are others which are less easy to see at first. The important thing is that you begin to see what is happening around you. For instance, there are many books about what animals mean when you notice them. Snakes are about change, hummingbirds are about happiness, mice are about seeing the details of what you are confronting more clearly and so on. What matters is that they appear before you, maybe more than once or in an obvious way, and the timing of their appearances relates to what you are dealing with at the time. The key to understanding the message they offer is to be able to examine yourself first: how you are feeling when you notice the animal, what is on your mind, how you feel about seeing it, and so on. Only then, when you have a baseline of your own response, can you begin to understand the message it offers.

First, you need to think back to any example when an animal showed up and had meaning for you in some fashion. One woman, for instance, whose mother had died, always saw a blackbird close to the back door on her mother's birthday. The blackbird had been her mother's favorite bird. It was a reminder to her of a continuing connection.

Similarly with dreams. The content of dreams can often have meaning in relation to your current circumstances. They do not have to be purely premonitions or warnings, but can be contributing information via the imagery or sensations within them.

With dreams, you pay attention to the really striking ones or to repetitions of images. An example would be if you are always having dreams about water flooding places, then you need to examine what emotions you are not expressing, as water is a symbol of emotions.

To benefit from such energetic connections, there are suggestions for you to follow in the Resources section.

Remember, intuition is always about information. How it arrives varies. You have to be ready to see it and to understand or interpret it.

To this end, go back to your notes or journal you began in an earlier section about how you thought about intuition. Look back over what you have recalled and see how much of it was due to synchronicities. Spend some time thinking about this aspect of intuition, how information comes to you in your daily life, in both big and small ways. The more you allow yourself to see it in operation, the more you will see it in the future.

Other examples could be getting lost in a town, or even in a large store, and ending up with a special or helpful purchase you could never have made by going about your normal routine. You are having trouble buying a gift for a friend or relative when you stumble across a new store or a new site online and there it is, the most obvious, best present imaginable. It could even be something so simple that only later do you realize how helpful it was. Or it could be something like a time when you were stressed and worried and were out walking when you followed a footpath and ended up at a spot where you could sit and take in the view. You relaxed there for the first time for a long time. That's help. That's the universe communicating with you. It can be just that simple. All you have to do is recognize it for what it is: intuition at work.

Summary

1. Take the time to examine how you feel about your body being more than merely the physical aspect. Learn more about how to care for the energetic aspect in a way which resonates with you.
2. Although you have looked earlier at synchronicities in your life, take the time to see how many events could be ascribed to them now you have a greater understanding of them.

7

INTUITION ON DEMAND

Mother Nature is always speaking. She speaks in a language understood within the peaceful mind of the sincere observer.
Radhanath Swami (Clergyman)

Intuition, when it happens to us, can often seem unconnected with what we are doing. You're fully involved in making a meal when you suddenly realize what piece of information is missing from a project you're working on. It's useful, but you have to go out of your way to record it before you lose the idea. And you're really busy right now! Or you are driving in traffic when you get the best idea you have ever had for your business, but you know it needs working on, and you're afraid that the details will vanish before you get a chance to make notes.

Often, we would really like to be able to have an intuitive 'hit' when we need it. It can be done, but to do so, our intuitive sense requires training. Making the physical changes to help clean out our system and using the mental and energetic techniques to gain a closer appreciation of the world beyond our senses is valuable and will provide results for the simple reason that you are focusing more on your connection with the world beyond your body. Our intuitive awareness improves the more we use it. Going through the previous exercises will certainly help. Learning to read and understand the information being brought to you is wonderful. However, it can seem slow and without any obvious progress being made.

But there is another way of accessing our intuition in a meaningful way every day of our lives. One way of describing this would be to call it focused intuition, intuition about a specific object of inquiry gained at the time of requiring it, instead of waiting for some haphazard intuitive 'hit' at a less convenient time when you are not able to give it your full attention, or, at least, the attention it deserves.

Consider what a British physician, Dr. T. Aubrey Westlake, wrote concerning this skill or activity, "…it gives indirect access to the super-sensible world, thus raising our level of consciousness and extending our awareness and knowledge. The faculty should be regarded as a special and peculiar sense halfway between our ordinary physical senses which apprehend the material world, and our to-be-developed future occult senses which in due course will apprehend the super-sensible world directly." (The reference to occult senses is an echo of Wilson's Faculty X, or the seventh and highest level of consciousness he postulated we all had access to.)

The continued exercise of such a faculty does certainly improve your ability to sense what is beyond your senses, as Westlake said. In fact, both Maggie and I have noticed a considerable increase in our intuition since we committed to developing the necessary skill. It is not some esoteric or arcane thing, but something commonplace, particularly in France and Russia, to take but two examples where this skill has been accepted as useful in widely differing fields. The following story illustrates the commonality of this.

The Reverend Smyth of San Jose in California tells the story of when he was a young boy in Colorado. He helped his great-grandfather and two uncles drive cattle the old-fashioned way, on horseback, from Fort Morgan to Cheyenne Wells, a distance of about 200 miles. It took them eight days. One morning, Uncle Dan, the cook, said that they needed more water for themselves and the cattle. In the Reverend's words, "He slowly moved his hand in an arc, with his palm out, starting in the southwest and ending in the southeast direction, and said, 'There is a creek about 5 miles down yonder. Ride over and see if the water is clear enough so we can filter it for the water barrel and the cattle can drink it.' I was puzzled, but rode over in that direction to find the creek was bank full. Then I rode back (about an hour, maybe hour and a half— didn't have a watch at that age—at a lope), and told Uncle Dan, 'Yeah, enough water, and clean enough to filter for the barrel.' Then I asked him how he knew about the creek and had he been this way before? He said 'No, never been here as far as I can recollect.' So I asked him how he knew the water was there, and he said, 'I felt it in my hand.' I said, 'No, that isn't possible.' He said, 'Sure it is, and anyone can do it. You try it.' I swung my hand rapidly in a half circle and he said, 'No, dummy, slow. See if you feel the palm of your hand gets a wet feeling or a feeling change.' I tried again, slowly, and he was right. I felt a tingle in the palm of my hand. So that is how I learned to find running water in a creek."

Finding water is probably the most common association people have with the simple and natural skill of dowsing. Uncle Dan in the story above was simply using the sensitivity of the body, together with the connection with everything that we discussed in Part One and that we all share.

It is interesting that Westlake wrote that dowsing was, he thought, a halfway sense, bridging the material and the super-sensible worlds, for it means that, when used correctly, it is an incredibly effective tool for developing a greater and deeper connection with that other world. Christopher Bird, in his extensive survey of dowsing, *The Divining Hand*, says that dowsers frequently are excellent intuitives. The inference is that by practicing the skill of dowsing, where there is a definite and focused intent to interact with the world beyond the senses, there is an increase in the faculty which shows itself in 'knowing' more about that world. It is an indication of our omnipresent connection and feedback.

Dowsing is, to put it simply, a search. It can be a search for anything. As Bird notes in the opening of his book, you can use it to search for "subterranean water flowing in a narrow underground fissure, a pool of oil or a vein of mineral ore, a buried sewer pipe or electrical cable, an airplane downed in a mountain wilderness, a disabled ship helplessly adrift in a gale, a lost wallet or dog, a missing person, perhaps a buried treasure."

This is not something frivolous, but a serious and useful tool which will, if used properly, certainly develop and enhance the natural intuition we all have. In France, for example, dowsers, particularly clerics, made use of dowsing for medical purposes. One practitioner, Abbé Bouly, was awarded the highest decoration in France. He was made Chevalier de La Legion d'Honneur and made it clear he was accepting it on behalf of all the dowsers in France. He started as a water dowser, then was contacted after World War I to locate unexploded shells and to determine whether they were French, German or Austrian, which he did successfully. After that, he turned his attention to health and to the study and identification of microbes, being able to identify various cultures through dowsing. His story is just one of several examples of the use of dowsing to explore the "super-sensible world." Medical dowsers in France are officially recognized as a professional group by the Ministry of Labor.

In Russia, dowsing is referred to as the 'biophysical method' and is the subject of investigation by government-accredited organizations, such as the Academy of Sciences' Institute of Biophysics and Institute for the Problems of Information Transmission. (Although the names of some of the institutions change, the research continues.) In particular, dowsing is used for the location and identification of mineral deposits, as well as for locating wells or identifying leaks.

Even such a commercial behemoth as Hoffman-La Roche uses dowsing to locate vital water for its plants. The in-house journal stated, "…with this unscientific method, Roche has been 100 percent successful in places where it has sought water all over the world."

Why is it that this skill can help intuition? Put simply, it is because to use it effectively requires an ability (which is acquired and developed through practice) of 'tuning in' to the world of intuition.

Jan Merta, a Czech-born physiologist, examined dowsers' reactions and tested himself by being blindfolded and still was able to sense water in a vial in front of him. He was convinced that, although tools were helpful, many dowsers use them when there is no need. They learned to dowse using them and then became reliant upon them. The best way to learn dowsing, he said, was to do away with any device and rely upon the body. "It's all a question," he said, "of being able to pick up a signal, a symbol, an idea or a thought extrasensorially. It doesn't matter in which form it's expressed. But it does require extensive training." Again, we have the association of thoughts, ideas, and symbols (pictures) with intuition, exactly as was noted in the first chapter of Part One.

It is clear that although there are many types of dowsing tools available, the simplest method, and the one which will encourage intuition on demand to develop most quickly, is to use the body itself. After all, that was the common element in all of the examples shown; people perceived their intuitions with their body. The use of dowsing is simply a way of forcing the body and its reactions to take center stage.

Exercise: Deviceless Dowsing (Dowsing Without A Tool)

ALTHOUGH THERE ARE at least 20 ways in which your body can be used in dowsing, we will look at only one here, that of blink dowsing. Therefore, if this particular method does not work for you, be assured that there will be one which does. (See the Resources section for further information on dowsing.) Because everything is connected, it is easier to take one body reaction as a focus of that connection and develop it so that it becomes responsive and therefore able to provide information (intuition) upon demand.

In this case, the focus will be on your blink response. Begin by soft-focusing your eyes so you are not aware of any details in what is before you; a plain wall works well, for instance. You should be relaxed as far as possible, so that your eyelids almost droop. Try not to expect or look forward to a specific response.

When you are ready, think clearly or say out loud the following statement; "I was born in _____. " (adding the location of your birth).

Be aware of what your eyelids do. Often there will be a blink or multiple blinks, or it will feel as if you want to blink. As this is your first time, the response might be a little 'muddy' or unclear. Don't worry.

Go back to the soft-focus, and this time you are going to think or speak an *incorrect* location of your place of birth. "I was born in _____. " (and add an incorrect place).

Again, be aware of what your eyelids do or want to do.

For most people, a true statement would be a blink or even a series of blinks. And the most common reaction to a false statement is not to blink at all. Your reactions might differ, but the most important thing is that there should be a difference in your eyelids' reactions to the two statements. The difference might be small at first, but that will improve with practice and awareness.

This is a simple method of dowsing using the body. You can use it in a number of ways. For example, you could use it to select the food you would enjoy most from a menu, to help decide which vitamins would be most effective for your goals, or where you should plant seedlings in your garden for best results, or to choose a dentist or doctor most helpful or sympathetic to you. All of these require a question which can be answered with a 'yes' or a 'no,' or 'true' or 'false.'

As we have seen with repeated examples in Part One, the human body is incredibly sensitive to a wide range of subtle influences. Dowsing is simply taking that sensitivity and using it repeatedly in a disciplined fashion on one aspect at a time so that the body, especially the mind, becomes used to 'listening' or receiving the slight impulses which arise from the correct use of a dowsing search query.

As with all the various intuitions in Part One, where different people had different results—visions, sensations, gut feelings, and so on—so it is with dowsing. Where one person might prove to be superb at finding water, another might be equally brilliant at finding lost objects or locating minerals. However, in all cases, for those who learn to use it well, it is always the same connection, but this time in a controlled state.

The more you use your body for dowsing, the more you are tuning it to allow intuition to arrive. To learn to dowse without a tool is to allow your body and mind to develop in ways which will encourage intuition in all its forms. It is a way of forcing yourself to be aware of and listen to your intuition by using a regulated approach, the constant use of which naturally allows your intuitive connection to become strengthened. Check the resources section at the end of the book if you want to explore dowsing further.

Earlier, dowsing was referred to as a skill. And, although the dowsing response is a natural one, the process of forming good, helpful questions and then being in a detached state of mind is where the skill becomes apparent. Therefore, it does not mean that learning to dowse will be the most appropriate way of using this type of focused intuition for you, although it is one which works very well indeed for a large number of people after they have practiced the skill.

If this approach does not resonate with you, then there are other methods which might provide an easier way of focusing your intuition. For example, Tarot cards are popular and use images to stimulate thoughts, associations, and ideas to provide answers to inquiries. If the thought of using the traditional tarot deck is too daunting because of all the associated concepts, there are any number of decks available using a wide variety of symbols. Simply choose the one which resonates the most with you. And then practice. Like any skill, time devoted to it will prove beneficial.

Similarly, the I Ching can be used to help you 'tune in' to your intuition. Indeed, it has been used as an oracle for thousands of years. Getting to know it takes time, but it operates in the same way as any other method, by providing stimuli to your mind to help it move past the rational and analytical modes and allow the non-rational, the intuitional, to come to the fore. Neither, however, give such definite answers as does dowsing. It is more a matter of preference.

No matter what your particular strength might be, there are one or more ways to help focus your intuition. These three—dowsing, tarot and the I Ching—are simply methods to discipline your mind in such a way that you are more receptive to your intuition. They are not the only ways of doing this. No matter which you end up with, a study of dowsing would prove to be hugely beneficial, as it is the most flexible method of all and can be used in all situations both quickly, effectively and privately (in that no one need even know you are using it). Be sure to look in the resources section for more details.

WHY INTUITION MATTERS IN YOUR LIFE

In some sense man is a microcosm of the universe; therefore what man is, is a clue to the universe.
David Bohm (Scientist)

We have seen how complex intuition is, and how we are always in contact with the wider universe, and how we can appreciate that connection and access the information it brings to us. But a good question to ask at this point is, 'What is the point of all this if everyone already has intuition?' Surely you will still have intuitive hits? Nothing's changed, has it?

It is true. Intuition is always present, whether or not you acknowledge it. It is only possible to stop recognizing its presence. It is impossible to switch it off. And that fact makes it important to remember that most of us live without giving anything beyond our routine much thought or attention. But, once we begin to accept, acknowledge and use the information, then our lives change as a result.

As humans, we are very good at accepting routine, of keeping within certain guidelines of behavior and thought. It is much easier and less stressful for us. At least, it appears to be. If you recall, Colin Wilson described seven levels of consciousness, with dream consciousness at level 1 and his Faculty X "when the mind seems so energized—or deeply relaxed—that other times and places are as real as the present" at the other end of the spectrum.

He believed that we spend most of our time at normal everyday consciousness (which he referred to as level 4), where nothing really stands out, but it is only slightly better than what he called the "grayness and boredom" of level 3. There is nothing sparkling in life at these levels, only routine with occasional punctuations of interest and excitement.

It is like looking out of a window at a familiar view, and we struggle to see anything fascinating or new, only the same everyday objects. In such a state, we attend to our intuition as an abnormal state of affairs— something like knowing who is calling before you pick up the phone. It's swift, doesn't convey much and is gone just as quickly without it being given much thought, and then we go back to being submerged in the day-to-day commonplace world again. Intuition, for most people, is a brief break from normality, a time when something intrudes into our awareness. It is not, in this common view, consistent or ongoing, and certainly not sufficient in itself to warrant further consideration.

But, instead of that haphazard approach, where you live as always with the occasional intuition which doesn't alter the course of your life, consider the effect of actively seeking to listen to your intuition each day, of using it consistently. Such use might be called 'living intuitively,' because you are using your natural receptivity in an enhanced way, so that it illuminates and guides you in your life. Dowsing, as we have seen, is one clearly defined way of doing just that and is a useful path to take in order to develop the awareness of your intuition more clearly.

Generally speaking, our lives are made up of a constant stream of planning and decisions placed against a background of a seemingly inexhaustible stream of data—news, photos, adverts, emails and so on— all clamoring for our attention or asking us to choose in some fashion. Such an overload can make even seemingly simple choices appear difficult or impossible. What to wear today? Where to eat? What to eat? Go here or there for vacation? Watch this film or go shopping? Or maybe just take a walk? And what about my health? Should I really be eating this? Would it help to go to this gym or that gym? Is that job advert something I should pay attention to? And so on and on.

In the light of this constant pressure, it's no wonder we stay at the ordinary and everyday level 4 consciousness. The overwhelm is constant. Most of the time we make the same decisions, go the same way, live without too much concentration on our lives. When it lets up, it's only going to be for a short while before we plunge back into it again. We watch TV or do something else to gain a bit of peace and quiet. As John Lennon said, "Life is what happens to you while you are busy making other plans." We take so little notice of it day to day.

But take a step back a moment. Certainly all those decisions you have to make or confront each day are exhausting. The reason they are exhausting is because all they seem to do is keep you doing the same sorts of things all the time. Their goal is to get you through the day and on to the next one. Of course, there are punctuations in this constant stream: starting a new job, buying a home, living with or marrying someone. But by and large, those punctuations in your life are just that; you keep on having to deal with the everyday issues all the time.

Given that scenario of life, yes, it would be absolutely wonderful to have your intuition fully on tap, the receptivity knob turned up to its highest level so that you always, *always* receive the most important and helpful nudges in the way which works best for you. I'm sure we'd all love to have that. But there is one problem with that. If you are open all the time to your intuition, and you always get those 'hits,' then how do you know which to follow, which one is most important? Being open like that would just add even more stress and strain to your life, because you'd be surging from one thing to another. It would seem most likely that would be the case.

Except for one thing.

If you were living at such an intuitive level, it is highly unlikely that you would be anything like the person you are now. After all, you wouldn't be at the everyday level of consciousness, you'd be pushing out of that toward something happier, richer, deeper, and more fulfilling. The analogy would be of having a different language; the world will be different because of it.

Being more open to intuition would not be adding yet another layer of information to your life, demanding you make more and more choices. Instead, such an approach to intuition would expand your life, pushing away the unnecessary and the unneeded and allowing more space, more freedom into your life.

Your intuitive systems, the ones that we examined in Part One, would be actively clearing the way for you, making your passage through life far less stressful, because you are seeing the signs, understanding the messages, reacting in the right way at the right time, and sliding more easily through life instead of combating it at every turn.

Take a moment to picture that in your mind right now: an easier life because you always know what to do, where to go, when to act. And then picture how, with so much more ease in your life, that could translate into really living your life, having the space and time to actually enjoy the days.

So why aren't you doing that, living intuitively, if it sounds so good?

To make the most of your intuition, there has to be something changing in you. Our everyday consciousness, the level at which we are just escaping boredom, is enough to push us through the day. Yet the role of intuition is to add to your rational experience of life and enrich it. But how can that happen if you are determined to remain at the level of coping and getting by? Intuition is a connection to our Neanderthal past whereby we have the ability to interact with the world in a different and more fulfilling way, a way which provides more information than our five senses offer, a way which is helping and guiding us every day.

To truly exploit the full potential of intuition and to allow it to bring to you what you need, it is necessary to have a goal you are working towards. Several goals, in fact. Without a goal, you are directionless, pushed along the rails of what you believe and how you perceive the world. If you are an angry person, you will see the world in ways that irritate you. If you see life as always being a struggle, that will be reinforced by all you see and do. If you are a loving person, you will see many ways in which you can express or experience that love. If you feel life is unfair, for whatever reasons, you will always see that belief playing out in what you see, read, or hear as well as how you perceive you are treated by others. That's how perceptions work; they bring us what our biases and beliefs are continually transmitting to the universe. Recall that what we perceive is always being filtered. Which filters operate determine what you perceive. But perceptions are not goals. They only show you what you are predisposed to see. If you have no goals, you have little focus.

Tony Robbins, the hugely successful life coach and motivational speaker says, "Setting goals is the first step in turning the invisible into the visible." The invisible is hugely important to us all, as we have seen. The zero point field, the implicate order, the superposition of the quantum field, the Pleroma—no matter how you refer to it, we coalesce our lives from the potential of the universe, bringing into our reality those events which are the response of the universe to the information we continually transmit. Therefore, it is hugely important to have an understanding of what it is we are actually telling the universe. What do you want out of life?

According to Maslow, there are the basic needs, such as being able to feed, clothe and house yourself, followed by the need to feel secure emotionally, financially, in terms of health and so on. Above these are the need to feel that you belong somewhere, with family and friends. But you also need to feel accepted in those social areas.

Beyond those, you need to feel a sense of accomplishment, a sense of pride in yourself before you can then reach the peak experiences he wrote of, where you get to have, "rare, exciting, oceanic, deeply moving, exhilarating, elevating experiences." But to get there, to get a sense of accomplishment, of pride and prestige, you require goals. Living from day to day is to live without a goal, and without a goal, intuitive hits happen only now and then, because your intuition has no focus from you, no information coming from you to which it can respond. Your intuition cannot be of great help if you don't know what you want, where you want to go, how you want to arrive. Without goals, you are transmitting 'white noise,' so you get very little back to help you.

Of course, there are the short term wants such as those listed earlier, all the small questions. But there are also the long term wants: What do you really want from your life? What would you have to do now in order to feel good about yourself in, say, five years? What is it that you keep putting away from yourself that you think you don't have the time or the money to do now, but you know it's what you really want to try, because you know you feel good about it? Writing? Painting? Sculpting? Composing music? Making music? Decorating? Directing or writing plays? Gardening? Starting a charity? Dressmaking? Embroidery? Becoming a pastry chef? Organizing kid's parties? What creative aspect is missing from your life?

Knowing what you want is to have a goal. And, if you are sincere about it, you will be able to focus on it so that it is always there in the back of your head. And if that is the case, then you can be certain that, because you are connected with everything around you in all sorts of ways, the world will help you. You transmit that information to the universe. And the universe responds. It could direct you to someone influential for you, or to the right store where there is the right helpful assistant for you, or to the right vacation where you meet, or see, or hear what you need to move forward, or to reassure you that you are on the right track.

That is how intuition fits into your life: having a goal and working toward it. Intuition won't do it all for you, but it will be there with you, as a support.

Having taken that step back to look at your life in the broader context, there is also a role for intuition in your normal life, the 'daily round.' In fact, it is the role which most people provide for it: as a consistent and regular helpmate. But here, the way to allow your intuition to speak to you, to help it help you, is not to step back and wait for it to happen. Instead, you must actively seek it out and be aware of it regularly. Hence the need to discipline your mind. Just as the yogic masters, through discipline, achieved their siddhi powers, so you can attain a level of mastery over your intuition.

As we have seen, instead of being overwhelmed by all the decisions, it would be a great deal more fun and much easier if you were able to navigate through them all by listening to your intuition. At the most basic level, that means feeling your way through life. The Ngan'gikurunggurr and Ngen'giwumirri languages of the Aboriginal people of the Daly River region, about 135 miles (220 kilometers) south of Darwin, in Australia's Northern Territory, for example, have a word for the way they live in a much closer relationship with the Earth than we do. They listen to it. The term they use for this mental approach is 'dadirri,' which loosely translates as 'deep listening.' An Aboriginal Elder, Uncle Bob Randall, says, "We do not separate the material world of objects we see around us with our ordinary eyes, and the sacred world of creative energy that we can learn to see with our inner eye. …. We work through 'feeling', what white people call intuitive awareness." It's really about a feeling of being a part of the land, nothing separating you from it in terms of both the physical (the trees and the rocks) and the energetic (the fields of life surrounding and intertwining with yours).

Such a connection is something much easier to consider in the Outback than in the city center, yet the essence of it is true no matter where you are. It is that connection between all things which is where intuition lives and arises from. It is what causes those nudges of feelings that something is right or wrong for you. The connection provides the basis for you hearing a word to help you, bringing an advert to your attention with the phrase you need, making you suddenly realize something you had overlooked before—all the varieties we have looked at in Part One.

That connection cannot be strong if you do not give it space and you do not practice giving it space. Think back to the gorilla on the basketball court. It was there in plain sight but unnoticed by most. The reticular activating system acts as a doorman to your perceptions, filtering out much of what is here in the world. What is necessary is to make a conscious decision to pay closer attention and allow ourselves to become aware of what is always around us.

One example of being open to the connections around us concerns a National Geographic explorer, writer, and photographer, Loren McIntyre. Back in the 1960s, he was dropped off in the Amazon to find a previously un-contacted tribe. Instead of a short stay, he ended up spending two months with them, because he missed his flight out, eventually using a raft during a flood which destroyed the camp. He was finally rescued by a pilot after floating down the river. During his time with the tribe, he had no common language, and yet he found he was able to clearly communicate with the chief using telepathy. McIntyre called it 'beaming,' and it was called the 'other language' by the tribal members. He told few people about it (as we have seen, it is difficult to persuade others of your own experiences), but tracking the tribe, the Mayoruna, several years later, he recognized one of the men he had known previously and asked him if they still used the 'other language.' He was assured it was so. McIntyre's experience was such that he had no other option than to open himself to a connection with what was around him, and by so doing, he gained a great deal more than he had thought possible. He was able to communicate without spoken language.

Then again, there is the example of the Bushmen of the Kalahari Desert described by the South African author, Laurens van der Post. One day they had killed an eland many miles from their camp. He helped them by driving them back with the carcass on his vehicle. He asked them what the others would think of such a kill and was told, "They already know—we Bushmen have a wire here...it brings us news." And as he spoke, the Bushman tapped his chest, using the white man's term—wire —for their form of communication.

Similar ideas exist in Scandinavia, which has a term, 'vardoger,' for sensing someone's arrival before they actually arrive. The Celts of the British Isles also refer to what they call 'the sight of the seer' which is an involuntary ability to see the future or distant events, just as Swedenborg did with the fire near his home.

In other words, there are many examples of people exhibiting different forms of communication without formal training at all. It is something, it seems, which is inherent in all of us.

Being open to the connection we have with everything in whatever form that connection reveals itself to us, despite it being a natural part of us all, seems to be a rare thing. We trap ourselves within a world limited by what we think we can do and what we believe will give us security, and we ignore the possibilities which every intuition presents us with. If there is one important thing which can be learned from Part One, it is that life does not happen to us. It is something created by us in every moment. We have the ability to live how we want, but we stay within the tram-lines of our normal life.

Nietzsche, who never turned away from questioning common attitudes and beliefs and condemning that which he saw as holding us within the limits and bounds of society, said, "The individual has always had to struggle to keep from being overwhelmed by the tribe (society as a whole). If you try it, you will be lonely often, and sometimes frightened. But no price is too high to pay for the privilege of owning yourself." And to that he added, "Today as always, men fall into two groups: slaves and free men. Whoever does not have two-thirds of his day for himself, is a slave, whatever he may be: a statesman, a businessman, an official, or a scholar."

You may feel that such a target of two-thirds of a day to yourself is too much or simply impossible. Nevertheless, the principle holds true: that of taking time for yourself. Nietzsche wrote passionately about individual freedom, and how by following others and how they acted and thought became a brake on "owning yourself."

Tending to the growth of intuitive awareness, allowing yourself to see and interact more closely with the world, will, inevitably, bring about the freedom in your life which Nietzsche and so many other writers on the human condition all agree as being worthy of attaining. To 'feel' the way ahead, to gain an understanding of the results of a decision, to allow the world you are creating to bring to your attention that which is necessary for you; those are worthy goals. But, in order to achieve them, you must also be willing to change. Goethe, the German writer, said, quite truly, "Everybody wants to *be* somebody: nobody wants to grow." Most people want to have superpowers right now, but hardly anybody wants to change what they do or how they think in order to attain them.

You can already, without even trying, access the future and the past and bend space to your will. Why stop there? Why limit yourself? Why wait for an intuition? Why not be able to call upon it when it is needed most? Why not learn to understand the messages you are being sent each and every day? Why are we burying ourselves in restrictive, microscopic lives when there is a much bigger, more challenging, far more engaging version of life simply waiting for us to decide to access it?

We only allow ourselves limited and occasional access to who we truly are, when our daily intuition tells us again and again that we are more than we think and are capable of far greater things. Intuition is really only a taste of what is possible for us all. It is something which gives us a glimpse of a world full of potential waiting for us to enter into it. Comic book superheroes are nothing more than enlarging mirrors of who we really are.

If we wish to avoid being the 'lazy gods' that Colin Wilson spoke of, then we can, perhaps, begin to be our own superheroes. As Luc de Clapiers, Marquis de Vauvenargue, an eighteenth-century French writer, so aptly put it, "Consciousness of our powers augments them." After reading this book, you are more conscious of your powers than before, and that knowledge means you are more intrigued by them and interested in them than before.

Now use them.

REFERENCES & RESOURCES

What follows are some of the main works which have been consulted. In order to keep this to a reasonable size and allow the reader to follow the lines of reasoning in the book, I have only listed those which provided the most complete or most useful information on any particular topic.

There are many others which were consulted, but which added little further detail. The few websites listed are merely the most solidly useful, although many, many others were accessed for cross-checking purposes.

Where journals have been acknowledged in the text, I have generally not added them here, with one or two exceptions where the information contained was essential in the argument or contained further corroboration or information.

Aveni, Anthony F. *Empires Of Time: Calendars, Clocks and Cultures*. New York: Basic Books, 1989.

Babayev, Elchin S. *Solar and Geomagnetic Activities and Related Effects on the Human physiological and Cardio-Health State: Some Results of Azerbaijani and Collaborative Studies*. First Middle East and Africa IAU-Regional Meeting Proceedings MEARIM No. 1 2008.

Bentov, Itzhak. *Stalking The Wild Pendulum: On the Mechanics of Consciousness.* Rochester, Vermont: Destiny Books, 1988.

Bentov, Itzhak. *A Brief Tour Of Higher Consciousness.* Rochester, Vermont: Destiny Books, 2000.

Bird, Christopher. *The Divining Hand.* Atglen, PA: Whitford Press, 1993.

Campbell, Robert. *Intuition and Logic in Human Evolution. Communicative and Integrative Biology* vol. 5(5) Sept 1 2012.

Copleston, Frederick, SJ. *A History Of Philosophy (Three Books Comprising Volumes I to IX).* New York: Image, 1985.

Dale, Cyndi. *The Subtle Body: An Encyclopedia of Your Energy Anatomy.* Boulder, Colorado: Sounds True, 1985.

Davies, P.C.W. and Brown, J.R. (eds). *The Ghost In The Atom.* Cambridge, UK: Cambridge University Press, 1986.

Dossey, Larry, MD. *Space, Time and Medicine.* Boston: Shambhala, 1982.

Gladwell, Malcom. *Blink: The Power of Thinking Without Thinking.* New York: Little, Brown, 2005.

Gore, Julie and Sadler-Smith, Eugene. *Unpacking Intuition: A Process and Outcome Framework. Review of General Psychology* 2011.

Goswami, Amit, PhD with Reed, Richard and Goswami, Maggie. *The Self-Aware Universe: How Consciousness Creates The Material World.* New York: Tarcher Penguin, 1993.

Lachman, Gary. *A Secret History Of Consciousness.* Great Barrington, MA: Lindisfarne, 2003.

Lanza, Robert, MD, and Berman, Bob. *Beyond Biocentrism: Rethinking Time, Space, Consciousness, and the Illusion of Death.* Dallas: Benbella Books, 2016.

Lecouteux, Claude. *Witches, Werewolves and Fairies: Shapeshifters and Astral Doubles in the Middle Ages.* Rochester, Vermont: Inner Traditions, 2003.

Lipsey, Roger (ed). *Coomaraswamy 2: Selected Papers: Metaphysics.* Princeton: Princeton University Press (Bollingen Series LXXXIX) 1977.

Lorber, John. *Is Your Brain Really Necessary? Science* Vol 210 1980.

Mayer, Emeran. *Gut feelings: The Emerging Biology of Gut-Brain Communication. Nature Reviews Neuroscience* Vol 12 2011.

McCraty, Rollin, PhD, Atkinson, Mike and Bradley, Raymond Trevor, PhD. *Electrophysiological Evidence of Intuition: Part 1. The Surprising Role of the Heart. The Journal of Alternative and Complementary Medicine* Vol. 10 No. 1 2004.

McTaggart, Lynne. *The Intention Experiment.* New York: Free Press, 2007.

McTaggart, Lynne. *The Field: The Quest For The Secret Force Of The Universe.* New York: Harper, 2008.

Perry, Whitall N. *A. Treasury Of Traditional Wisdom.* Louisville: Fons Vitae, 2000.

Radin, Dean. *The Conscious Universe: The Scientific Truth Of Psychic Phenomena.* New York: Harper Collins, 1997.

Radin, Dean. *Entangled Minds.* New York: Paraview, 2006.

Radin, Dean I., PhD and Schlitz, Marylin J, PhD. *Gut Feelings, Intuitions and Emotions: An Exploratory Study. The Journal of Alternative and Complementary Medicine* Vol 11 No. 1 2005.

Ranquet, Joan. *Communication With All Life.* Carlsbad: Hay House, Inc, 2007.

Ravelli, Carlo. *The Order of Time.* London: Penguin, 2018.

Sinclair, Marta and Ashkanasy, Neal M. *Intuition: Myth or a Decision-Making Tool? Management Learning* 36 (3) 2005.

Sinclair, Marta. *Misconceptions About Intuition. Psychological Inquiry* 21 2010.

Sitvarin, Michael I. and Rypstra, Ann L. *Fear and Predation Alters Soil*

Carbon Dioxide Flux and Nitrogen Content. The Royal Society, Biology Letters, June 2014.

Surowiecki, James. *The Wisdom Of Crowds.* New York: Anchor Books, 2005.

Tiller, William A., PhD. *Science and Human Transformation: Subtle Energies, Intentionality and Consciousness.* Walnut Creek, California: Pavior, 1997.

Watson, Lyall. *Supernature: A Natural History Of The Supernatural.* London: Hodder and Stoughton, 1973.

Watson, Lyall. *Lifetide.* London: Hodder and Stoughton, 1979.

Wilson, Colin. *Mysteries.* New York: Putnam's, 1978.

Wilson, Colin. *The Occult.* London: Watkins, 2003.

Wilson, Colin. *Beyond The Occult: Twenty Years' Research into the Paranormal.* London: Watkins, 2008.

Wolf, Fred Alan, PhD. *Mind into Matter: A New Alchemy of Science and Spirit.* Needham, MA: Moment Point Press, 2001.

Zarkeshian, Sourabh, Tuszyński, Barclay and Simon. *Are There Optical Communication Channels in the Brain? Frontiers in Bioscience* March 2018.

The following websites, although useful, cannot be guaranteed to remain always available, nor to always contain the same information.

GreenMedInfo: http://greenmedinfo.com

HeartMath Institute: http://heartmath.com

Dr. Jack Kruse, Reversing Disease For Optimal Health: http://jackkruse.com

National Institutes of Health: http://nlm.nih.gov

Water Structure and Science: http://lsbu.ac.uk/water

For the biochemical complexity within us see:

http://bit.ly/pathwaydiagram

or

http://biochemical-pathways.com/#/map/1

Interviews with Sayer Ji, Dr Sachin Patel, and Kiran Krishnan were obtained via the Human Longevity Project website at www. humanlongevityfilm.com.

What follows are some suggested tools and books you can use to better understand your intuitive sensing and to further develop your awareness which add to the exercises in each chapter. Please bear in mind these are only a selection of what is available and are generally the most popular in their field. However, you may find other sources which suit you more closely.

Supplements:

www.westonaprice.org (for details on healthy diets)

www.perfectsupplements.com (for details about better quality supplements)

About Dowsing:

Learn dowsing (particularly without a tool):

www.discoveringdowsing.com/dowsing-course

The website www.discoveringdowsing.com contains a huge amount of free information on this subject

To learn more about what you can do with dowsing:

Percy, Maggie and Percy, Nigel. *101 Amazing Things You Can Do With Dowsing.* (Free ebook) Arizona: Sixth Sense Books, 2017. (You can download a copy at Amazon or other online retailers for free.)

―――――――

Alternatives to intuition on demand:

Baynes, Cary F (translator) and Wilhelm, Richard. *I Ching or Book of Changes.* London: Arkana, 1966

Dean, Liz. *The Ultimate Guide to Tarot: A Beginner's Guide to the Cards, Spreads, and Revealing the Mystery of the Tarot.* Vancouver: Fair Winds Press, 2015.

Wing, R L. *The I Ching Workbook.* New York: Doubleday, 1979.

―――――――

The chakras:

Bruyere, Rosalyn L. *Wheels of Light: Chakras, Auras and the Healing Energy of the Body.* New York: Fireside, 1989.

McLaren, Carla. *Your Aura and Chakras.* Maine: Samuel Weiser, 1998.

Simpson, Liz. *The Book of Chakra Healing.* London: Gaia Books, 1998.

Tansley, David V. *Subtle Body: Essence and Shadow.* London: Thames and Hudson, 1977.

―――――――

Your creativity:

Cameron, Julia. *The Artist's Way.* New York: Joseph P. Tarcher / Putnam, 1992.

Synchronicities brought to you:

Andrews, Ted. *Animal Speak.* Minnesota: Llewellyn, 2007.

Your dreams as a source of information:

Cheung, Theresa. *The Dream Dictionary from A to Z: The Ultimate A-Z to Interpret the Secrets of Your Dreams.* London: Harper Collins, 2006.

Crisp, Tony. *Dream Dictionary: An A-to-Z Guide to Understanding Your Unconscious Mind.* London: Dell, 2002.

PLEASE LEAVE A REVIEW

The authors' goal is to advance knowledge of and interest in intuition and to offer a coherent theory of what intuition is and how it works, as well as to provide simple and easy ways to access intuition and strengthen one's awareness of it.

If you enjoyed the book, please help share this important message by posting a review wherever you bought the book.

ABOUT NIGEL & MAGGIE PERCY

Nigel and Maggie Percy of Sixth Sense Books and Discovering Dowsing met online in 2000 through their shared interest in dowsing, an intuitive skill for focusing intuition.

Over the years, they have written over twenty nonfiction books about dowsing and related subjects and taught dowsing to thousands of students around the world.

They continue to present about dowsing and intuition in free online events that attract a global audience and through their Discovering Dowsing website, the largest free dowsing website on the internet.

For information about their work, visit:

http://discoveringdowsing.com

http://sixthsensebooks.com

Made in the USA
Middletown, DE
24 September 2020